Captain Lee Hall of Texas

CAPTAIN LEE HALL
OF TEXAS

By Dora Neill Raymond

With Illustrations by
LOUIS LUNDEAN and
FREDERIC REMINGTON

NORMAN
University of Oklahoma Press

To

Jean Campbell Myers

1912—1937

Preface

IN WRITING two earlier biographies I have had to strain my eyes towards Parnassus in an effort to chronicle the means by which Milton and Byron strove to transmute the politics of their time into the gold of their desires. Neither poet has cost me more arduous days than my present subject, a Texas Ranger who lived through the "smoking seventies" and on into the hectic century we call our own. His trail has led through the length of Texas and into Mexico, to the Kiowa-Comanche Reservation, to New Orleans, and across the Pacific to the Philippines. On the long journey I have received deeply appreciated assistance.

For furnishing me with family data on Captain Hall, his reports to Texas adjutant generals, his records in the Philippines, as well as with informative letters and a unique collection of newspaper clippings, I wish to thank his daughter and namesake, Mrs. Isham Keith (née Jessie Lee Hall), of New York City. Without these and her personal reminiscences, it would have been far more difficult to piece together the story of his life.

For valuable criticism of the manuscript while yet in preparation, I wish to thank my brother, Mr. Robert T. Neill, of San Angelo, Texas. His opinions have been of even greater help than the books in his western library. I thank also my son, Mr. Neill Raymond, and my kinsman by marriage, Mr. Charles Robb. Two busy authors, Mr. Duncan Aikman and Mr. Owen P. White, read and criticized the manuscript in its entirety. Colonel William O. Smith read and corrected chapters on service in the Philippines, and the western artist, Mr. Louis Lundean, rendered a similar service in connection with the early chapters on the Rangers.

For permitting me to use unpublished manuscripts of importance, I wish to thank Mr. Emmor Harston, San Antonio, Texas; Dr. William E. Howard, Dallas, Texas; and Mrs. Harriet Smither, Archives Division, State Library, Austin, Texas. I wish to thank the author, Mr. J. Frank Dobie, for the privilege of using his folder of newspapers dealing with the "rollicking seventies"; and Brother C. Raymond, who lent his clippings on the organization of the regiment of "Immunes" in Galveston.

Others who have given information on Ranger days, or assisted me in finding it elsewhere, are the following: Judge Duval West of San Antonio; Lieutenants Ben F. Riely of Charles Town, West Virginia, and Netteville Devine (since deceased); Judge J. A. Brooks of Falfurrias, Texas; Sergeant John W. Bracken, Austin; and Messrs. Sam Crowder of San Angelo, and George Talley of Falfurrias. I thank also the widow of Captain Hall's friend, Sergeant Sam Platt, of Austin.

For information on Captain Hall's army record and on the Philippine campaigns, the following officers and men of the famous Thirty-third U.S.V.I. have given me gallant assistance: Colonel Theodore Schultz; Captain Carroll Power; Lieutenant A. E. Gebert; Dr. B. A. Lieberman; Sergeant Rogers S. Clarke; Messrs. Carl Musgrove, W. J. McCamman, Robert R. Montgomery and G. C. Jones. In addition, for help on the same matters, I thank the artist (then war correspondent), Mr. John T. McCutcheon; Colonel William C. Harllee; and Mr. James A. Sheehan, editor of *The National Tribune*, Washington, D.C.

Others who have assisted are the late Colonel E. M. House; Mr. Charles Moore of the Commission of Fine Arts, Washington, D.C.; Senator Tom Connally; the Honorable R. E. Thomason, M.C.; Mr. Lawrence Miller, Okmulgee, Oklahoma; Mr. William H. Burges, El Paso, Texas; the late Mr. Rhodes Baker, Dallas; Judge W. A. Wright, San Angelo; Colonel Martin L. Crimmins, New York City; Mr. Silas Ragsdale, editor of the *Galveston News-Tribune*; Mr. Marvin Hunter, editor of *Frontier Times*; Mr. Meigs O. Frost of the New Orleans *Times-Picayune*; Dean C. S. Potts and Professor Herbert P. Gambrill of Southern Methodist University, Dallas; Mr. E. R. Dabney, Library of the University of Texas at Austin; Rabbi Henry Cohen of Galveston; Messrs. Kleber Miller, Frank M. Edwards, F. M. McCaleb, Edward S. Sears, and the author, Mr. Clyde Wantland, all of San Antonio; Mr. W. E. Sherrill of Haskell, Texas; Mr. Robert E. Hardwicke of Fort Worth; Mr. Max H. Bickler of Austin; Mrs. S. E. Ragsdale of Dallas; Mr. John Abbot of Lynchburg, Virginia; Mr. Robert J. Usher of

PREFACE

New Orleans; Mr. Thos. W. Streeter of New York City; Mr. C. J. Collins of Worcester, Mass.; and Mr. Fred C. Dolcater of Washington, D.C.

The four drawings by Frederic Remington contained in the book are reproduced through the special courtesy of Harper and Brothers, publishers.

I end my record of indebtedness with the names of three alumnae of Sweet Briar College, who assisted me in research: Miss Adelaide Richardson of San Antonio; Mrs. L. C. Page of Austin; and the late Miss Jean Myers of New Orleans.

DORA NEILL RAYMOND

Sweet Briar, Virginia

Contents

Illustrations

Map

I
Rangers Are Born
(1849-1869)

"The true point of view in the history of this nation is not the Atlantic Coast, it is the great West."—FREDERICK J. TURNER, "The Significance of the Frontier in American History."

I

Rangers Are Born

"TELL ME A STORY OF LEE HALL." In saloons, in camps, and on the trail, men have answered with tales of Lee Hall's Ranger days in Texas, his adventures in the Philippines, of escapes and escapades, and always of his understanding of the human breed. Only a few, and these few children in North Carolina, have asked on occasion what the man was like when he was still a boy. For the rare individual who may be curious about Lee's childhood, the beginning of the story is here recorded.[1]

Like many another "Texian," he was not native to the state. Begat of the strong loins of a Scotch-Irish surgeon, he saw the light of day on October 9, 1849, in Lexington, Iredell County, North Carolina. His Presbyterian parents, having no premonition of his destiny, brought forth with lusty prodigality four other sons as though extravagantly indifferent to the unique value of their first. The father was James King Hall, very tall, very florid, auburn-haired. Virile himself, he delighted in his profession of strengthening the bodies of his fellow men. In 1858, he moved with his family to Greensboro, Guilford County. From there, Leigh Hall as a boy of twelve watched his father ride away to serve as surgeon in Colonel Pettigrew's regiment, the Twenty-second North Carolina State Line. The operations that Dr. Hall performed during the Richmond campaign—amputations without anæsthetics, probing with makeshift implements for flesh-imbedded bullets—afforded copious testimony

---

[1] Material for this chapter is derived from family manuscripts in the possession of Mrs. Isham Keith, eldest daughter of Captain Lee Hall, and from his obituary in the *San Antonio Express*, March 18, 1911.

to the heights of heroism. Until he broke beneath the strain, he strove to mend the shattered bodies of the old, the mature, and of boy soldiers in their teens. His Civil War experience imparted an abiding respect for humankind. He could not tell at first who was of hero-stuff. It was well to respect all. Throughout his life he served with equal care the owners of plantations and the poorest of the "darkies" who sent small pickaninnies after him with mandatory messages. Had he been forced to describe himself, he would have said he was an average country doctor. Others pronounced him "grand in his simplicity."

His wife, the mother of Leigh Hall, was Frances Mebane Rankin, Scotch, and of Revolutionary lineage, as was her husband. One ancestor, Robert Mebane, had fought as a colonel against the British. Robert's son, Alexander, had been a general of militia and a congressman in the period of the young republic. Her father was the Reverend Jesse Rankin, who supplemented his salary by coaching young gentlemen for entrance to the University at Chapel Hill. "Fan," as they called her, had studied in girlhood with the young gentlemen, and at fourteen passed the entrance examinations, though she knew that to women the University closed its doors. Throughout her life she continued her intercourse with books, preferring library to kitchen, to the contentment of her husband and the amazement of all neighbors. She had a nimble wit that made her more companionable than many who excelled as housewives. She had, too, a sharp tongue, and those who criticized took care to do it furtively. In height, she was small—five feet two—a good twelve inches shorter than her husband. Her coloring was Scotch—blue eyes, fair skin, brown hair.

During the first years of her husband's absence, Frances Hall remained at Cotton Grove, the family plantation. Leigh was the man of the family and was consulted on the management of the plantation before he reached his teens. His brothers, Dick, Jim, and Will, looked up to him. Towards little Frank he acted like a father. During the war, the home was burned and the family found refuge with relatives. There was no longer occasion for Leigh to give advice to a mother who preferred flowerbeds and poetry to accounts of the plantation. The time had come for him to leave her whimsical and tender tutelage for the regimen of his grandfather at Lenoir.

The Reverend Jesse Rankin, theologian and disciplinarian, believed instruction should be formal. At the manse, Leigh was initiated into the routine of academic learning. When he raised his eyes from his book in the evening, it was to listen to talk of the discipline of this world which was a necessary preparation for the next. His grandfather and his Uncle Nat discussed with gusto problems of education. What he understood of their conversations, he disagreed with. He knew that he and his brothers were not alike and that his mother accorded individual treatment to each son. In small matters, she was lenient. From the vantage point of an interested witness, he decided that it was well to spare the child from being spoiled by the rod.

Sometimes pupil and elderly preceptor climbed the Nuntahula Mountains, Leigh outdistancing the portly minister who puffed behind.

"My son," warned the grandfather, "you will live to see a day when you are afraid of that which is high."

Very well! Till then, the boy would climb. If one must come at last to feel black fear and choose to sit securely in the shadow of a mountain, he would at least have gathered first arbutus and found an eagle's nest.

There was much church-going, and more condemnation of evil than praise of good. Leigh was chilled by a glimpse of the theology of Calvin. He did not like the God worshipped by his uncle, his grandsire, and his austere aunts. He did not like to sit straight in a pew and hear of punishments when there were blessings in the out-of-doors. The boy's world that he knew, he loved: sunshine and bird-song, mountain streams with leaping trout, ponies that nuzzled soft noses up and down his sleeve and begged for sugar, colts that flung high their heads to sniff the morning, kicked and scampered to show that life was good. They knew better than to eat too much—these animals. They never theorized. When they were old enough, they submitted to saddles and to shafts. Leigh Hall, unfavorably and irreverently, compared them to his uncle and grandfather.

He achieved at Lenoir, none too willingly, some knowledge

of the classics. He came to appreciate much that was good in literature. For Robert Burns he developed true devotion. The Scotch poet loved animals, even a little mouse, and, more than other animals, Burns loved the highest of the creatures, man —the essence of man, the honest worth beneath gewgaws of dress and rank. The boy understood the joy of the cotter returning from the fields. He would have a home too—a home to sleep in. There were a hundred things to do in the daytime, and he had inclinations for them all. At day's end Burns, Tom Moore, and Byron would be good to read in lamplight before a drowsing fire. They had a way, somehow, of making a fellow see beyond the walls. They made him look at things within that he had thought familiar and see these things as strange, sometimes as beautiful.

Songs were like that. He could sing "Flow Gently, Sweet Afton" and "Annie Laurie" with the rest, but when he tried the songs of the clansmen, the Paisley blood, the Moore and Mebane strains that mingled in his veins, ran hot, his auburn hair flamed to an aureole. When the spell cracked, life flattened into dullness. He learned "I'm a Pilgrim and I'm a Stranger." It meant little then, but in years to come it echoed and re-echoed and supplied the vagrant rhythm of his life.

Arduously, he penned his compositions for Uncle Nat. It was only Brother Dick who was studious. For Leigh, the schoolroom tasks were painful and unnecessary. Punishments were frequent. He was thrashed for laughing on the Sabbath, since Seventhday joy was an emotion most untimely. Finally, he begged that he be sent home and Brother Dick sent to replace him.

Ed and Martha, freed slaves, and all his dogs, ran out to welcome him. In the doorway stood his mother. The days passed pleasantly. While "Fan" read, or worked in helter-skelter fashion in her garden, Martha cooked and at irregular intervals placed excellent food upon the table. Ed hunted and fished with Leigh and Dick, and told the smaller brothers stories of Cotton Grove when it was in its glory. There was work to be done, but this offered only an exchange of physical routine for the mental discipline of Lenoir. Yet for a season home was sweet—the gently wayward garden of his mother, good talk in firelight,

[6]

hunting in the rose of early dawn. These, he could see, made satisfying the small world of his young brothers.

Leigh had what they had and, in addition, the zest of leadership. This was his natural gift, innate and owing nothing to seniority. He could outdare them all. None rode so well. None shot so quickly and with so true an aim. None equalled him in trailing and taking directions from the language of the forest. He could be tender when there were ugly accidents, could tell amusing stories to a brother who was ill, could rock the boys with laughter by his mimicry. Wherever Leigh was, things happened. In the center of every group bobbed his dominant red head.

His father aspired to make of him a physician. His grandfather regretted that the boy had no inclination for the ministry. His mother regarded him in silence, thinking of the family's soldier-blood, and of stories that, reluctantly, her husband told of waste of battle fields. Leigh was the eldest, and he was of the breed of pioneers. Pennsylvania, North Carolina, Tennessee had known the prowess of his forebears. His period was one of nostalgic longing for the largesse and indolence of days before the war, but this boy was hopelessly alien to reminiscence. He was of today and of tomorrow. Of memories, he cherished none, and he fashioned no dreams of rainbow's end. His blue-gray eyes looked straight to far horizons. Nothing they encountered was so dramatic, so compellingly promising, as the flaming colors of the sunset. Such colors taunted with their ribald vigor the faintly pretty posies of his mother's garden. They lured him and they challenged, and Leigh Hall's eyes followed the golden streamers that sped among the clouds from the great flaming ball that found the world too tame, too wearily quiescent, and left it quickly, carrying lucent glory far into the west. And for a little while it seemed a patch of western light had lingered on the boy's young head as though to mark him for its own.

Surely he had been touched, for day and night his thoughts were western thoughts. And the call he heard was a call as clear as the one that had come to the Presbyterian who was his grandsire. It was a call to the West, to Texas, where life that was free and fresh could be had for the asking; where life that was old and vapid could be a thing forgotten; where fortunes could be made and where mere living was itself the greatest fortune. Leigh Hall was not yet twenty, but a boy matured soon in the period that followed on the war and could depend on danger to bring him early to full stature. Danger there was to be in plenty in Texas in the smoking seventies. In 1869, Leigh Hall went forth to meet it.

II
"G— T— T—"
(1869-1873)

When all the world is young, lads,
And all the trees are green,
With every goose a swan, lads,
And every lass a queen,
Then, Hey for boot and horse, lads,
And round the world away,
Young blood will have its course, lads,
And every dog his day.

—Charles Kingsley

II

"G——— T——— T———"

WHEN LEIGH HALL left North Carolina, "G———T———T———"
was the commonly used phrase that stood for "Gone to Texas."
It was a phrase that shut off questions, explained why a warrant could not be served, why a family lacked news of an errant
son. To some, Texas offered largesse for the future; to some, it
promised oblivion for the past. In an earlier century, Spaniards
had searched the land for gold and silver, and the French had
striven to replenish from its wealth the war-lean treasury of the
Bourbons. Priests of both countries dared its dangers to redeem
lost souls. The treasure and the lost souls still remained.

Leigh Hall, on his dusty journey, thought of its vivid history,
of how it had shaken off the shackles of old Mexico to pursue
its course as a proud republic; of how it had become one of the
United States of America, only to separate from these at the
time of the Civil War; of how it had opposed the Union with
troops difficult to discipline but fired with Confederate zeal.
Now in the post-war period, he knew the state was keenly suffering the pangs of reconstruction. Never before had it so needed
able citizens.

Perhaps because a slender purse called "Halt!" Leigh Hall,
after crossing the Red River, began his career in the northeast frontier. The nineteen-year-old North Carolinian became a
schoolmaster in Grayson County. Young tow-heads, who under
his direction studied *Webster's Blue-back Speller, McGuffey's
Readers, Ray's Mental Arithmetic,* wondered whether they
would grow to be as strong and handsome as Leigh Hall. Their
sisters parsed sentences from *Smith's Grammar,* wrinkled their
pretty foreheads over problems in *Monteith's Algebra,* and

[11]

hoped he would insist on instruction after school. Parents, spelling out the signature at the end of the schoolmaster's bills, pronounced his name "Lay Hall." Forthwith he changed the spelling to L-E-E. He was not a man to be labeled with a supine cognomen. Many with inclinations less innocent were changing both Christian and surnames. Such men did not remain in one place long enough to acquire nicknames. Lee did. His wavy, colorful hair marked him as "Red" Hall, and his reputation made the name appropriate.

It was a reputation speedily acquired. During the two years of his teaching he often gave assistance to peace officers, and then left his school to become City Marshal of Sherman. It was a county seat admirably located for the realization of his ambitions. Depredations by Indians across Red River were constant. Fugitives, arriving at the terminus of the railroad, regarded Grayson County as their particular Land's End. The strapping newcomer, unencumbered with family, dowered with a clear head and a steady aim, was the right man in the right place. As law officer, he dealt constantly with men who traveled their fastest "to keep the news behind them," and, if this was not fast enough, exchanged gunshots instead of explanations. From tar heels to the top of his Stetson-covered head, the North Carolinian preferred John Law to John Bullet. He recognized, none the less, that sometimes the latter had jurisdiction. On such occasions his aim was prompt and true. His story is not of arms and the man, but rather of the man whose arms were a necessary auxiliary.

The life of the county revolved around the county seat, the life of Sherman, around Court House Square. At its center stood the most imposing of its citizens, the big Negro who guarded the portals of justice and twirled their keys with ruminative majesty. From his point of vantage he saw pass and repass city fathers, desperadoes, and the poke bonnets and bustles that obscured housewife and harlot. Above the crowd he could pick out with ease the Stetson of Lee Hall. Often the crowd around an auction or medicine show overflowed plank sidewalks and spilled into the Square. Boys in homespun and ragged little darkies stopped to listen.[1] Gamblers, loan sharks, and certain furtive gentry with shifty eyes, sped on. The big Negro noted that their pace was always accelerated when they caught sight of the City Marshal. He noted, too, that sunbonnets turned, like sunflowers to the sun, in Hall's direction, that small boys cocked their hats at a Lee Hall angle. Even in a crowd, no one jostled this gentleman from North Carolina. The very pigs, lazy and fat from gutter-pilferings, allowed clear passage to the well shined boots of young Red Hall. Unobtrusive as he tried to be, he created more attention than the last horse added to the common hitching frame, though the whinnying of fifty roans and pintos gave notice of the horse's coming. Sleepy men in wagons heavy with lumber from the northern timber belt, and cowboys driving cattle from the prairies to the south noted his presence with satisfaction. Lumber, cattle—these were true wealth that attracted those who toiled not, yet gained from the toil of others. When changed to specie, lumber and cattle were "easy pickings" for light-fingered gentry from the older states.

In such dubious characters Lee Hall exhibited an interest amply reciprocated. More than once the "tin horn gamblers" thought they had his "name in the pot." In 1871, a certain J. D. Whitney attempted assassination. For seven years the assailant escaped justice. He scarcely met it when he was sentenced to two years.[2]

Three Sherman papers, the *Courier, Register,* and *Weekly Patriot,* chronicled Hall's activities and the bad luck of the men who occasioned them.[3] The editor of the *Gainesville Gazette* described him as "intelligent, shrewd, sociable," and possessed of extraordinary qualifications for detection and arrest.[4] Loungers in tilted chairs at Binkley House watched the tall Marshal stride by with careless grace and seeming negligence, told of his trigger-quick reactions, nodded approval of stories of his bravery,

[1] Edward King, *The Great South* (Serialized in *Scribner's Magazine,* 1874; published in book form by American Publishing Company, Hartford, 1875), 1180.
[2] *The Daily Democratic Statesman,* Austin, Texas, May 5, 1878.
[3] James L. Rock and W. I. Smith, *Guide to Southern and Western Texas* (St. Louis, A. H. Granger, 1878).
[4] Quoted in *The Denison Weekly News,* August 14, 1873.

boasted that he had the riff raff "jumping down the trail at the toe of his boot."

The City Marshal of Sherman was bone-seasoned for later work, winning in the process the reputation of a man of mettle who could not be "cold-decked." Already he knew and was contributing to the code of the southwest: he did not shoot from ambush; he knew better than to linger in saloons, where to refuse a drink was rejection of frontier courtesy, and to accept too many caused a loosening of the tongue; he staged his arrests far from the vision of womenfolk; he preferred solo work to the chorus of a *posse comitatus*; he was modest, close-lipped. Already he could qualify as a wheel horse, a true-steel "Texian."

III
Railroads Bring Civilization
(1873-1874)

"The sheriff followed hard and fast,
a muy hombre *he."*

III

Railroads Bring Civilization

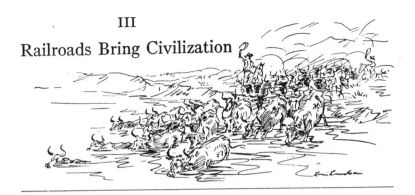

FROM HIS OFFICE of City Marshal of Sherman, Lee Hall was advanced, in 1873, to the office of Deputy Sheriff of Dension, where "top hands" for the herding and cutting out of criminals were as badly needed as in any locality within the state. The year before Lee's arrival, the Denison Townsite Company had used a rowel spur on competition by offering free right-of-way, lands for commercial trackage, switchyards and machine shops to the first railroad company that would run a train over its own tracks into the "city limits." Thereupon, the Houston and Texas Central set a thousand men to laying tracks from Houston. The Missouri, Kansas and Texas set another thousand to rush its line through from Sedalia. It was the latter, the "Katy," that entered Denison first. Tooting across the bridge that newly spanned Red River, bell ringing, whistle screaming, smoke belching from wood-burning locomotive, and with proud Pat Tobin in the cab, Number 15 entered Denison. From his locomotive Pat looked out on a wooded tract and grass-land that soon would be a town. Band music resounded and speeches waked the echoes, for no man failed to recognize the significance of the straight-backed Grant engine drawing baggage-express car, day-coaches, and a single Pullman.[1]

It was civilization, open-throttled, making its advance.

When Lee Hall took office, the town had been incorporated and was advertising itself as the "Gateway to Texas"—gate-

---

[1] W. W. Hornbeck, "Big Celebration at Denison in 1874," *Frontier Times* (Bandera, Texas), December, 1936; "Arrival of First Train in Denison," *op. cit.,* April, 1933; C. M. Hammond, "How Railroads Peopled Texas," quoted in *Frontier Times,* May, 1933, from *The Texas Weekly.*

[17]

way to freedom, gateway to opportunity, to license, to adventure. Many men of many minds were in search of gateways. In September, 1873, the banking house of Jay Cooke suspended payment, and lesser banks throughout the nation had to follow suit—as sequel to the railroad and banking rivalry of Gould and Vanderbilt. In New York, legislators and judges had been bribed and a private militia organized. Whichever captain of industry might win, it was in the cards that the people would lose. The depression that followed threw hundreds of thousands out of work. Industry had balked. A short corn crop in the Mississippi states increased the woes of cattle breeders. In short, the great westward movement had received a striking impetus. Texas gained citizens.[2]

They came at a time when northers were unusually severe and unusually frequent. Lee Hall was far too busy to discuss with the loafers the effects of the weather. He knew that stock loss was heavy, that men were butchering beef cattle for hides, horns, and tallow. His business was to keep down recklessness bred by want and disaster. The multitude that entered Denison could be divided into two groups—those who needed protection, and those who needed watching. Some strays were as helpless as any sad-eyed, kettle-bellied, little dogie struggling to get his share and crushed by the herds that milled around the waterholes. These human dogies were most pathetic and necessitous when they attempted the bravado of shootin' irons and the tall talk of frontiersmen. Towns like Denison, "at the end of steel," had the common characteristic of a flourishing cemetery for those who made their exit informally and rapidly. "Boot Hill" became the permanent address, alike, of the brave and the cowardly.

From April to November was a busy season for Lee Hall, for then a dozen or so herds awaited shipment; and the men who had driven them in from below Gonzales, from the San Antonio country, and Fredericksburg, were prankish and guileless. Gamblers, knowing that Denison was the only distributing point in Texas with railroad pens, chose the town as head-

2 W. MacL. Raine and W. C. Barnes, *Cattle* (New York, Doubleday, Doran and Co., 1930), 153.

[18]

quarters. They were eager to assist in celebrations staged at the end of the trail. Sometimes the gains of the sharpers were postponed by the cowboys' awesome interest in the oratory of the Diamond King. Enthroned in his wagon, the "King" praised the cure-alls that had won him friendship on a social scale ascending from lone sheep herders to the president of Mexico. Buttons of ten- and twenty-dollar gold pieces shone against the scarlet velvet of the "King's" apparel. They would have made excellent targets, but men respected the curious prejudice Lee Hall exhibited against the shooting up of shows. When the medicine man of the Great Mohawk Herb Remedy was in town, the cowboys fared better. Negro minstrels played "tooth-pulling tunes" to drown the cries of the victims of the unctuous professor's dentistry. Sometimes the cowboys egged on a farmer to try to get his money back, and rejoiced themselves with a good sized ruckus. Sometimes there was a chance to see what acting really was. Westerners, who knew not Byron, still approached him by memories of imitations of Ada Mencken in "Mazeppa's Ride." But the shows were over while yet the night was young.

It was in places less public and more lurid that Lee Hall searched for wanted men. Saloons with women in them, dance and gambling houses, were demanded as civic rights, and with tumultuous gusto the demand was supplied. Three notorious resorts—the Palace, the Park, and the Sazerack[3]—made one back street a bedlam. The Sazerack was run by the unholy team of Red Joe and Rowdy Kate. Their place had been burned out by the soldiers in Wichita—customers usually of unbounded tolerance. On the other side of the railroad tracks were houses of prostitution. Choctaws drifted in from the lands across Red River to mingle in dingle-dangle theatres with avid, pleasure-seeking whites. Bootleggers were everywhere, filth of the off-scourings, eager to contract for the sale of murderous "white mule." Bad men in Denison were "thick as fiddlers in hell," and heavy odds gave zest to the struggle to maintain the law.

Prosperity was garishly apparent; peace and propriety delayed their advent. The Denison Townsite Company in its first

[3] Major A. B. Ostrander, "Old Days in Denison," *Frontier Times*, June, 1930.

two years sold $90,000 worth of building lots. Demand for lumber rushed the loading of freight trains hundreds of miles away. The planks were used for homes within the town and in the fertile farming country for which the town was an outlet.[4] If the land was to be made a good land, homes must be built and homes protected. It was a problem often pondered, and never more anxiously than when Hall shared a hotel room with an assorted group of strangers. The hastily clapboarded buildings with their leaky roofs engendered the wish for home and fireside. Marriage was a frequent ceremony. Brides were at a premium. A comely waitress, before she had soiled her first white apron, could be expected to pin store orange blossoms in her hair. The pink-frilled bareback riders in Mollie Bailie's circus deserted to become prim matrons. They swept and garnished their little homes of one story, and carried market baskets into stores that proudly reared their fronts a story-and-a-half, but from the rear revealed the "half" to be a gross deception.

The advent of the Texas Central increased the sheriff's problem. The road connected Denison with the great route to the south and ended the career of rival Red River City. Roustabouts from there increased the number of undesirables in Denison. They boasted with the earlier citizens that the Gulf of Mexico and the Atlantic and the Pacific Oceans were now connected by road and wire with Denison![5] Lee Hall viewed the road's coming with less opulent vision. He could see that the sprawling freight houses were wrenched and twisted by their added merchandise, as though they writhed in the birth throes of prosperity; that loan sharks and terminus gamblers plied their trades with greater profits. The new road was always months behind with pay. Its men cashed their checks for what they could and tried to even up by wooing Lady Luck. The town was wide open, running full tilt, as if it knew the vivid present would dim into a stable, placid future.

To Edward King, visiting the place in 1873 to write of it

---

[4] Edward King, *The Great South*, 175-77.

[5] F. M. McCaleb, "Happenings in Texas Sixty Years Ago," quoted in *Frontier Times*, May, 1935, from *San Antonio Express*.

for *Scribner's* in "The Great South," Lee Hall stood out as one of the town's chief wonders. King had him sketched by the artist, J. Wells Champney, and recorded with gusto his activities. Hall had just captured a horse-thief, who with two companions, armed to the teeth, were waiting for the ferry at Red River. So many times had Hall been assaulted from ambush that King believed his life was charmed. His enemies, since they could not kill him, conspired to deprive him of office. One morning, Hall was awakened by the prodding of a pistol, to find himself surrounded by armed men and confronted by a warrant served at the instance of the United States Marshal. He was detained only till afternoon when the Marshal, satisfied that the charges were false, restored him to authority. All of these events *Scribner's* recounted for its readers.[6]

One story of Denison days, Hall himself related: Men calling themselves buffalo hunters were terrorizing the nearby ranches. Hall gathered together a posse, "neither hipped nor crippled," and pursued. During the chase, his party clambered through the brush to the top of a low hill. There, silhouetted against the sky, they saw a line of motionless Comanches! The braves were riding half-wild horses, bridled and bitted with rawhide. Their bows were of Osage orange wood and their lances of ash. For greater execution some carried bowie knives and Mexican machetes. On their faces were daubs of paint and streaks of clay. The whites reined in their horses in amazement. Both sides were tensely quiet. A little breeze stirred the stiff feathers in war bonnets. The rustling sounded ominous. Suddenly Hall on his gaited thoroughbred shot out full tilt towards the Comanches. The Indians were so amazed that no man aimed his arrow. Riding low in the saddle, the sheriff circled the foremost warrior and galloped back unscathed to his posse. Long afterward Hall explained that his bravery was unintentional. His Kentucky mare had never before been close to Indians. When she smelled them, she bolted.[7]

The *Denison News* chronicled deeds of more genuine brav-

---

6 King, *op. cit.*, 178-79.
7 The story has been retold by Jeff Davis in his column "Around the Plaza," *San Antonio Daily Light,* July 26, 1935.

ery; Deputy Sheriff Hall had returned from Muskogee in the Nation, where he had "put the cuffs" on W. A. I. Posey, mule thief and fratricide; Hall was in from Jack County where he had captured two horse thieves wanted in Denison; he had brought back from the Choctaw Nation a man who, behind the shelter of a horse, had tried to fight it out. On one raw day in November he returned to Denison bringing one prisoner from Dallas, one from Austin, and a certain Charlie Williams from New Orleans, to which city the latter had fled after attempting the life of Hall.[8]

Sometimes the Deputy Sheriff stalked his man for months. One of his hunts took him to Little Rock, which, he had learned by grapevine telegraph, was the hiding place of a notorious outlaw. Rather than wait for extradition papers and risk the claiming of the reward by Arkansas officials, Hall undertook the capture by himself. He left Denison in a buggy, and on reaching Little Rock captured his man. With one handcuff he coupled the prisoner's right hand to his own left, and with the other he fastened the prisoner's left hand to the side of the buggy. United in such twinship, and keeping a lookout for attempts at rescue, he drove day and night until he had his man across the state line at Texarkana. There he saw his prisoner jailed, found a bed, and slept the clock round.[9]

On another occasion when he had trouble in making a capture, a man under many indictments sent word that he would meet Lee Hall for a duel on horseback. "Red" accepted; when he had dismounted his adversary, the man challenged him to fight on foot. Al Jennings says that he accepted. The shooting attracted to the scene two cowboys. They found Hall unconscious, his horse standing sentinel beside him. In front lay the desperado—dead.[10]

[8] *Denison News,* issues of April 3, July 3, and November 14, 1873; February 28, April 21, and August 13, 1874. The story of the outlaw who attacked from behind his horse is told in *Glamorous Days,* by Frank Bushick (San Antonio, Naylor Publishing Co., 1934); also in Hall's obituary, *San Antonio Express,* March 18, 1911.

[9] This story was repeated to me by Captain Hall's daughter, Mrs. Isham Keith, who had it from her father himself.

[10] N. A. Jennings, "Lee Hall, Fighting Man," *Saturday Evening Post,* January, 1900.

The Deputy Sheriff learned a needed lesson from this incident, and another from Mike Gormly and his band. Mike and his men had arranged to meet at Widow McCoy's in the Chickasaw Nation, twenty miles from Red River on the Tishomingo Road. In the gray of dawn, "Red" Hall stationed his men near the house. With one companion he began his watch. Scarcely had they taken their positions when Gormly and three desperadoes, double armed with six-shooters, rose from the brush some sixty steps behind. Hall covered Gormly with a Winchester. His companion took aim at one of the others. Both fired and Gormly fell. More shots and the outlaws fled, Hall and his posse pursuing. The Sheriff proved with gory certainty the value of his .44 center-fire Winchester, but he lost Gormly who was carried from the field by a brother outlaw. On the tablets of his memory Hall indited a new maxim: Don't leave a wounded mountain lion and run after coyotes.

On his way back from this fracas, he had an experience of a different sort—the capture of a thief, fresh from robbing the till at Maupin's store. The man was half insane from terror, eyes twitching, face like wax, and dank hair matted black upon his forehead. With a quick movement, the thief raised a bottle of morphine to his lips and drained it.[11] He was young in crime. Hall watched him die in agony and felt remorse that he had not managed to see the man alone and gain his confidence. The memory of the self-imposed death sentence caused the peace officer in later years to use, sometimes, the method of persuasion. Words that were exchanged in midnight conferences were not revealed by Hall, but men to whom he had given a second chance were less reticent, and reports of his reforming efforts reached the press.

By many, leniency was not regarded as a virtue. At the time that Hall turned over the member of an outlaw band to the guard at Collinsville, the *Dallas Herald* stated that there had been no news of the man's detention and surmised that his thieving days were over. The *Herald* advocated recruiting of minute men and the stretching of some necks. Due to confi-

[11] The fracas with Gormly and his men, and the escape by suicide, are chronicled in *The Denison News*, June 6, 1874.

dence in Hall and his kind, this advice was disregarded. The conviction was formed—and the conviction endured—that when the Deputy Sheriff went after a man, he got him.

As for Denison when Edward King paid it a second visit in 1874, citizens pointed out an "opry house" and churches, and invited him to attend Sunday service. He told the readers of *Scribner's* that the place could not again be called "the worst town in East Texas."[12]

In truth, the times were changing. Richard Coke's inauguration in January, 1874, ended the dictatorial régime of Governor Davis, strongest of the carpetbaggers. The State hoped to assure, through its laws, its judges, and the bravery of its officers, security of person and of property. For this, there was need of scores of men of such caliber as Lee Hall.

In October, 1874, the Deputy Sheriff was in Denison when President Grant, General Sherman, General Augur, and General Babcock, "ventured across the dead line" and visited Texas. They had come to study the condition of frontier defenses.[13] There followed organization of scouting expeditions under General Shafter. Lee Hall began hearing of the work of a company of Negro-Seminoles commanded by Lieutenant John L. Bullis. Surveys were made and an account of springs, lakes, and water-roads was submitted to the adjutant general of the newly created Department of Texas.[14] At last it was recognized by the federal government that redemption was too great a task to be accomplished alone by a state that was overburdened with criminals from outside its borders. Texans welcomed the promise of Uncle Sam's assistance, but they realized, also, that their own men had certain advantages over the men in uniform. Austin was closer than Washington, and its executive could be more safely depended upon to give support.

After 1874 the coöperation of scout, commander, and peace

12 King, *op. cit.*, 181.

13 W. A. Adair, "Denison, Wild Town in 1872," *Frontier Times*, February, 1930. *The Dallas News*, October 13, 1874. The article quotes the account of the visit of President Grant and his party.

14 Colonel M. L. Crimmins, "The Twenty-fourth Infantry in Texas," and "Shafter's Exploration in Western Texas, 1875," *West Texas Historical Association Year Book*, October, 1933.

officer was needed less on the banks of the Red River than on the border of the Rio Grande. Denison yielded priority in crime and the trail of danger led southward. With a few belongings, and the refrain of an old song on his lips, Red Hall set out. Again he was a pilgrim, again, a wanderer.

IV
Smoke of the Seventies
(1874-1876)

"The men who made Texas
Rode West with dazzled eyes
On the hot trail of the Future,
To take her by surprise:

. . . .
. . . .

"Old men and young men, little men and tall,
Bad men and good men—but strong men all."

—KARLE WILSON BAKER
"Song of the Forerunners."

Smoke of the Seventies

THE WORK of carrying the law into the domain of the ranch-men, into the mushroom construction camps that forged ahead of railroads, and into the matted bosque on the Rio Grande, was not work to be done in the space of three cigarettes.

On his journey south from Denison, Lee Hall found that a reputation for straight shooting and fair dealing had preceded him. His prowess was known to gentry more important than the mouthers of cowboy windies, since, over four others, he was elected Sergeant-at-Arms of the Twentieth Legislature.[1] The sessions of the spring and summer of 1876 were held under the small dome of the simple old Capitol facing south on a knoll bisecting Congress Avenue. Standing in its portico, Hall faced the Colorado and looked beyond it to blue hills that merged into a bluer sky. On one side stood the Governor's mansion, where many times the Sergeant-at-Arms was entertained. On the other, was the old Land Office, where his brother was to serve as commissioner and give employment to an odd young stripling, famous later as "O. Henry."

To reach the chamber, Hall ascended a flight of stairs and passed a grim monument recording the heroism of defenders of the Alamo. Inside the chamber, he observed and appraised the law makers.

Ranged into semicircular ranks, they presented a picture decorously somber: string ties of black, black suits, pants laxly wrinkled over legislative paunches, or, on the rangy men of the plains, held taut by galluses that could be thumped to give re-

---

[1] *Daily Democratic Statesman*, April 19, 1876.

sounding emphasis to oratory. Men from east Texas were better tailored and conscious of amenities marking the progress of their districts upward from the level of pioneer settlements. Much tobacco was used. Hall watched the solons' skill and energy in masticating and expectorating. He was man enough to overlook quiddities and oddities and, in addition to the fools and knaves, he recognized the presence of fine men—men who were brilliant and spoke much, and men who were silent—prudent, thoughtful men, who registered wisdom in committee rooms and by their votes.

The legislators considered the problem of security. Hitherto, Texas had been less able than Wells Fargo to make good the property losses of its citizens.[2] Nor had it adequately protected human life.

Lee Hall heard much of commissions sent in 1872 and 1873 by the United States to investigate border claims of theft of stock, and of the alarming figures, sworn to by scores of reputable citizens, which they accepted. The commissions held that local civil authorities were effete, corrupt, and powerless; that on the frontier demoralization was complete; that legislation on the part of the Republic of Mexico was unfriendly; that the *Zona Libre* was a zone for the free deposit and trans-shipment of smuggled goods; that General Juan Cortina, commander of the Mexican line of the Rio Grande since 1870, had established a venal and anti-American dictatorship.[3]

What was the *Zona Libre?* And who was General Cortina? It was only because Hall was fresh from north Texas that he did not know. The *Zona Libre* was a stretch of land on the farther side of the Rio Grande. From six to eight miles wide and five hundred long, it had been established in the fifties by a

[2] From 1870 to 1884, customers of Wells Fargo lost to highwaymen and train robbers $415,312. The company made good these losses. See Neill C. Wilson, *Treasure Express* (New York, Macmillan, 1936).

[3] *House Exec. Doc. 257, Series No. 1615, 43 Cong., 1 sess., Final Report of the U. S. Commission to Texas, Depredations on the Frontiers of Texas,* May 26, 1874; *Misc. Doc. No. 64, Serial No. 1820, 45 Cong., 2 sess., 1878, Testimony taken by Commission on Military Affairs in Relation to the Texas Border Troubles.* This latter document will be referred to hereafter as *House Misc. Doc. No. 64.* Summaries of the reports of the U. S. Committee and the Mexican Committee of Investigation in *Twentieth Century History of Southwest Texas* (Chicago, Lewis Publishing Co., 1907), I.

Mexican rebel of Tamaulipas, assisted by interested Texans. As a result, traffic in the district was customs free. The zone attracted smugglers and raiders, and served as a refuge for criminals.

General Cortina (Juan Nepomuceno Cortina) was the most successful of those descendants of Spanish grandees, who, in defiance of all treaties, still claimed Texas territory. His boast was that he held true title to the land between the Rio Grande and Nueces rivers. In 1870, a million steers ranged there, and Cortina and his bravos—his *muchachos*—asserted these were the cattle of his grandmother. Regularly his raiders rounded up "Nanita's" cattle, good steers of King and Kennedy branding that grazed in the triangle bounded by the Gulf and the two rivers. For himself, as inexorably as any Spanish viceroy, he levied the *quinta,* or royal fifth. At various times he held Matamoros, Brownsville, and Corpus Christi, and raided as far as the San Antonio River. He flew the Mexican flag on Texas soil, stocked four *ranchos* with Texas cattle, and shipped "wet stock" to Havana for the provisioning of Spanish troops.[4]

The claims of the United States commissions were countered by those of Mexico. Not denying the crimes of its citizens, the commissioners of Mexico placed responsibility on citizens of the United States: American citizens of Mexican blood interfered in Mexican politics; under the patronage of influential statesmen, Texas traders at regular intervals for twenty-five years had collected droves of horses, systematically stolen by organized bands from Mexico, and they had branded hundreds of head of cattle, abandoned during the Civil War—cattle to which they had no title. The Mexicans claimed that their countrymen suffered from the antipathy and persecution of Texans; that certain counties in Texas, notably DeWitt, Goliad, Karnes,

---

[4] *House Report No. 701, Serial No. 1824, 45 Cong., 2 sess., Report and Accompanying Documents of the Committee on Foreign Affairs on the Relation of the United States with Mexico.* This document will be referred to hereafter as *House Report No. 701.* Accuracy is difficult to attain in dealing with Cortina, or Cortinas, for he signed his proclamations variously, and cannot certainly be said to be a citizen of the United States or of Mexico. Truth and legend blend in tales of him. He was not a personage who could be remembered objectively. Recommended as escaping customary inaccuracy is F. C. Pierce's *Brief History of the Lower Rio Grande Valley* (Menasha, Wisconsin, 1917).

and Victoria, abounded in criminals to such an extent that the public press admitted the need of vigilance committees. To be a stock raiser in Texas, the committee averred, was to have a passport for robbery, since any cattleman could sell entire herds in which his brand could not be found.

As for the northern Rio Grande country, Mexican commissioners declared that there the Indians had been thrust back upon the frontier and forced to prey upon the *haciendas* for their livelihood. Raids from the Mexican side, allegedly by Lipans, Kickapoos, and Comanches, the commissioners claimed were raids of American bandits in Indian disguise.[5]

In part, the Mexicans were right. A former Ranger, Captain Dan Roberts, states that many came to Texas who, not owning cattle, made their wealth by thefts carried out by their rustlers. Such thieves and their *juntas* were too powerful to be intimidated by the civil authorities.[6] Equipped with branding irons, shooting irons, and rope, these long-loop men could be disciplined solely through the use of force. Only a fool or a very brave man would have dared to question ownership of such herds as those of Shanghai Pierce. State legislators knew that he had contracted with the Cuban Government for the delivery of 100,000 head of bulls for the provisioning of its army. Because the moss-horned cattle proved too tough, Cubans refused to carry out a contract endangering international good will.[7] Even without this his activities within the state "resulted in a small war." Rival ranchmen developed into feudists due to quarrels arising from the employment of gunmen and rustlers to brand on the open range. In addition to law-breakers who pretended to respectability, there were hundreds of outright criminals from older states—too old to leave their past behind.

---

[5] *Un Siglo de Relaciones Internacionales de Mexico (á traves de los mensajes presidenciales), Archivo Historico Diplomatico Mexicano, Publicaciones de la Secretaria de Relaciones Exteriores, Mexico, 1935.* This contains President Carranza's message to the National Congress, September, 1919, listing border raids into Mexico. This message, with the list of raids omitted, appears in *Papers Relating to the Foreign Relations of the U. S., 1919* (Washington Government Printing Office, 1934).

[6] Captain Dan Roberts, *Rangers and Sovereignty*, 143.

[7] Owen P. White, *Them Was the Days* (New York, Minton, Balch and Co., 1925).

The answer to the international problem and to the civil problem was the Ranger. Such men as had served in her companies before, Texas wished to bring again into her service—hoping not so much to revive the old as to salvage all that was good and weld a new force capable of making precedents. In 1874 a bill was passed for the reorganization and maintenance of regularly constituted Rangers for frontier defense. Major John B. Jones of Corsicana, veteran of the Civil War, was made commander and recruited six companies of seventy-five men each—the Frontier Battalion of Texas Rangers. Its duty was to protect the Texas frontier from Jacksboro in Jack County to the Rio Grande, a distance of six hundred miles.[8]

Much of the danger in this stretch of territory was due to the Comanches, who raided from the west, and to the Lipans and Apaches, who raided into Texas from their hunting grounds in *Tierra Desconocida*, south of the Big Bend, and from their reservations in the Territory. This unknown country had only a single village, San Carlos, on the Rio Grande.[9] Kickapoos, on a peaceful journey from their reservation to Mexico in 1864, had been mistaken for a raiding party and attacked at Dove Creek by the Southern troops.[10] Other Indians took up their grievance and added it to loss of land, destruction of buffalo, and denial of the privilege of taking for themselves longhorns and mustangs. At the time of full moon, they raided. For preliminary spy work in locating desirable Texas herds and *caballadas*, for the furnishing of relays, and places of refuge, they depended on Mexicans. The two races had a common hatred for the conquering "gringos." It was the Americans who had limited Indians to the confines of reservations, and, by the treaty of 1848, had deprived Mexican border towns of their common lands for grazing.

Criminals, who entered Texas from the older states, consti-

---

[8] H. S. Thrall, *A Pictorial History of Texas* (St. Louis, Thomas & Co., 1879), 437-38; J. M. Callahan, *American Foreign Policy in Mexican Relations* (New York, Macmillan Co., 1932), x, xi.

[9] Irving Stahala, quoting Ranger Will Snearly in "Living Forty Days," *Dallas News*, December 18, 1932.

[10] King, *The Great South*, 168-170; Roberts, *op. cit.*, 55-56. J. B. Gillett, *Six Years with the Texas Rangers* (New Haven, Yale University Press, 1925), 17.

[33]

tuted the second source of trouble in the territory to be policed by the Frontier Battalion. At the beginning of Coke's campaign for law enforcement, three thousand men were listed as fugitives from justice. By January, 1876, seventeen hundred of these had been imprisoned, but additions were so rapidly made that the next year's list had expanded to five thousand. Of these, about 250 were Texans. Governor Hubbard increased the offer of rewards to a maximum of $10,000.[11] A gray, paper-backed booklet, compiled from information sent by sheriffs to the Adjutant General, was furnished to each camp.[12] The Rangers called it the "Crime Book," sometimes "Bible Two," and studied its descriptions more diligently than its names. For names fluctuated from Thompson, to Smith, to Williams, and Jones, with confusing rapidity. Peculiarities of speech, scars, height, color of eyes, were more dependable.

A Jones by any other name was as sweet to a Ranger, if he could be captured and bring the Jones reward. But to capture Jones was not so simple as to capture an individual. If he was a horse or cattle thief, he was, most probably, one link in a chain that stretched loosely from Mexico to some state that bordered on the Mississippi. The chain was strengthened by the protection of isolated ranchers who trafficked in "wet stock." In three years, 1875 to 1878, it is claimed that no less than 100,000 head of horses were stolen.[13] If Jones was a bank or train robber, he did not travel singly. If he was a murderer, his crime might have been committed in the line of filial duty to a feudist father; or at the behest of a ranchman who wished to rid his range of nesters and the cowboys and bravos of his rival; or simply as an incident necessary for the successful completion of some other crime. Murder and theft were seldom personal. They were institutional.

When a Ranger captured "Jones," his duty was to secure

[11] W. P. Webb, *The Texas Rangers* (New York, Macmillan Co., 1935) ; Frederic Remington, "How the Law Got into the Chaparral," *Harpers New Monthly Magazine*, December, 1896.
[12] Roberts, *op. cit.*, 39; N. A. Jennings, *A Texas Ranger* (New York, Scribner, 1899), 22.
[13] J. Frank Dobie, *A Vaquero of the Brush Country* (Dallas, Southwest Press, 1929), 82. Mr. Dobie gives as authority an early statement in the *Galveston News*.

him against lynching and jail delivery. He had, also, to safeguard the witnesses who could testify against Jones, and to convince them of their safety so that their memories would function. Further, the Rangers occasionally had to police the court, protect the judge during the trial and after adjournment. Whether Jones was captured in a railroad construction camp, in the brush country or in some mountain hide-out, there was always the probability that he would be granted "strawbail" —set at liberty by an intimidated or corrupt official. Sometimes a "writ of rouster," or the forcible decision of "Judge Colt," seemed a better answer to social needs than did recourse to due process of law. There were notorious counties where justice was the best that money could buy!

The order to Rangers, however, was to follow the law. Preferably, each man of the force was to act in response to a *capias*, a legal command to arrest and make due diligence in doing so. In case of necessity, he knew he need not be punctilious. Request for a *capias* often went to the Adjutant General after the arrest had been made. Very seldom did an outlaw quibble over legal forms. He accepted the statement that he was under arrest, or, if desperate, he shot it out.

There were times when he had the laugh on the Rangers by enlisting in one of their companies. He never remained long, for a new fugitive list was sure to appear with a dangerously accurate description. Then before the morning star ascended and the horse wrangler brought in the *remuda*, "Jones" "fanned out" for the Rio Grande.[14] Until he reached the river he was in danger, for Rangers could pursue through as many counties as they wished. They were not impeded, as were sheriffs, by territorial restrictions. Each member of the company had a roving commission that justified his appearance wherever there was need.[15]

Such were the duties and privileges of members of the Frontier Battalion. No citizen of the state doubted the necessity for

---

[14] Eugene Cunningham, "Rangers Tell of Old Days," *Houston Post Dispatch,* October 23, 1927.

[15] White, *op. cit.,* 118-19; N. A. Jennings, *op. cit.,* 110-11.

[35]

its creation. No citizen of the state was more proud of the Battalion than was Lee Hall.

Because of the anarchical condition of DeWitt and adjacent counties, as referred to in the report of the Mexican commissioners, it was enacted that, in addition to the Frontier Battalion, there should be another company. Its fifty men were to be known as Special State Troops and were to operate in the counties mentioned until order had been restored.[16] The second duty was to suppress the Mexican bandits on the southwestern Rio Grande. For if "Jones" was a slippery customer, his Mexican equivalent, "Treviño," was even more so. The odds in the latter's favor were multiplied by a river that treacherously changed its course; by one of the poorest extradition laws on record; and by the connivance and protection of a neighboring people, who regarded the Americans as predatory enemies. All territory bordering the Rio Grande on the Texas side had once belonged to Mexico. Land titles having their origin in royal grants from Spain, the Mexican *hidalgo* still believed to be valid. And even the lowly peons felt shame at the defeat of their country by Texans and by the United States.

The bill creating the Ranger force provided for a "mounted, armed, and movable constabulary"—one "not immediately under nor responsible to county officers" anywhere. Due to difficulties on the border, Governor Coke, in August, 1874, gave his Rangers a right of way still more unique. He ordered that, in consideration of the great loss of life and property during the previous twenty years, these Texas troops, when in "hot pursuit," should cross the Rio Grande for the recovery of stolen property.[17]

The next year, 1875, the Constitutional Convention of Texas memorialized the Federal Congress on border depredations and

[16] Roberts, *op. cit.*, 15. Mrs. G. C. Mayfield, "Oldest Texas Ranger an Englishman," *San Antonio Express*, March 20, 1937.

[17] *Correspondencia diplomatica relativa á las invasiones del territorio Mexicano por fuerza de los estados-unidos de 1873 á 1877* (Mexico, 1878), letter of August 6, 1874, Governor Coke to George Williams, Attorney General of the United States. The Governor's letter is quoted also in J. M. Callahan, *op. cit.* See Chaps. X, XI, for this and references to House Report No. 701, p. 161, and House Report No. 343, pp. 161-167; see also G. L. Rives, "United States and Mexico," *Texas Historical Quarterly, IX*.

atrocities, and on the evil influence of the *Zona Libre,* whereupon the lower house of Congress appointed an investigating committee. Its report in February, 1876, described conditions on the Rio Grande as intolerable, recommended a larger defensive force and authority for its officers to cross in "hot pursuit" of robbers in possession of stolen goods. Congress failed to act upon the recommendations of its committee. As Captain Dan Roberts puts it, the people of Texas did not want to pick a quarrel with as big an *hombre* as Uncle Sam, but they came to realize that his striped trousers did sag on him when there was need of help.[18]

The Special State Troops, on whose bravery security of life and property on the border depended, and on whose discretion maintenance of good relations with Mexico depended, were entrusted to the command of a former Virginian, Captain L. H. McNelly.[19] He had been one of the bravest officers of the Confederacy—a captain at seventeen. Later, under Governor Davis, he commanded the white and Negro State Police. This the Texans forgave, since, though he was in the service, he had shown he was not of it, and on one noteworthy occasion had denied the Governor's need of proclaiming martial law. Captain McNelly was slight and lacked the robust physique expected in a Ranger, but his stamina was proven. A reputation for bravery and skill in leadership enabled him to take his pick of state recruits.

Service was popular. A Ranger was paid forty dollars a month, quarterly—three times, plus, what any private received in the army, and the Ranger, unlike the private, could leave the service on request. Any state captain preferred a depleted company to a full one containing unwilling men. Ranks could be speedily filled, for besides high pay there was the lure of adventure and distinction.[20]

In the nine years since the Civil War, Rangers had not existed.

[18] Roberts, *op. cit.,* 55; Alex. Sweet and J. Amory Knox, *On a Mexican Mustang Through Texas* (Marshalltown, Iowa, Barnes & Ballou, 1884), 538-40.

[19] N. A. Jennings, *A Texas Ranger,* 106-107; Dudley G. Wooten, *A Comprehensive History of Texas* (Dallas, Scarff, 1898), II, 350.

[20] Mrs. L. Roberts (wife of Captain Dan Roberts) *A Woman's Reminiscences of Six Years in Camp with the Texas Rangers* (Austin, Texas); Sarah E. Davidge, "Texas Rangers were Rough and Ready Fighters," *Galveston Tribune,* quoted in *Frontier Times,* November, 1935.

The Captain had the opportunity of making his own pattern for his force. Former service in the Confederate Army caused him to see the benefit of discipline, and he introduced this to a degree greater than usual. He did not believe in praise, but a laconic expression of approval sometimes escaped him, always to be treasured. He regarded his troops as social equals, eating with them, talking with them, permitting them to saunter up and listen when he conferred with army officers. On one requirement he was severe—the men were not to waste ammunition.

From its beginning, the Company was destined for distinction. Debarred by legislators from service east of the Colorado, it found sufficient field for its activities in the vast and turbulent territory to the west. There, each of the Rangers had the right of arrest and the right of summoning good men and true to serve as guides and as members of a *posse comitatus.*

The Company excited the envy of Lee Hall. When its name was mentioned in debate, the young Sergeant-at-Arms forgot that he was in attendance in a legislative chamber. In imagination, he scouted with the Rangers, using the woodlore of his boyhood and the methods of his days in Denison and Sherman. He was a man of the out-of-doors, the mere thought of McNelly's Company seemed to free him from confinement in the little Capitol.

Citizens of the Southwest shared his admiration and hoped that there would always be captains, like McNelly, willing to "play a lone hand and play it strong." Citizens of eastern Texas, whose representatives opposed the creation of the Special Troops, believed distrust was justified by the daring raids McNelly undertook across the Rio Grande. They hoped that other captains would add discretion to such bravery as McNelly's. Rangers must be suave as well as sure. It was due to the breed of men who became Rangers that the dual purpose of the State was realized—that Texas, in the seventies, evolved "an active, potent, and reliable force," the envy of her neighbors.

Of this breed was Lee Hall. Governor Coke was happy to appoint him second lieutenant and assign him to Special State Troops—to McNelly's Company. Before receiving his office on

August 10, 1876, Hall swore that he did not owe his appointment to pecuniary considerations; that he had fought no duels or given assistance to any other so offending; that he would faithfully and impartially discharge his duties and act always in conformity with State and Federal laws.

The oath was more than a form. For the new Lieutenant, its meaning was deeper than its words. The country of which he was a citizen was too vast for him to know and love in its entirety. The oath meant that he would know immediately, and so possess, one part of it—more rocks than rills, woods and their Spanish moss, hills without temples, a land to be made sweet for ordered liberty. And the winds and the rains of southwest Texas, its heady northers, the southern blue of its skies, the virile heat of its sunshine, would give him, in exchange for service rendered, a characer more elemental than that of common men—would take him for their own, would merge into his being, *hasta sus entrañas.*

V
"There Was a Noble Ranger"

(August-December, 1876)

"He left his home when but a youth,
Went ranging far away."—From the
"Ballad of Mustang Gray."

V
"There Was a Noble Ranger"

McNelly's Company, to which, in August, 1876, the Governor assigned Lee Hall, was stationed south of Oakville, the county seat of Live Oak. The village had a population of one hundred, and a flourishing mortality rate. Forty of its citizens, in the decade just past, had met with violent death. Its women, as well as its men, were expert and ready with six-shooters. Outside the jail, oaks served as nature's gallows. A few miles south of the place were larger trees. So often had their branches been weighted down with gasping, choking, humankind, that when men passed that way their blood ran cold. Live Oak was a county that keenly needed Ranger services.[1]

Being in a locality so dangerous, it was characteristic of the force that its camp should suggest an Eden of contentment. On the afternoon when Hall was expected, some of the men were stretched out near a fire, not that they needed warmth, but that the smoke kept away the mosquitoes. They had unbuttoned the vests that took the place of coats—vests made with small lapels for ornament and with plenty of pockets for use. The higher left-hand pocket of each held cigarette papers and a sack of Bull Durham with round white tag and yellow drawstring hanging outside. In other pockets were two-bit pieces, nickels and dimes, pencil stubs, and memo pads filled with sketches of cattle brands, and descriptions from the Fugitive List of criminals for whom Governor Coke was offering rewards. The vests were about the only articles of apparel that showed

[1] Mrs. S. G. Miller, *Sixty Years in the Nueces Valley*, "The Passing of Oakville, (San Antonio, Freeman, 1930).

uniformity. For "the Rangers had no uniforms and wore no ten-gallon hats—they wore just what they could get, and didn't have much of that."[2] Down at the creek, some younger members of the Company were washing dark flannel shirts. They had bought neckties at a village store and their intentions were to "go gallin' " as soon as they could dry their laundry on mesquite bushes close to the fire. Their positions appeared precarious, for Rangers wore their trousers tight, but since these were of buckskin or corduroy, the danger was not real. The men could easily bend their legs at the ankle, for the leather of their boots was pliant. A Ranger had to be extravagant in buying boots. He got the kind that were seventeen inches high, cut straight across the top, with straps outside, or those with tops that curved to a point in front and had their straps concealed.[3]

The men wore their hats on the back of their heads—Stetsons with wide, stiff brims. One had taken his off to measure a leather band that he had braided to go around its crown. Others were watching and offering humorous advice. When the Company returned from its first scout into Mexico, there had been more than one bullion trimmed *sombrero* in camp, and a brace of braid-sewn buckskin jackets. These, proving cumbersome, were left behind as souvenirs for *baile señoritas*. Ever since, the men had been skeptical of adornment. A gold watch chain that brightened up the vest was permissible because it was handy in pulling out a watch. From anything that savored of the Mexican gusto for finery, McNelly's Rangers shied.

Horsemen, riding in from a late scout, looked decidedly more businesslike than the men at the creek or around the fire. Their low-slung cartridge belts were weighted down by ammunition and the contents of pistol holsters and scabbards for bowie knives. The pistols that they carried were .45 Colt's, distributed by the State. The most desired saddle carbines were the 1873 model Winchesters, such as Lee Hall had used when scouting

[2] The Company was so described by the late Ranger, John W. Bracken, who talked with me at his home in Austin in the summer of 1934.

[3] I have been assisted in my description of the horses, saddles, and outfits of the Rangers, by the artist, Louis Lundean. Mr. Lundean has known intimately many veterans of the service. See also Sweet and Knox, *On a Mexican Mustang Through Texas*, 63, 246.

after Gormly. Only a few had these and they were not paid for. The money for them, plus $40 for ammunition, would be deducted from salaries. There was the difference of $33.50 between the Winchester and the Sharps, or "muley carbine," furnished by the State, but McNelly encouraged his force to spend the extra money. The Sharps heated easily and was not accurate. The Winchester carried more shells and was quicker to handle.[4] The difference might be the difference between life and death. The men were returning with full cartridge belts. Nor was this unusual. Instructions were not to shoot, "unless somebody needed killin' and needed it bad." On this occasion, prisoners had been delivered peaceably at the Oakville jail. They would be safe from lynching or from jail-delivery as long as Rangers were in the county.

As he reached camp, each Ranger dismounted, almost in a single motion, and began unsaddling. Any one who watched could see why he rode with graceful comfort. His horse's bit was light, his bridle light. The ox-bow stirrups, slipped through saddle-loops, were light also. Spurs were the kind a man uses who rides much and has an agreeable understanding with his horse. Double girths were loosened and the apple-horned saddle and the Navajo beneath were lifted off together. From behind the saddle, a ground-blanket was unfastened and unrolled. The hair stake-rope had been slipped over the horse's head, where it had hung in a loose loop, and now, from its fastening at the side of the saddle, trailed upon the ground. It was long enough to allow the horse a grazing radius of about thirty feet. *Morrals* were left around the saddle horn and not untied from rawhide thongs, but the thongs that had held a *serape* were left to swing empty from the leather saddle rosettes to which they were attached. The *serape* was a concession to the superiority, in some respects, of Mexican equipment. The Rangers admitted that it made a better slicker than those for sale in village stores. The saddles, as is seen, were full-rigged, but nothing on them was unnecessary.

The men who had returned demanded "grub *muy pronto*," and, angered by the absence of the Negro cook, disregarded

[4] N. A. Jennings, *A Texas Ranger*, 111-12.

McNelly's order against swearing. Then they saw him coming in, followed by Mack, the little pack mule. Cook had been gathering "squaw-wood" and Mack was almost hidden by the pannier-like load that covered both his sides and jutted high above his head. The Rangers eased him of his burden and he trotted off with the horses to the *remuda*. Every man in the Company was fond of Mack. The little mule followed with equal eagerness, whether to a "shindig" or a skirmish. He seemed to understand, even better than the horses, what kind of spirit was expected of an animal of the Special State Troops.[5]

The Rangers had brought in a mess of perch from Christoval Creek and bought lard at a country store. Good smells came from skillets and the huge camp coffee pot—better than the fragrance of the myriad golden balls of the huisache. Cook had "wrastled" with flour and soda and bacon grease, and bread was in the Dutch oven. The boys had brought molasses from the town so he had made "a plenty." He was glad when they began to talk of the new Lieutenant, for they became so interested that there was rest from their jokes and lazy scoldings.

The men were curious about Lee Hall. They knew of his captures in northeast Texas, that he had proved to be a hard man for criminals to deal with. A horse and rider appeared, silhouetted against a sunset sky that seemed to send a streak of its color between the man's hat and his brow. No one but Red Hall could have hair like that! They liked him at first sight. From the easy way he rode, they knew he "savvied" horses. His voice was as warm and colorful as his hair.

"Say," he sang out, "have any of you boys got a chaw of tobacco? I'm Hall."

He spoke their language. He was a man come to serve with men, as well as an officer come to lead them. They told him to 'light.

He ate with them—bread from the Dutch oven, perch and fried beefsteak—and drank the Ranger coffee, a brew that could "float iron and would eat holes in the coffee pot, if left to stand." They beguiled him into telling of his days as Sergeant-at-Arms. Without knowing it, he was undergoing a Ranger initi-

[5] Another of John W. Bracken's descriptions.

[46]

ation. Hardly had he begun to talk before one of the thirty got up and strolled away; another rose, lazily stretched himself, and followed; a third almost sprang the hinges of his mouth with a great yawn, and walked off into the brush. In the space of a few minutes, Hall and a somnolent campfire were alone. The red headed young lieutenant stopped. From different parts of the gloom, came the uproarious laughter of thirty lusty throats. Hall grinned and kept his temper.

"You're a tough lot," he drawled to the returning Rangers.[6] They could hardly have chosen a better plan to prove his fellowship. He told a story supremely well. Where he went, his magnetic personality gave him center stage. Frederic Remington has described him as a "gentleman of the romantic Southern soldier type," a man of high ideals with whom it would be extremely unsafe to trifle.[7] But this first afternoon his men held him up to ridicule and lived to laugh at his discomfiture.

After the initiation, they tried him out on horse talk. They had to admit that Hall's mount was just about right, and that was fortunate, for in the Company the mount almost determined the value of the man. The horse had a good short head—a sensible head—a strong muscular neck, sloping shoulders and a deep chest that meant sound wind, meant that the horse could smash through brush of the Brasada. The legs were solid, their bones flat; the hooves large enough not to sink and flounder in country that was sandy. The talk disclosed that Hall had chosen the horse for just these points, and because, too, it had "plenty of bottom" so that the Lieutenant could sit close in his saddle and ride deep, as did Comanches. From sensitive nose to his flat hocks, the horse was good. The men would have trusted its owner to select even their own mounts. Confidence could go no farther. Each man in his talk made it a point to underrate his own nag, but obviously did not expect agreement. Each in the past had had "a real horse," one that could turn on a dime, one that could scale a vertical cliff that dropped sheer into the Rio Grande. If a horse was lost or killed on duty, the owner

---

[6] Jennings took part in the initiation and describes it in *A Texas Ranger*.
[7] Frederic Remington, "How the Law Got into the Chaparral," *Harper's New Monthly Magazine*, December, 1896.

[47]

was reimbursed by the State. Since Hall was a newcomer, the men boasted of the money they had collected, due to the estimates civilians had placed on their mounts. As a matter of fact, the recognition by civilians of Ranger worth and Ranger needs did much to heighten appraisal of the horses.[8]

Red Hall liked his company. Most of them, he knew, had been recruited at Burton, near McNelly's home in Washington County. They were not native, for McNelly wanted no men who had acquaintance with the fugitives or kin for whose safety a Ranger might turn cautious.[9] The men were young, and although it could not be said of any one that he was typical, certain characteristics each shared: these were a keen sense of direction, enough knowledge of woodcraft and plainscraft to follow a trail and make for water, ability to win or lose at monte with carelessness of fortune. Some could tell a story with point and humor. Some could add to rations by their skill at hunting and fishing. A few were good natured enough to bring in mesquite chunks for a busy cook, but they were sheepish about being caught at it. When scouting, if the trail was long, they knew how to get the most out of their horses. When a horse had to swim, they loosened flank girths and indicated direction by splashing water at either side. In one hand, the Ranger held his carbine so that if the horse should founder, the gun would not be drawn under and ruined by the water.

If Hall was to be successful, it was the individual traits and capacities of each of his men that he must study. Captain McNelly was in San Antonio receiving medical treatment, so the Lieutenant formed opinions of his own. He did not record judgments of his "boys," but many of the men we know through names they made in border history. Some became captains in the Frontier Battalion, one an assistant adjutant general. There were two poets in the camp, S. G. Adams and Horace Rowe. Unfortunately, Ranger service did not seem to them a fit subject to hobnob with the Muse and they left no

[8] N. A. Jennings, *A Texas Ranger*, 110.

[9] Clyde Wantland obtained a good description of the Company from George Durham, one of its members; Wantland, "Taking the Law to the Rio Grande," *Frontier Times*, January, 1936; N. A. Jennings, *op. cit.*, 120.

rhythmical description of the Company. Rowe had attended the University at Waco, and his "original poems" had been published by Lippincott's. He regarded himself as Cupid's victim, driven to seek fame by the cruelty of woman. He adjured youth to follow his example and

> *"Look thoughtful down the future*
> *With a proud defiant heart."*[10]

It will be seen that he had a better chance of making a name for himself with a Colt .45 than with a pen.

The cavalier of the Company was a tall Kentuckian, Sergeant John B. Armstrong.[11] He was well built, his full face marked by heavy brows and made distinguished by a finely modeled nose and deep-set, languid eyes. Like McNelly, he wore both beard and mustachios. When the exigencies of camp permitted, like Hall, he was a dandy in his dress. His nickname was "McNelly's bulldog." All had nicknames, from the smallest Ranger, "Colorado Chico," to Hall, who soon was known as "Colorado Grande." "Little Red" was English and was accused of dropping his H's all over the plains when he sang that

> *"The 'orn of the 'unter is 'eard on the 'ill."*

He was red-faced, as well as red-headed, sat the largest horse in the troop and, on duty, assumed much dignity as corporal. In camp, high spirits made him a favorite.[12]

The man who came to be best known outside the State was Napoleon Augustus Jennings. On his first attempt to join the troop, he had amused Captain McNelly by proposing to use a mare as his mount. Western stories read inside his textbooks at St. Paul's in Concord, and the mendacious writings of J. Amory Knox, had lured him to Texas from Philadelphia. His grandfather had been a publisher, his grand-uncle, Morton

[10] D. W. C. Baker, *A Texas Scrapbook* (New York, Barnes & Co., 1875), 438-39.
[11] A description of Sergeant John B. Armstrong, by Captain V. O. Weed of Austin, appears in Thomas Ripley's *They Died with their Boots on* (New York, Doubleday, Doran & Co., 1935), Chapter xix. In his old age, I knew this former member of the Company as the debonair and still gallant Major Armstrong of San Antonio.
[12] Mrs. G. C. Mayfield, "Oldest Texas Ranger," etc., *San Antonio Express*, March 20, 1937.

MacMichael, had fought for civic reform and been honored by a statue. When Jennings left Texas he became a newspaperman in New York. Once, when he needed money, he remembered that he had a good story to tell and wrote *A Texas Ranger*. Not letting facts stand in the way of his effort to embody the essence of the past, his book remains an authentic bit of the saga of Special State Troops.

John Young was the guide. He was under age and so debarred from taking the Ranger oath, but because he knew the brush country and was recommended by the sheriff, he received equal pay with those who were enlisted. An outlaw, he claimed, had hearing as keen as a buck deer. Young could stalk his man without disturbing the silence by the breaking of a twig.[13]

Sam M. Platt, another member of the Company, was the son of one of Rip Ford's sergeants in the War with Mexico. Four of Sam's brothers were Rangers, "men, all of them!"[14] McKay was the Company's Adonis, proud only of his strength. He had a tenor voice and sang Scotch songs to Hall's delight. G. W. Arrington, a Virginian, was destined to win fame as the man to bring the law to the Panhandle. Already, he had an enviable reputation for bravery. The Georgian of the Company was George Durham, who had attached himself to the Rangers at fifteen. Men say that he used to go into action with one leg crooked around his saddle horn and a cigarette drooping from the corner of his mouth. To him, McNelly still is "Cap'n" and will always be.[15]

Most dangerous of the group to Mexicans was their former compatriot, Jesus Sandoval.[16] Once he had lived at the ranch of

[13] J. Frank Dobie, *A Vaquero of the Brush Country*, gives a picturesque account of a picturesque character.

[14] John W. Bracken's appraisal in his obituary of Tom Platt, *Frontier Times*, December, 1929.

[15] I have frequently visited the lower King Ranch, "El Sauz," which was managed by my father-in-law, the late E. B. Raymond. George Durham was foreman. Though I saw him several times, I did not have any conversations with him. His reminiscences, "On the Trail of 5,000 Outlaws," as told to Clyde Wantland and published serially in *West*, have shown me what an opportunity I missed.

[16] W. P. Webb, *The Texas Rangers*, 242-43; testimony given by Sandoval, *House Report No. 343*, 84, is quoted by Paul S. Taylor, *An American Mexican Frontier* (Chapel Hill, University of North Carolina Press, 1934) ; see also *House*

Estero Grande, fifteen miles above Brownsville. He had served in the U. S. Quartermaster's Department throughout the war with Mexico. From 1853, he had been a citizen of the United States, regarded across the Rio Grande as Americanized, a "gringado," a traitor. Attempts against his life had been so frequent that for months he spent his nights hidden in the chaparral, a solitary sentinel over his own person. He had a personal vendetta which accounted for his hatred of his race and for the assaults that won him a name as the scourge of the border. When McNelly instituted his spy system, Sandoval helped by using cruelly unique methods of gaining information from the spies of his opponents. The Captain preferred not to witness all of the activities of Jesus, nor to ask what became of Mexican scouts when they had been drained of their secrets. Officers of the Regular Army, debarred from using such men as Sandoval, could not compete with Rangers in accuracy of information. The year before Hall joined the troop, Sandoval had earned himself more hatred by testifying before commissioners of the United States that the Mexicans meant to drive away Americans in the southwest region of the Rio Grande and reclaim the district as their own. He was McNelly's man, and Hall was glad to see him dropped when there was an opportunity to reorganize the Company.

The Lieutenant acquired as his personal servant another Jesus, surnamed Seguira.[17] He had fought as an officer under the famous bandit, Cortina, and after that as a member of an irregular Texas guerilla force that sometimes worked for Captain King and was disbanded after the organization of McNelly's men. Due to over-indulgence in mescal, Seguira had killed a cook in the other company. To secure protection, he had taken service with Red Hall, who neglected to inquire as to his past.

Report No. 701, 88. In this Sandoval claims to have been "a peaceable citizen since 1853," with many enemies in Mexico who hated him and threatened to kill him as a traitor to Mexico. "For several months," he claims in this affidavit of May 3, 1875, "I have not slept in my house; I have slept in the chaparral— and have been a solitary sentinel over my own person."

17 J. B. Dunn, *Perilous Trails of Texas* (Dallas, Southwest Press, 1932), Chapter xi.

[51]

Young men with walrus mustaches, young men with mustaches that twirled upward in finely pointed tips, and young men who could not even tease into existence a mustache of virgin softness, looked now for guidance to a red-headed young lieutenant. Under him the Company won praise for vigilance in Live Oak, and reduced crime to such an extent that details could be spared for service elsewhere. The mortality rate in Oakville dropped, bad men behaved like deacons, and picnics could be sweetly held under the trees that once were sinister.

One detachment was summoned to San Antonio to act directly under McNelly. The Captain brought about a great change in the men's appearance, having them outfitted by Pancoast, the tailor who made uniforms for the highest officers at Fort Sam Houston. The Captain sent them to Lucchese, who measured them for the finest boots. They "drove their whiskers in," bought neckties and wore them. George Durham boasted, "Unless you knowed our faces, you couldn't tell us from a store clerk."

Meanwhile, the Adjutant General noted the increasing expense of medical treatments for McNelly. Scouting on the Rio Grande in rough weather had aggravated the weakness of the Captain's lungs. He had contracted tuberculosis and had few years to live. Perhaps it was because he foresaw this that he indulged his wish to see his men well dressed.

In camp, the Rangers raced horses, played poker and monte, and practiced drawing guns from holsters and trying at full gallop to plant all their revolver shots into a single tree. They became adept, too, at dropping a can on the run, shooting it before it hit the ground, and picking it up by a swerve from the saddle.

In the late afternoon of August 24, news came that a bank had been robbed fifty miles away in Goliad.[18] Hall set out with a detachment of eleven. Overhead, when he brought his men

[18] N. A. Jennings, *A Texas Ranger,* 215; Lieutenant Hall's report to Adjutant General William Steele, October 4, 1876. This and other reports of the Ranger, letters and petitions of citizens regarding his Company, muster rolls, etc., are owned by Mrs. Isham Keith, the Captain's daughter, and were lent to me by her. The originals are in the files of the Adjutant General's offices in the Capitol of Texas. These papers will be referred to hereafter as *Hall Ms.*

into town, were still, sharp stars, crystal clear in the dry air. On the way, he had added to his number a young hot-blood with the very American name of George Washington Talley. Citizens told Hall that the men accused of robbing the bank were wanted, also, for horse and cattle theft and for murder. The sheriff was the protector of the criminals, and prospects for law and order were dark indeed. Companies of Vigilantes, or Regulators, had ridden in from nearby counties, and added to the terror. For this self-authorized militia was made up of stock owners and their bravos, whose real purpose was to rid the county of men who had no property and might become nesters. The Vigilantes had ordered off all transients and given force to their order by killing two who questioned their authority. Business was brought to a standstill and citizens remained indoors.

Hall informed the Vigilantes with Ranger emphasis that he did not need them. They returned to their ranches. He instilled such courage in the citizens that they deprived the lenient sheriff of authority. Until some one could be discovered bold enough to accept appointment to the vacant office, Hall and the Rangers undertook the work of bringing criminals to justice. When McNelly ordered four of the men back to Oakville, the eight who remained did their work so ably that, by October 4, the Lieutenant reported to the Adjutant General that the county was orderly, quiet, and without crime since his arrival.[19] The bank robbers had fled towards Mexico and a detachment was in pursuit. Their names, the Lieutenant had sent to McNelly. He himself needed to remain in Goliad to give assistance during court week. While there, he succeeded in arresting one of the bank robbers and getting a confession from him that implicated eleven others. Another report from Hall told of arrests in San Patricio and Refugio. Sergeant Armstrong was sending to McNelly reports on his detachment. The night of September 30, near Lake Espinosa, they had killed four Americans and one Mexican and recovered horses and cattle. Hall's reports told of many prisoners but only one killing, and that due to bungling of a sheriff who had mismanaged an arrest.

The Adjutant General valued the accuracy, clarity and

[19] Hall's report to Adjutant General William Steele, October 4, 1876, *Hall Ms.*

modesty of Hall's statements. The Governor received a letter recording Goliad's appreciation of the new Lieutenant. It described Hall as courteous, efficient and gallant: "We don't think that as an officer he has an equal in our state."[20] When he was ordered to return to Oakville, the citizens petitioned the Adjutant General: the sheriff was new to his office and did not yet inspire fear; if the Ranger was removed, bands of criminals would resume their activities and scatter before a posse could be organized.[21]

The petition was not granted, for on November 14, Hall again reported from Oakville. He had located some of the Goliad bank robbers in Karnes and Gonzales Counties and planned to set off for their arrests. Obviously, they were well organized and responding to orders from men unusually intelligent. And these men, Hall found, were William Brooking, Bill Taylor and King Fisher. Against Brooking and his brothers, there were at this time more than twenty indictments. More were added the next month when again his gang infested hapless Goliad. Bill Taylor was a criminal and feudist, a dandy in dress, with one eye out for a lady and one for a good horse. His light, wiry body responded dangerously to the dictates of a hot temper. The angrier he became, the cooler and more pitiless were his eyes. They were the eyes of a killer, snake eyes, through which he appraised and enjoyed his victim's agony. So far, though he had not escaped capture, he had escaped punishment, due to certain vagaries of nature and of man-made law. But luck was a fickle jade, and he had still a feud to carry on, and certain other activities, in conflict with the Governor's campaign for law and order; so he associated himself with two of the state's most powerful desperados, one of whom was John Wesley Hardin, the man who had started his criminal career by sending two Negro soldiers "to hell on a shutter," and who had become the foremost practitioner of the murderous "border roll."

Bill Taylor's second associate was a gentleman redoubtable and most elusive. He was a ranchman, handsome, tall, lean, and

<hr />

[20] Letter from E. R. Lane to Governor Richard Coke, October 22, 1876, *Hall Ms.*

[21] Petition drafted by Charles Roberts, attorney, October 27, 1876, *Hall Ms.*

dark—his name, King Fisher. He was twenty-six, and boasted that he had killed a man for each year of his life. And yet with a woman he could talk very pleasantly of his wife and babies, as he did on the Mott Ranch with Mrs. Albert Maverick, before she took fright on hearing who he was.[22] Not as a family man, however, did his career become legendary and his figure come to glisten with romantic trappings. The legend has it that he wore apparel auriferous enough to satisfy King Midas. His favorite hat was wide and white, festooned with gold and silver braid and banded with a golden snake. His chaps were of tiger skin, seamed with gold, and hung with rippling buckskin fringe. To get the tiger skin, his bravos had undertaken the little matter of capturing a circus! Golden embroidery glinted from his buckskin jacket. His shirt was very plain, of thinly fine, white linen. At his neck, he wore a knotted handkerchief of silk, around his waist a crimson sash. And thrust inside the silken sash were pistols plated with silver, their ivory handles full displayed. On his boots were silver spurs, adorned with little bells that advertised his presence. When men heard their tinkle, it was good policy to back out! They were in the presence of the royalty of crime.

His home ranch was in Dimmit County, ten miles northwest of Carrizo. From that point to Oakville, no man dared testify against him. Earlier in the year, he and most of his band had been captured by McNelly. They had to be taken to Maverick County to be jailed, for, in accordance with its ruler's wish, Dimmit was not organized for judicial purposes and lacked accommodations for confinement. When King Fisher wished to punish, he used methods more summary than imprisonment. Two days after his capture, the Rangers captured more of his men, and as they brought them in they met King Fisher and the first batch riding back to Carrizo Springs. He vouchsafed the information that he had been released on $20,000 bail, and that it would be well to consider that any member of his party could be furnished any amount of bail.[23] He spoke the truth

[22] Mrs. Albert Maverick, "Ranch Life in Bandera County," *Frontier Times,* April, 1928.
[23] N. A. Jennings, *A Texas Ranger,* 218-31.

and McNelly knew it, for, many times before, King Fisher had collected by duress from local merchants. The Ranger Captain released the prisoners whom his troops had labored to apprehend. He threatened that, if King Fisher continued his practices, he would return, and return to kill. King Fisher, with a bow, replied that he would be delighted to see the Rangers at any time. He would entertain them to the best of his ability.

The entertainment, McNelly estimated, would be extended by from one to five hundred of his bravos. Fifty of them were always in attendance on their leader. The County Judge of Maverick and others like him, who were not of the royal following, were in constant fear of death. The desperado flaunted his power with a daring that infuriated the Rangers. He used his straw bail method to defeat Lee Hall, as he had used it with McNelly. Wherever details scouted, the insolence of the desperado was camp gossip. This was King Fisher, who, when men demanded too high a price for smuggled cattle, ended the matter by murder and theft, or, in another mood, paid the price, then waylaid the vendors, killed them, and recovered the money from their silent bodies. This was King Fisher, who dictated how long a man might live in Dimmit County, and the direction of his travels. On his *Camino Real,* a sign was placed giving fair warning:

"This is King Fisher's Road. Take the other."

So it was that Hall's initial scout to detect and punish the robbers of a bank at Goliad projected him into a struggle with some of the darkest characters of his time: William Brooking of the twenty indictments; Bill Taylor and Wes Hardin, killers; and King Fisher, criminal-at-large.

VI
A Texas Cattle Feud
(1866-1876)

"Since the days of Lot and Abram
Split the Jordan range in halves
Just to fix it so their punchers wouldn't fight
. . . .

"There has been a taste for battle
'Mong the men who follow cattle,
And a love for doing things that's wild and strange,
And the warmth of Laban's words
When he missed his speckled herds
Still is useful in the language of the range."

—BADGER CLARK, *Sun and Saddle Leather.*

A Texas Cattle Feud

THE NAMES of John Wesley Hardin and Bill Taylor occur in every record of events leading to a crime the consequences of which long claimed the attention of Lee Hall. This was the murder of Dr. Brazell and his eldest son, one more killing—and that the most atrocious—in the gory record of the Taylor-Sutton feud.[1] The feud involved scores of families and was virulent in many counties, developing from an affair of the clans into a community enterprise. According to the accounts that Lee Hall heard, the trouble started in the Carolinas, flourished in Georgia in the forties, and was brought to Texas with the household goods of the Taylors and the Suttons, who, oddly enough, elected to settle in DeWitt as neighbors. After the Civil War, this county, as well as Victoria, Calhoun, Karnes, Goliad and Gonzales (in all of which the feud took toll), was overrun by unbranded cattle. To natural increase were added herds of strays from farther north that drifted down in search of milder weather and better grazing. As yet there was no barbed wire to obstruct them, for this was the era of the open range.

When the Texans found that markets could be gained by driving cattle northward or shipping them to New Orleans, branding of mavericks became a hectic enterprise in which the men of the Sutton and Taylor families were keen rivals. Chance for wealth from the cattle industry greatly increased after St.

---

[1] De Witt Reddick, "The Taylor-Sutton Feud," taken from historical data compiled in the Texas Collection of Library of the University of Texas, quoted in *Frontier Times*, June, 1925; "The Taylor-Sutton Feud in Early Days," *San Antonio Light*, June 29, 1913; Sweet and Knox, *On a Mexican Mustang through Texas*, 239.

Louis and Kansas City recovered from the panic of 1873, after the Indians had been driven into reservations, and after destruction of the buffaloes had left a richer range. Both Suttons and Taylors drove large herds to Indianola for gulf shipment to Louisiana and thence up the Mississippi. Their outfits for branding mavericks were numerous and energetic. Strictly speaking, the term, maverick, can be applied only to an unbranded animal over a year old, and not following a branded cow. Such an animal was considered the property of the man on whose range it was found. Brands of the Taylors and Suttons, like those of other ranchmen, were sometimes scorched into cattle that could not qualify as mavericks and were of doubtful ownership.

Rival claims as to cattle, shootings, arrests, the exercise of *la ley de fuga* by interested peace officers, jail deliveries, lynchings, were Sutton-Taylor practices that, taken together, created a veritable training school for crime. From it John Wesley Hardin was said to have graduated "with a diploma as a sure and careless shooter." The son of a Methodist preacher, he had not a single Wesleyan trait in all his make-up. When he walked the streets of Cuero with his friend, Jim Taylor, he wore his .45 shoved into his sash, its handle far protruding, where all might see. In later years, he invented the shoulder holster, known as the "Hardin jacket." He was of average height, five feet nine, was faintly blond, and wore a drooping mustache. His goatskin leggings, silk handkerchief, and jacket of velveteen could have been matched by many of the young Texans who cared for masculine adornment. In manner he was mild, and he was sparing of his words. His presence was conducive of reticence in others also. No one cared to express an opinion that might prove contrary to Wes Hardin's, nor did one care to be near him overlong. For Hardin was a killer—one of those few men who kill with actual and unreasoning pleasure. He had signalized his entry into the Taylor-Sutton fray by killing Marshal Jack Helms in retaliation for the Marshal's killing of two members of the other faction. And this was but an incident in his career.[2]

[2] James Hatch, "More about the Career of John W. Hardin," *San Antonio Express*, quoted in *Frontier Times*, June, 1924; Hardin's account of the feud ap-

A TEXAS CATTLE FEUD

No one on the Sutton side was fated to such preëminence in crime as Hardin, but among the two hundred men organized as Regulators by the former Indian fighter, Joe Tumlinson, the Suttons found a tower of strength in Shanghai Pierce. Six feet four was Shanghai, generous and peaceful when sober, but an ugly customer when he tanked liquor beneath his belt. This Yankee owner of Tres Palacios bragged of his record in the Confederate Army and of methods that had gained for him in a single year the branding of 15,800 calves and mavericks.[3] Count and examine, he who'd dare! When he was angry, his voice would rise to the shrill scream of a calliope or a locomotive whistle. If this did not drown arguments, he would adopt methods more definitive. One morning, half a dozen Mexican cowboys were found hanging to a tree in one of his pastures. Joseph McCoy, the pioneer cattle shipper, who has told the tale, records that Shanghai claims, had the tree been alive and green, the crop at the end of its hempen stems would have been larger. "Old Shang's" reputation made it safe for him to ride the range with a pack horse loaded with gold and silver for purchase of mixed stock. He was as secure from robbers as from arrest by the respectful and terrified sheriff of his county. When the grand jury became too officious regarding his activities, the native Rhode Islander, Virginian, and Texan, by successive adoptions, moved on to enliven the history of Kansas City.

In the decade, 1866-1876, the feud grew in intensity. The motto of the Taylor family was, "Who sheds a Taylor's blood, by a Taylor's hand must fall." The practice of the Suttons demonstrated that the rule they followed was equally rigorous. With such human dynamite as Wes Hardin and "Old Shang" in either faction, the fact that Sutton and Taylor principals decreased in number was a fact of importance only to their respective families. Regulators, Vigilantes, and local peace officers finding it impossible to stop the feud, Governor Coke

pears in his autobiography, *Life of John Wesley Hardin*, reprinted by *Frontier Times*, October, 1925; Webb, *The Texas Rangers*, 297-98; Dobie, *Vaquero of the Brush Country, 9, 10.*

[3] Joseph McCoy, *Historical Sketches of the Cattle Trade of the West and Southwest* (reprinted from 1874 edition, Washington, Rare Book Shop, 1932), 142-44.

himself took the matter under advisement. He sent for Captain McNelly and instructed him to take his men into the feudists' territory, not to fight and kill, but to help the leaders to make peace.

The Ranger Captain and his force arrived in Clinton in the summer of 1874. The little Englishman, Rudd, was quartered first in the home of Captain Joe Tumlinson, head of the Sutton party, and then in that of Bolivar Pridgen, State Senator from Victoria County and a member of the Taylor faction. The more facts he and others reported to McNelly, the less confident was the Captain that the affair could be settled by the pacific method recommended by the Governor. Trouble on the border offered chance for action and more tangible success. There the Company went, and for fourteen months McNelly burned himself out in service on the Rio Grande. Long days and nights in the saddle wore the Captain to a shadow. Gaunt, hollow-eyed, and gray with dust, his men rode with him, a phantom troop.

Meanwhile the feud continued. When Lee Hall joined the Company, its lurid incidents made the flame of the campfire seem pallid in comparison. Tragedy had followed tragedy. A last one, pitiful and somber, occurred on the night of September 19, 1876, its victims, a physician and his eldest son. Dr. Philip Brazell, who in Georgia had been a member of the state legislature, during his seven years in Clinton had made an enviable reputation as a Christian gentleman, skilled in his profession, impartial and law-abiding. He had treated the men of both factions when bullets left any life for treatment. More than once, blindfolded, he had been led into the brush to minister to a wounded man, and then led out again. Perhaps he would have echoed McNelly's judgment, that Suttons and Taylors were all alike, "turbulent, treacherous, and reckless." He would have agreed with George Durham that death ran a race with the stork in DeWitt County. Sometimes the stork, with the Doctor's aid, would get a few laps ahead, but then the men-folk on the stronger side would be thinned out. Male babies would begin arriving to receive the welcome of the other faction—not that one among them might be president, but that each might live to carry on the feud.

[62]

A TEXAS CATTLE FEUD

On the September night of the crime, the Doctor was tired, and he was ill from heavy demands made on his strength. In his primitive home there slept himself, his wife, a grown daughter, his eldest son, George, and the smaller children. Two other sons of this patriarchal family, Theodore, aged eighteen, and Sylvanus, seventeen, were sleeping on the gallery. They were awakened by the barking of their dogs and by men hallooing in the yard. The strangers demanded that the house be lit, and Mrs. Brazell rose and put a match to the wicks of the two lamps. She saw her younger boys taken from the gallery to the smokehouse and put under guard. She heard orders given to search the house, and then the order to her husband:

"Old man, get up and come out of there! Come out, old man!"

The two women were ordered to dress and come out also. Dr. Brazell went out, and George went with him, not waiting to put on hat, shoes or coat. The man called "Mr. Sheriff" searched the house. The wife was told not to be alarmed. The search was made for some one they did not think could be there. Then the boys were allowed to return to slip on shirts and pants, and George whispered to his mother the names of three men. He said he knew the others also; there were seven or ten. Some one was on the gallery and the boy could not tell more. Then the wife watched from the door and saw the men start off—her husband and her sons being marched ahead. The men were asking the way to the Ainsworths'. She knew her men had done nothing to be killed for, and she went back to the little children. As the clock was striking ten, she heard shooting, and she went out in the yard and called to the men not to shoot any more. The little children were afraid, and clustered around her, asking if their father might not have been killed. She "reckoned not." But at midnight, Mr. Humphreys and Mr. Ainsworth came to her to say that Sylvanus had brought word that the men had killed the Doctor and George—he thought brother Theodore, also. Then she went out and found her husband's body about 250 yards from the house, shot through the chest and through one leg. Later, she found the body of her eldest son, with a bullet hole between the eyes.

The neighbors, bearing what was left of her husband and her son, went into the house. It was a little house for death to come to. There was no chance of closing away in a dark room the young body and the old one with their ugly wounds. The little children saw. They were never very much like children after that.

The testimony of Sylvanus gives the details of the murder. He had run, and they had called after him to learn which boy he was. When they found he was Sylvanus, they let him go. Theodore had escaped by running towards the Ainsworths' and climbing a high tree. At the coroner's inquest, Sylvanus had been afraid to name the men in the group. Later he said that it was Dave Augustine who shot his father, and Bill Meador who had killed George. George had been defiant. He said if they would take him to court, they could find nothing against him. Meador declared that George had robbed his neighbors. He shot him full in the face.

Now, the statement of the case says that there was some evidence that Theodore "had shot at a man named Hardin," and that a prosecution of him for this was contemplated, but Meador, who was Deputy Sheriff, had, on the night of the murder, no warrant for the arrest of Theodore or any of the family. Addison Kilgore's testimony, accepted in one court and thrown out in another, told of conversations in which Meador stated his intention of taking the lives of Theodore Brazell and the two Ainsworth boys. Claiming to have two writs for the arrest of Theodore and for William Humphreys, he had summoned Kilgore and others to serve him as a posse. The writ for Theodore, Meador said, had been issued at the instance of Hardin, who claimed that Theodore had shot at him. To Hardin's house the posse went, but after Hardin, Meador, and Augustine had talked together privately, Kilgore was told that the arrest was not to be made because Hardin would not testify against the party. Still later, Kilgore heard Meador say he would go with a posse and kill all four.[4]

---

[4] The best account of the murder can be gained from reading the testimony of the Brazell family, *Texas Court of Appeals Reports*, edited by Jackson and Jackson, (St. Louis, F. H. Thomas Co., 1880), VIII, 254-310. For the use of this and other legal works necessary for the writing of this biography, I am indebted to Judge W. A. Wright, of San Angelo, Texas.

Mention of the name, Hardin, makes the testimony stricken out become of more interest than that which was accepted. Initials of the Christian names were not included. At this time, a price of $4,000 had been placed on the head of John Wesley Hardin. In September, 1874, he had been captured in Louisiana, but had escaped and returned to Texas. From then till the summer of 1877, he was in hiding. It was a time when he would not have cared to come forward as a witness against any man, and a time when it would have been most injudicious to add another to his many crimes. In his autobiography, Hardin claims that members of the Sutton faction, on an earlier occasion, had tried to win his support, and failing, had promised, none the less, to give him warning should he be threatened with danger.

At the time of the Brazell murders, the feud was no longer led by members of the two chief families and it is conceivable that, after his Louisiana experience, Hardin might have considered joining the faction which he had earlier opposed, for now the Suttons seemed desirable as friends since they had filled the peace offices of the county with their own men. The sheriff could be trusted not to execute any writs against them or their followers. The deputy sheriff, also of this faction, was notoriously corrupt, a man who constantly drank, and, as the Brazell case showed, one who was quite willing to take human life. But the young men of the neighborhood—the Ainsworth boys, young Humphreys, and Dr. Brazell's son, Theodore— were vigorous and indiscreet. It would seem that the fugitive Hardin may have had some part in a plan that would rid him of the danger from these young men, a plan by which, also, he might ally himself with the Suttons.

However this may be, the killing of good Dr. Brazell aroused such dangerous indignation that there no longer existed any advantage in alliance with the faction responsible for his murder.

There was need for a long scout and an arduous one. Captain McNelly was no longer able to assume command. Lee Hall and his Special State Troops took the trail for DeWitt County to reëstablish law and order.

VII
The Brazell Case and the Law
(1876-1899)

"My father, sixty years of age,
The best of lawyers did engage,
To see if something could be done
To save his vile and wicked son."

—CHARLES FINGER, *Frontier Ballads*.

VII

The Brazell Case and the Law

ON DECEMBER 10, 1876, Lee Hall reported to Adjutant General Steele that he was on duty with six men at Clinton, county seat of DeWitt. The next day the District Court would begin its session, and Hall expected all of his Rangers to be on hand. There were thirty-one cases of murder on the docket, besides many of other felonies. In no case in which members of the Sutton faction were defendants could the sheriff be trusted to execute the process. Half of the county were so "mixed up in deeds of blood" that they could not afford to have any member of the brotherhood imprisoned, for fear he might divulge the secrets of the rest. Hall believed that, in the event of a conviction of the murderers of Dr. Brazell, the Rangers should be concentrated at the county seat to prevent attempts at rescue.

The Lieutenant scouted for witnesses. All but three—and these women—had left the county. Threats had been sent to Mrs. Brazell and her daughter that, if they testified, their home would be burned and themselves killed. Hall let it be known that they must not, even in the slightest degree, be molested. The male witnesses he protected by taking into his own camp. To the others he promised an armed guard if they would return to the county. He realized the need of a larger force and requested the Adjutant General to keep ready eight or ten more men. A very present need for arms caused Hall to write:

"I would be glad if you would send us about four breech-loading shotguns and about two improved Winchester carbines in place of the Sharps carbines we have; at least I would be glad to have a Winchester carbine for myself."[1]

---

[1] Lieutenant Hall's report to Adjutant General Steele, dated Clinton, Texas, December 10, 1876, *Hall Ms.*

On December 18, the criminal docket of the court was reached. The murderers of Dr. Brazell and his son were still at large. At the coroner's inquest, even the relatives of the dead men had fearfully withheld the names of those they knew were guilty. Due to Hall's exertions, the grand jury had evidence for the indictment of seven men: Bill Meador, Deputy Sheriff of DeWitt and City Marshal of Cuero; Joe Sitterlie, Deputy Marshal and Deputy Sheriff of DeWitt; William Cox; Jacob Ryan; David Augustine; Frank Heister and Charles Heissig. Receiving the capiases on December 20, Hall executed them at once.

In a cold drizzle he galloped to his camp at Clinton and ordered his men to saddle their horses for a scout—a short one— no need for blankets. They would return that night. (Would return? He hoped they would return.) He promised "fun." Two men of the detachment were ill and had gone to a house in town. The sixteen others were eager to set out. Hall had a bottle of whiskey and gave them each a swig—short rations for seventeen men, but they were Rangers and must be steady and quick of eye and movement. As they rode, Hall spoke of the luck he expected. By good fortune, all of the Sutton faction could be found at one time and one place. Joe Sitterlie, for whom Hall held a warrant, was being married at the home of the bride's father near Cuero. The rest would be present for the festivities. A short ride revealed the house, brilliantly lighted and animated by the sound of squeaking fiddles that came through the windows. The troop could see gay couples whirling in a waltz. As pretty a "pat-a-foot" was in progress as any Ranger who liked to "go gallin' " might hope to witness.

Hall gave quick orders for surrounding the house, which was a double one with a gallery at either end. He stationed four men at the ends of the galleries, the others in a wide circle outside. Making a rapid round in the darkness, he saw that each was in his place and said enough to recall to these sentinels the crime for which the guilty must be brought to punishment. He ordered that no unnecessary shots be fired, but that none of the indicted be permitted to escape. Then, lone as a *paisano*, he walked away into the night.

When next they saw him, he was standing at the door of the

room where couples were dancing. He was unarmed. He had in his hands nothing more deadly for stopping bullets than a white handkerchief. The music stopped. Warm hands were dropped by hands that sought cold handles of revolvers.

"D'you want any one here, Hall?" called the groom.

"Yes," came the answer, "I want seven men. I want you and William Meador, David Augustine, Jacob Ryan, William Cox, Frank Heister, and Charles Heissig, charged with the murder of Philip Brazell and son, indicted this day."

There was an uproar. The men surged forward and pushed Hall from the door into the gallery. The trigger fingers of his Rangers came to position.

"How many men you got, Hall?" shouted Meador.

"Seventeen, counting myself," was the response.

Counting himself, Red Hall of Denison and Sherman; Red Hall in command of sixteen of McNelly's Rangers!

"We've got seventy. I guess we'll have to fight it out."

"That's the talk!" Hall's voice was jubilant. He had promised his men some fun, did not care to disappoint. Three minutes he'd give them to move out their women and children. He had no wish to kill them.

Not shifting his gaze, he gave orders to the Rangers outside.

"Ready, men! You with the shotguns, sweep the porches when I give the word. The rest shoot to kill. They're moving out women and children, then we'll have it!"

To those inside, "Now, gentlemen, you can go to killing Rangers, but if you don't surrender, Rangers will go to killing you."

But Meador, half drunk on bridal liquor, had broken down.

"We don't want to kill you all," he blubbered.

"Then give me your gun, quick!" Hall grabbed it before the Deputy regained his courage. With both hands, the Lieutenant reached out for the six-shooters of the astounded wedding guests. Calling two of his men to help, he disarmed a dozen feudists. Then the rest of the force strode in, and in short minutes were walking arsenals of Sutton arms.

The women at the party were feudist women, and they did not scatter. The children gazed in wide-eyed curiosity. The

[71]

bride made a request: she hoped that now the party could go on; and Red Hall honored her request. He detailed men for guard duty, changing them every two hours, and permitting those who were free to join in the celebration. The prettiest girls favored the men indicted for murder, but good-natured Rangers enjoyed the second prettiest.

In the gray morning, when fiddlers had played "Money Musk" and "Old Dan Tucker" for the latest encores, a cavalcade of Rangers and dance-worn captives set out for Clinton. When the prisoners, with Ranger escort, reached the county seat, Hall lodged them in jail.[2] Afterwards, he marched them to the upper floor of the Court House, where danger of rescue was slight. The arrest and the guard mount were Hall's response to Judge Pleasants' command and promise:

"You do your part and I will see that the courts deal justice. Together we can bring order out of chaos."

The Judge was a Virginian of old school, dignified and courtly, and a man of signal bravery. The accused, each under two indictments, one for the murder of Dr. Brazell and one for that of his son, sued out and were brought before the court upon a writ of habeas corpus. Judge Pleasants reinvestigated the cases without haste and in impartial fashion. The Rangers felt honored by being his associates. Members of Sutton and of Taylor factions attended also, but not before they had submitted to disarming. In the Judge's pockets were letters commanding him to set the prisoners free, threatening his life

---

[2] The story of the famous arrest has been told by many; N. A. Jennings describes the incident in his *A Texas Ranger,* 281-88, and in "Lee Hall, Fighting Man," *Saturday Evening Post,* January, 1900; Judge Duval West kindly retold the story in a letter to me dated San Antonio, Texas, February 27, 1935; I have it also from the Frances Weir Hall manuscript, lent me by Dr. Howard of Dallas. Frances Wier Hall often visited at the home of Captain Hall after his marriage and heard the story either from him or from his wife. Clyde Wantland reproduces George Durham's version of the affair. Frank Bushick, who may have heard the story from Captain Hall in San Antonio, retells it in *Glamorous Days,* 235, 236. Frederic Remington, to whom Hall recounted it on a memorable evening at the San Antonio Club, uses it in "How the Law Got into the Chaparral," *Harper's,* December, 1896; G. W. Talley, one of the Rangers who assisted Lieutenant Hall in the arrest, told the story to Kleber Miller at Falfurrias, Texas, in April, 1935, and Mr. Miller's uncle, Lawrence Miller, kindly sent the account of the interview to me.

should he refuse them bail.[3] Information that a rescue would be attempted caused Hall to telegraph for additional men.[4]

When the Judge had heard the last of the cases based on the fourteen indictments, and was prepared to render decision on granting bail, the stairway groaned under the booted feet of the crowd that pushed and clambered to the court room. Former lords of the county, when they entered, found Hall and his enlarged detachment of Rangers in position near the Bench. It was apparent that if violence was threatened toward the officials, or any attempt made at rescue, a goodly number of those present would face an extra-judicial sentence of death. When the Judge sat to render his decision, Rangers with ready Winchesters stood at each side. The silence was heavy—as heavy as though the shattered bodies of Dr. Brazell and George had quietly been brought within. Lee Hall's eyes were very blue, very serene, while he regarded the hostile gathering.

Judge Pleasants spoke, clearly, deliberately, and with conviction. His words constituted an informal indictment against the lawless audience crowded within his court. He described those who listened to him—and he did not mean the prisoners at the bar—as "murderers, bush-whackers, and midnight assassins." He acknowledged the receipt of threatening letters. Such letters had been used, without success, to intimidate also the foreman of the grand jury. The Court had been forced to call in Rangers, and intended to keep them until the county had become as law-abiding as any in the Union. He denied the prisoners bail. His intention was to send them to a secure jail, one outside the boundaries of DeWitt. There they would await their trials for crimes as wicked and as cowardly as ever had disgraced the state.

The Judge ceased speaking, but all men's eyes remained upon him. It seemed that for a time the majesty of the law, the scorn and hatred of things evil, had become incarnate in his person. Those who hated justice, hated him. From his flashing

[3] W. P. Webb, *The Texas Rangers*, 290, 291.
[4] Lieutenant Hall's telegram to Adjutant General Steele, Clinton, Texas, via Victoria, December 10, 1876; the telegram to Lieutenant Wright is referred to in Lieutenant Hall's letter to Adjutant General Steele, Clinton De Witt Co., December 16, 1876, *Hall Ms.*

[73]

eyes, the men shifted their gaze. There was a pause, then an uneasy rustling, a dangerous murmuring.

"Lieutenant Hall, clear the room, sir!"

Sutton and Taylor Vigilantes, as they made for the door, were in strange agreement. They smarted from a verbal lashing. They shared a strange fear that the old order, before their very eyes, was changing.[5]

It was. After this, Hall and his Rangers arrested scores of criminals in DeWitt. Where the Judge went, they formed his escort. They guarded jails. They induced—sometimes compelled—witnesses to return, and gave them assurance that they could safely testify.

But the story of the duel between justice and the Brazell murderers had just begun. Its chronology offers strong proof of the forbearance of Rangers who sought to work *with* the law rather than *as* the law. After the Judge's denial of bail, Hall was joined by Captain McNelly, who rendered his last service to the State by commanding the guard that accompanied the prisoners to Galveston.[6] There, on January 5, 1877, they were committed to the county jail for one day, after which Lieutenant Hall transferred them to Austin. In December, 1877, the Rangers brought them back to DeWitt. On the way, at Lockhart in Caldwell County, a rescue was attempted. Shots were fired, but none took effect. The Rangers captured three of the assailants and lodged them in jail before continuing to Cuero. There they were met by a tearful and angry delegation of prisoners' wives, sweethearts, and relatives. Some, doubtless, were among those who had attended the wedding at which the Rangers were uninvited guests. In December, 1877, Hall reported that the trials had begun and all was quiet.

The case of Charles Heissig was dismissed. A severance having been granted Dave Augustine and Frank Heister, they came to trial for the murder of George Brazell and were acquitted.[7] Indignant at an obvious miscarriage of justice, Judge

---

[5] N. A. Jennings, *A Texas Ranger,* 248-59.

[6] Lieutenant Hall to Adjutant General Steele, Flatonia, January 4, 1877, *Hall Ms.; Galveston News,* January 6, 1877.

[7] From the history of the Brazell case as it is briefed in *Texas Court of Appeals Reports,* VIII.

Pleasants on the same day, on his own motion, changed the venue of the other defendants to Bexar.[8]

"There exists in this county," he declared, "influences resulting from the terrorism prevailing among the good people of the county which will prevent a trial alike fair and impartial to the accused and the State."

Lawyers of the defense objected and were overruled.

The State had now an additional witness. On the night of November 23, Hall had set out from Sherman to bring back a man named Jacobs, who had taken up his residence in Columbia, Missouri. He located him and traveled home with him the following day. The case against Bill Meador was scheduled for February, 1878, in the District Court of Bexar. Hall requested the Adjutant General to send Jacobs there under the guard of J. E. Lucy. The trial was not conclusive, and Meador's case, "No. 440," continued to appear upon the docket until 1894, when the district attorney informed the court that he saw no reason for pressing the trial, and the prisoner was discharged.

In April, 1878, Cox, Ryan, and Sitterlie, having severed from their co-defendant Meador, were brought to trial before the same court. Again Lieutenant Hall was present. He assisted the prosecuting attorney in preparing his case and in rounding up the witnesses, having the Rangers bring some in from Cuero after the trial began. Hall reported to the Adjutant General that the State's case was strong, the jury good, and prospects for conviction were bright.

On April 17, he telegraphed, "Cox, Ryan and Sitterlie convicted of murder in first degree."

On appeal, judgment was affirmed at the Austin term of the Court of Appeals. And then there was a strange occurrence. The clerk of the court mislaid the opinion affirming judgment of the lower court. The opinion had not been entirely recorded and was never found.[9]

In 1880, a rehearing was granted. The opinion of Judge J. P. White was most gratifying to the distinguished counsel engaged

8 The date, December 29, 1877.
9 The strangely negligent clerk was a Mr. Feris, *Texas Court of Appeals Reports,* VIII.

for the defense, among whom were Messrs. Waelder, former Congressman Upson, J. W. Stayton, later Chief Justice of the Supreme Court, and John Ireland, later Governor. The Judge held that illegal and inadmissible evidence had been allowed to go before the jury: Kilgore's relation of conversations with Meador revealed no intention to take the life of George Brazell. The attack on George had been unpremeditated, and his assailants could be guilty only of murder in the second degree. Further, the Court held that the Texas Constitution provided that an indictment should conclude with the words "against the peace and dignity of the State," whereas, this indictment was fatally defective in that it concluded, "against the peace and dignity of the Statute"!

The judgment of the San Antonio District Court was reversed and the cases remanded. The defendants made bond. Their cases never came up again.

Hall had dreaded the verdict of the Court of Appeals. During the trial, the press quoted him as saying that, by 1879, he and his men had captured 420 offenders, most of them murderers, and gained only the convictions of Sitterlie, Ryan, and Cox, which were about to be set aside on a technicality.[10] Pilgrim in search of justice, stranger to rest, Hall had in this case alone for years marshaled witnesses, guarded courts, and transferred prisoners.

Twelve years later, December 31, 1891, a new indictment against David Augustine for the murder of Dr. Brazell was returned by the grand jury of DeWitt. In 1893, the venue of the case was changed to Gonzales County. In 1896, it was again transferred—this time to Hays. Though Augustine was condemned to twenty-five years penal servitude for second degree murder, the law on which he was condemned was repealed by an Act of June 19, 1897, which the defense held to be retroactive. Prosecution claimed that the Act of 1897, known as "mob law," was void, for it did not define mob violence. By this time in the court records, the spelling of the Doctor's name had been changed to Brassell and that of Meador to Meadows. The defense still was able to avail itself of excellent legal abil-

10 *Galveston Daily News*, June 28, 1879.

ity—being well served by Rudolph Kleberg. The prosecuting attorney pointed out that for twenty-two years Augustine had evaded justice, and that now justice should be done. Judge John N. Henderson, of the Court of Criminal Appeals, was like-minded. Again there had been a difficulty as to spelling. He held that it was not necessary to discuss the objection to the verdict of the jury, based on the ground that penitentiary was spelled "peintentiary," and duly cited authority for his opinion. On June 21, 1899, he affirmed the judgment and overruled the motion for rehearing.[11]

The date on which the murder had been committed was September 19, 1876. The year of the decision, 1899, was that of Judge Pleasants' death, the year in which Lee Hall sailed for Manila as an officer in the Thirty-third U. S. Volunteers. More than two decades had elapsed. The sentence imposed on Dave Augustine was one that, because of the prisoner's age, meant imprisonment for life.

A good lawyer could brief the history of the cases on a single sheet of legal foolscap. Any such account would have made them unrecognizable to members of Hall's company. To the Rangers, the cases meant court service in Clinton and in Cuero; escort of prisoners to safer jails in counties better organized than was DeWitt; they meant escort of the accused to various courts of law far from the locality of the crime, for there were many changes of venue, as well as appeals and rehearings. Detachments under Hall's command, or that of one of his men, shuttled the prisoners from Austin to Cuero, Cuero to Austin, Austin to Huntsville, back to Austin, again to Cuero, then to San Antonio. This traveling exhibit had a salutary effect in curbing desires of evil-doers. The cases meant the acquisition, whether consciously or not, of certain legal knowledge; they meant search for reluctant witnesses in mavericking outfits and in humble homes where frightened women feared the vengeance on their men-folk of the powerful Suttons.

For Lee Hall, the affair meant extended search within the

[11] *Texas Criminal Reports,* cases argued and adjudged in the Court of Criminal Appeals of the State of Texas (Austin, Gammel-Statesman Publishing Co., 1902), XLI.

state and, in addition, the hurried journey to Missouri. It meant prolonged and thoughtful conferences with a succession of prosecuting attorneys; and on the credit side, the forming of friendships with some of these men who valued his aid as far in excess of what the State required of any Ranger.[12] It meant the constant tapping of every resource for gaining information to stimulate the lagging memories of witnesses, or aid in the selection of juries. It meant, again and again, the weakening of his Company through the sending of detachments to guard prisoners, judges, witnesses—the interruption of important work that might be lucrative in winning rewards.

It was a service that called to mind a moving panorama of court house scenes and landscapes in all the seasons of the year —prairies and chaparral as seen by eyes stung by hot winds, heavy with sleep, or keenly vigilant in early morning northers. It did *not* call to mind scenes of lynchings, or jail deliveries, or the wounding or killing of any man.

The service of assisting in the prosecution of the murderers of Dr. Brazell and his son was carried on by Lee Hall persistently, quietly, and effectively. It was work discouraging to feudists and to self-styled Vigilantes. For Texas, it was work that made the prairies and the chaparral secure for simple families living in humble, isolated homes like that of the Brazells'— the very bone and sinew of the state.

[12] One of these friends, a prosecuting attorney, was the father of the Honorable William H. Burges of El Paso, Texas.

VIII
The Book of Knaves
(January, 1877-May, 1877)

"Oh, pray for the ranger, you kind-hearted stranger;
He hasn't seen home for many a year.
But he's chased the Comanches from off'n your ranches
And run all the outlaws clean off the frontier."

—Old Western Song.

.   .   .   .

"U. S. Mail and brave Wells Fargo!
Dancing harness, screeching brakes,
Reinsman bold, superb, loquacious,
Sawed-off shotgun disputations,
Miners, gamblers, dames flirtatious
Dusters, pokes and wide-awakes—
Storm and battle your companions,
    Glitter in your hold."

—Neill C. Wilson, *Treasure Express.*

By permission of the Macmillan Company, Publishers.

The Book of Knaves

THE last of January, 1877, McNelly's Company was reorganized for the short term of six months. The State was Lee Hall's debtor for several hundred dollars of back salary,[1] and his rank remained that of a lieutenant; but for the North Carolinian, the Texas stars shone with a greater luster, the winter sunshine held a warmer radiance, and life seemed vastly good, for he was given command of Special State Troops.[2] At the time of the Company's reorganization, Dr. Cupples of San Antonio found McNelly's physical condition no better than in the preceding October, when the doctor had certified "complete disability." Adjutant General Steele informed an inquiring press that the Captain's bills for medical attendance had amounted to a third of the amount expended on the Company. The subject matter of Lieutenant Hall's reports, their clarity and modesty, laudatory letters from citizens where the Company had served, and petitions that it be retained, convinced Steele that in giving Hall command, he was placing the right man in the right place.[3]

The reorganization was carried through at the height of the "hide and tallow war" in the Brasada, and the Company was sent to the worst part of that country, the Nueces Strip. This land, bounded by the Gulf and the Rio Grande and the Nueces rivers, teemed with cattle and wild horses—mustangs which gave the district a name on early maps. Through the three hundred miles of its length and the hundred of its width, cattle

[1] Certificate of service signed by Captain L. H. McNelly, February 1, 1877.
[2] *Denison Daily News*, January 25, 1877.
[3] Undated clipping from *The Galveston News* in the collection of clippings saved by Captain Hall's mother, now in the possession of Mrs. Isham Keith.

were being killed and skinned, and rebranding progressed at dare-devil pace. When possible, hides were shipped without inspection. Hall sent for copies of the List of Fugitives. He and his men thumbed them eagerly and to purpose. In the short month of February, they made more arrests than in any earlier month of the Company's existence.[4]

The Lieutenant's method was to station one squad in Refugio County and send two men to San Patricio, a center of "hide and tallow factories." St. Patrick's village possessed four stores, a Catholic Church, convent, two boarding houses, and a hotel. The Rangers stayed at the latter. They ate at a table set for thirty-five and slept in the hotel's upstairs room, a dormitory lined with cots and open to the stars. It was not a quiet sleeping place. When things became too noisy, the landlady restored quiet by using a bed slat with vim and impartiality. Rangers enjoyed the excitement indoors and out. They captured 1,250 hides, but thieves they failed to get. It was rumored that a third of the county, including the sheriff, his deputies, the county attorney, and most of the justices of the peace, were trafficking in hides of stolen cattle.[5] Those who favored the Rangers threatened a lynching bee to rid the county of corrupt officials. Hall reënforced his men. He wanted no illicit assistance for the cause of law and order.

His own scout led into the Brasada of the Frio and Nueces —"catclaw" country, where chaparral and prickly pear tall as a man's head provided natural defense for outlaws. The thickets were as they had been in 1856, when Robert E. Lee wrote from Ringgold Barracks: "Every branch and leaf in the country are armed with a point and seem to poison the flesh."

It followed that settlements were sparse and hunting of man and beast was good. In the Brasada were quail, wild turkey, deer, rattlesnakes, *javelinas,* and outlaws. At Dog Town on the Frio, in McMullen County, Hall found things at their worst, and arrested many for cattle thefts and skinning. Situated as it

[4] Lieutenant Hall's letter to Adjutant General Steele, Clinton, DeWitt County, February 22, 1877, *Hall Ms.*

[5] Lieutenant Hall to Adjutant General Steele, Clinton, DeWitt County, March 5, 1877, *Hall Ms.*

was on the stage route connecting San Antonio with Laredo and the Chihuahua Trail, the outside world had to acknowledge the town's existence. Until the G. H. & S. A. linked San Antonio with Laredo and connected both with the Mexican Central, Dog Town flourished according to its fashion. It took its name from the custom of using packs of dogs to catch Brasada cattle. When off duty, the dogs contributed to the noise and care-free character of the mangy town.[6]

Its clapboard houses, its pigs, the corrugated iron walls of its saloons, its Mexican *jacals,* seemed just a little filthier than any others. Mail bags, thrown from the stage into its dirty main street, were carried by the postmaster to Uncle Sam's weather-beaten building and therein dumped. The people scrambled for their letters on the floor, while the postmaster looked on. He was an individualist and believed in letting each man do his rooting for himself.

Many received no mail nor even entered the post office. Only when mosquitoes in the dense brush grew too bad, and cattle came in to bed on the open road, did outlaws seek furtive refuge in the town. Dogs there, as elsewhere, barked only at the unusual. In Dog Town, they barked at respectable men. Rangers worked as diligently as they had in the other Brasada town, Oakville of Live Oak. Although the Company was reduced in number by detaching men to guard judges, jurors, witnesses, and prisoners, its activities were notable in the hide wars of four counties: San Patricio, Victoria, Calhoun and Bee. So greatly did the Rangers improve conditions in Oakville and McMullen that no longer could it be said that the Nueces, which traversed the counties, was the "sheriff's dead-line."

Ranchmen of the district hoped Hall would carry the war against cattle thieves across the border and force Mexicans and Indians to surrender their "wet stock." And for this, Steele thought the time was almost ripe. He planned with Hall a "big round-up." In February and March, 1877, the Lieutenant conferred with the wealthiest ranchman in southwest Texas, Captain Richard King, who had suffered the greatest property loss

6 The best descriptions of the Brasada are scattered through J. Frank Dobie's *Vaquero of the Brush Country.*

from border depredations.[7] In May, he consulted with Lieutenant Colonel Shafter. Careful plans were necessary, for the "big round-up" entailed scouting across the border and a long absence from districts only recently made safe.

While the project took shape, Ham White, highwayman, furnished diversion. No common road agent was Ham, but a true knight of the road. He plied his trade between Austin and San Antonio on the *Camino Real,* a thoroughfare older than Texas itself. Spaniards had traveled it in journeying from Mexico to lands upon the Mississippi. Few *conquistadores* had surpassed in daring this outlaw of the seventies. Sometimes he enriched himself by looting two stagecoaches in a single day.

He had good pickings. Cattle, wool, faro, good air, and swift horses brought wealth in plenty to San Antonio. Ranchmen played at crack-loo on its cobbled sidewalks with double eagles, and gamblers backed their choice of a card with stacks of chips limited in height solely by the law of gravity. Lacking wool, cattle, and horses, but free as air and armed with daring, Ham White effected, to his own benefit, redistribution of the city's flowing wealth. His code and methods were his own. He worked alone. He did not rob women. If a man surrendered money from horny, work-chapped hands, Ham returned it, saying the owner looked as though he'd earned it—"better keep it." At times, Ham showed consideration for the affluent by leaving coin enough for a meal and a night's lodging, and even returned watches and rings of sentimental value. But Judge Burts of Austin failed to wheedle back his greenbacks and his cherished meerschaum, and Ham entertained no sentiment that forbade his taking heavy toll from the heavy bags of old Wells Fargo.

He robbed without dismounting. Due to a game knee, caused by a gun wound, he preferred to sit his horse and have his victim slit the mail bags and pass to him the registered packages and letters. Meantime, he drawled a scolding at the passengers for their iniquity in taking property entrusted to the worthy express company and to Uncle Sam. He vowed that, had he time "to fool around the courts as witness," he would present formal

[7] Lieutenant Hall to Adjutant General Steele, Goliad, February 9, 1877; Clinton, DeWitt County, March 5, 1877, *Hall Ms.*

complaint against their thefts. In 1877, due, perhaps, to inconvenience caused by his stiff knee, he decided to take an assistant and enlisted young John Vaughan. He could afford to. Sometimes he got a thousand dollars at a haul. He was in his early twenties and his depredations threatened to be prolonged and costly. To end them, the state offered a reward of $1,250.[8]

In the latter part of March, 1877, Lee Hall with three Rangers and the young son of Major Thomas Purnell undertook pursuit. The little cavalcade clattered out of Austin at two in the morning. A stage had just been robbed and the men scouted a hot trail. For twenty-five miles, as rapidly as possible, they rode across country and on highways till their horses' legs were dyed to the knees with pollen of the wild flowers. Three or four miles from Blanco, they saw by the roadside the white of scattered papers. The men reined in, dismounted, and gathered from the dust post office bills that gave the numbers and particulars of letters registered at Bracketville and New Braunfels. From tracks on the road, Lee Hall found that the robber had changed his spent steed for a stage horse, and that his new mount had a broken shoe. The Rangers followed until the trail was lost in a confusion of tracks near Lockhart. From there, they relied on recurrent news of a man traveling ahead on a good bay horse.

Heavy with sleep, they entered Luling, and riding to a livery stable, slid gratefully from jaded horses. It was warm inside. There was a pleasant smell of grain and leather. The clean hay bedded in the stalls suggested slumber. Suddenly Lee Hall was alert. Half way down the stable, in the shadow, he saw a man tightening the cinches of a saddle, tugging and buckling hurriedly, uneasily. The horse that his fumbling hands made nervous was a bay—a good horse that had seen hard riding. Hall walked closer and, in casual fashion, addressed the stranger.

"Don't come near me," warned the horseman, and thrust his hand inside his coat.

"Why, you appear frightened," said Hall, still advancing.

"It's enough to frighten anyone to be surrounded by three or four men."

Hall was beside him now and seized his wrists. The Rangers

8 *The Daily Democratic Statesman* (Austin), March 29, 31, 1877.

drew their pistols. Others closed in, and the stranger was relieved of a six-shooter, a notebook with incriminating memoranda, and $900 in silver and bills. The packages of money and their amounts tallied with the numbers of the post office bills recovered from the roadside—black proof that the captive was Ham White! Some one asked if the Rangers were going to examine the "brother" as well, since he had been inquiring as to when the stages left. The "brother" was arrested and proved to be John Vaughan, just twenty-one, and of good parentage.[9]

To assist himself in breaking jail, Ham White had wound steel saws around both legs. These his captors removed before they turned their horses' heads towards Austin. News of the arrest sped ahead and lined the streets with people long before the horsemen crossed the Colorado and entered Congress Avenue. Ham White was under indictment for murder as well as robberies. His crimes were picturesque and notable, but whatever bravado he had, he lost when his steel saws became the property of Rangers. The lord of the highways was no fine figure on the Avenue! The crowds that jammed the curbings in front of the depots, the Avenue Hotel, the Senate Bar, looked rather at Lee Hall, erect in his saddle, fresh and debonaire, intent on getting his man to jail, indifferent to attention.[10]

Next to demand the Lieutenant's service was a trio of stage robbers known by description to all students of the Rangers' Book of Knaves. Joe Horner, Murray, and Jones, were the names that emerged most often from the cloud of their aliases. White's capture sent them on the run to Maverick County, in King Fisher's domain, and then across the Rio Grande into Mexico. There, too, were the cattle thieves and marauding Indians that Hall hoped to cut from honest men in one "big round-up." The trail of the Lieutenant was clear. He meant to follow to the border—perhaps beyond.

Dividing his Company into three squads, he instructed the one under Armstrong—now a lieutenant—and the one under

[9] Lieutenant Hall's telegrams to Adjutant General Steele, Eagle Pass, March 28, 1877; Jennings, *A Texas Ranger*, 262-65; Kleber Miller's interview with G. W. Talley, Falfurrias, Texas, April, 1935; *Daily Democratic Statesman*, March 29, 1877.
[10] *Daily Democratic Statesman*, March 30, 1877.

Sergeant Parrott, to converge with his at Eagle Pass on the Rio Grande. His subalterns arrived first, for Hall and his eight men had to police a hanging at Beeville, were delayed by a broken wagon near Pleasanton, and in Medina County stopped to make arrests. At Uvalde, he found conditions satisfactory and continued to Fort Clark, where he wished to see Lieutenant Colonel Shafter. In the stampede that followed the arrival in Eagle Pass of Armstrong and Parrott, these officers had succeeded in capturing three men across the River and having them jailed at Piedras Negras.[11] Hall's visit to Shafter was to arrange for extradition and to confer with the officer on how to work together for the "big round-up."

On May 11, the Lieutenant reached Eagle Pass with necessary papers and met the others of his Company. On the fourteenth, with Rangers Armstrong and Parrott, he crossed the river to negotiate the extradition. Striding across the plaza of Piedras Negras, they ran into a fourth criminal—one of Joe Horner's men, known as Jones when he was not known as Williams. Him, too, they gathered in. The four prisoners were citizens of the United States and the Rangers succeeded in getting them across the river by the end of the day, although in his dispatch to Steele, Hall had to admit that the exploit occasioned "a good deal of excitement." The Company at this time had a total of fifteen under arrest, several of whom were on their way to Mexico from Kimball County, where they had been flushed by Major Jones. Hall reported also that stolen stock was being held fifty miles up the river, and that Indian cattle thieves had moved their camp thirty miles into the interior. Ranger scouts and United States scouts were trying to secure accurate information of their location. Until this was received, nothing would be attempted by Colonel Shafter, but the Lieutenant reported that in Piedras Negras a revolution was expected in a few hours.[12]

The revolution did not take place, for the next day, May 15, Lee Hall quietly arrested the man most responsible for the dis-

[11] Lieutenant Hall's telegram to Adjutant General Steele, Eagle Pass, May 12, 1877, *Hall Ms.*
[12] Lieutenant Hall to Adjutant General Steele, Eagle Pass, May 14, 1877, *op. cit.*

order. This was King Fisher. In the winter and spring the desperado had been ruler of the county. At his ranch on Pendencia Creek, near the Nueces in Dimmit County, five hundred men from both sides of the Rio Grande reported for orders. Armstrong stated to the Adjutant General that he "could not persuade a man in the whole county to testify against King Fisher or any of his clan." Half the citizens of the border city he counted as his henchmen, the other half he scorned as cowards. Four successive grand juries had cautiously ignored the most recent and flagrant of his murders. He boasted that, if he were indicted, he could raise bail in any amount. He came and went freely and conspicuously. Hall did not have men enough in all his troop, King Fisher said, to catch him.[13]

But there had been a royal miscalculation. Three months earlier the Ranger, according to his dispatch of May 16 to Steele,[14] had named the grand jurors for the county and had assured each one that he would be amply protected in case he undertook to bring outlaws to justice. The district judge, Thomas Paschal, and the district attorney, were "able and fearless in the discharge of their duty." According to a dispatch in the *Galveston News*, a member of Hall's command was sworn in as deputy sheriff and the court was "virtually run by the company."[15]

The result was an unprecedented number of indictments. Interest in the rest was negligible compared to the amazement caused by the indictments of King Fisher, headed by one for murder in the first degree. The "King" was not amused. He was astounded when Hall entered a saloon, quietly placed him under arrest, and lodged him in the county jail.[16] On May 29, with three other prisoners, he made his ignominious appearance in

---

[13] King Fisher, it is said, not only kept an accurate record of past killings, but also a list of those that he planned for the future. A. H. Gregory in *Texas Argus*, quoted in *Frontier Times*, June, 1928.

[14] Lieutenant Hall to Adjutant General Steele, Eagle Pass, May 16, 1877, *Hall Ms*. This is a relatively long report, telling of the Lieutenant's activities, his relations with Colonel Shafter, and of the scouts of his men.

[15] *Galveston News*, May 25, 1877. The citizens are commended for their "unprecedented animation" in trying to make a clean sweep of the desperadoes who so long had terrorized the community.

[16] Lieutenant Hall's telegram to Adjutant General Steele, Eagle Pass, May 16, 1877, *Hall Ms*.

Austin under escort of a detachment of Hall's Company commanded by Private George Talley. Of the three, one was an associate in crime from Maverick County, one was Charles Thayer, a swindler wanted in Grimes, and the other was Jim Burdett, charged with Ben Thompson for a murder in Austin.[17]

During the summer months, the "King" became familiar with interiors of jails in Castroville and Uvalde, where he was conveyed under escort of Sergeant Parrott, chief witness for the State. His royal progresses were diversified by scouts who brought in companions for his captivity. He found that adventure and bravery were as necessary for enforcement of law as for its violation. The contrast was in the matter of rewards. Few loose coins jingled in the pockets of Rangers.

Settlers in Dimmit County and in Maverick, who through fear of King Fisher had deserted their homes and property, returned. Cattle and horses no longer were driven to the Pendencia from the pens of their owners. Men rode out in the morning without fear of meeting robbery or death before night. Women slept in their homes without fear of being awakened by a murderous fusillade. The county judge of Maverick dared sleep in his own home.

For good measure, the loop of the Rangers tightened around King Fisher's man, Bill Bruton, under some half dozen indictments, and around Bill's brother, Wes. They, too, became a traveling exhibit between Austin and Castroville. Twenty-one other criminals were delivered to sheriffs waiting in six separate counties.[18] *The San Antonio Express,* after recounting the exploits of the criminals, expressed the opinion that the white robbers and murderers were more dangerous than the "firm of

[17] Lieutenant Hall to Adjutant General Steele, May 25, 1877, *Hall Ms.; Daily Democratic Statesman,* May 29, 1877. In addition to these men mentioned in the text, *The San Antonio Herald* noted among Lieutenant Hall's recent captures: "Jones, alias Williams, connected with Joe Horner in his stage robberies; William C. Bruton, against whom a round dozen of indictments have been presented in Goliad County for cow stealing; Jim Lewis, connected with Bruton in sundry above cases; ... John Murray, who lately escaped from Atascosa County jail; Breck Dorn, alias Fitzpatrick, in whom the people of San Patricio are interested, and John West, another innocent young man of eighteen summers."
[18] *Austin Statesman,* May 18, 1877.

Lo and Hidalgo." The *Austin Statesman* regretted that Hall had no better mode of disposing of them than jailing.[19]

But conformity with law was Lee Hall's method. He was "peculiar that way." He depleted his Company to provide guards to take the men where they were wanted, just as he depleted his forces to shuttle back and forth the prisoners in the Brazell cases, and to provide security for jurors and for judges. On May 23, when he was on court duty in Castroville, with his Company still divided, he heard that Indian marauders had come within four miles of the town the night before. Unmounted, they had left no tracks that could be traced. Hall was the more eager to get his men together since the time of their service would soon expire. Legislative appropriations for the Company were exhausted. For some time the men had received no pay. Their leader's salary was two months overdue. He lacked the assistance of Lieutenant Armstrong and Sergeant Watson. The Sergeant had been wounded in Yorktown by the explosion of a pistol as it fell from the counter of a store. Armstrong had wounded himself while carelessly handling a gun in Goliad, and could no longer ride his horse. The loss of these two officers, Hall wrote Steele, was unfortunate. He had no men in the Company who could fill their places.[20]

And yet in this period of grave anxiety, there was much that he could be proud of. His men—all of them—agreed to serve for certificates of the State. Their spirit was exceptionally good. They were well informed through the work of the Company spies. They were lean and hard from covering thirty-five miles a day. They were well armed and well mounted. Altogether they constituted a flying squadron, so mobile and efficient that outlaws, who before had spread terror, now themselves were terrorized. It was such a company as the state could not afford to lose.

Petitions for the Rangers' increase and maintenance[21] on a

---

[19] *Daily Democratic Statesman,* May 29, 1877.

[20] Lieutenant Hall to Adjutant General Steele, May 31, 1877, *Hall Ms.*

[21] A memorial to the Governor on this subject was circulated at Eagle Pass and rapidly filled with signatures. The District Judge, District Attorney, and all of the county officials also addressed the Governor: *Petition presented to Gov. Hubbard by County Judges of Maverick County asking that a Detachment of*

permanent basis reached the Governor from the Brasada, the counties of the Taylor-Sutton feud, and more populous districts preyed on by highwaymen. From DeWitt County came an appeal signed by three hundred citizens, led by the county judge and Robert Kleberg, Clerk of the District Court. The petitioners claimed that unless the Company could be maintained until indicted men were tried, the organized bands in the county of the Brazell murders would never be suppressed. Newspapers pointed out that the good effects of the force were not confined to the western border, but felt by the state at large.

The Governor was in a quandary. He needed support from politicians of East Texas, who disapproved of the activities of the Rangers. He wished to maintain the force, and had authority to keep it intact, but lacked the funds to pay it. Ranchmen assisted. Until the time when the next legislature should meet and vote appropriations, the Southwest Texas Stock Association offered to keep Special State Troops in the field. Governor Hubbard agreed, and a meeting of the Association was called at Goliad for June 11.[22] The fact that Goliad was chosen was in itself a tribute to the Company. Until its service there of arresting outlaws, the town would have been an awkward place in which to hold a conference.

Hall went to Goliad to talk with his supporters and to listen. Already the stockmen had appraised the Ranger Lieutenant. They had opportunity now of seeing him in happy mood; of hearing him tell his inimitable stories; of noting, as judges of fine animals, the man's exceptional equipment in muscle coordination, his strength of limb and body. As judges of men, they admired the keenness of his mind, his ability to make quick decisions.

Rolling with one hand his inevitable brown cigarette, the

Special State Troops be stationed at Eagle Pass, May 17, 1877, *Hall Ms.; Petition to Governor Hubbard from citizens of Atascosa County asking that Lieut. Hall's Company be continued in service,* Pleasanton, Texas, June 1, 1877, *Hall Ms.; Petition presented to Governor Hubbard by citizens of Karnes County for retention of the Company of Special State Troops Commanded by Lieut. J. L. Hall, Hall Ms.*

[22] *Galveston Daily News,* May 25, 1877; clipping from *Goliad Guard,* forwarded to Adjutant General Steele by Lieutenant Hall, June 2, 1877.

Ranger also took stock. He knew that to call the roll of those who had undertaken to solicit for the fund in twenty-four adjacent counties was to call the roll of the lords of the southwest ranges: W. A. Pettus, J. N. Keeran, Robert Clark, A. J. West, Tom Coleman, J. M. Mathis, E. R. Lane, Captain Richard King, Tom Worsham.[23] The wealthiest of them was a familiar figure to Hall's Company, as he had been to McNelly's, Captain Richard King. His face was a strong one, somewhat square, the nose cleanly cut, the chin hidden by a beard that swept to the second button of his white shirt front. His eyes were eyes that could see a vision and yet not miss examination of such details as were necessary to bring the vision to reality.[24] He was a native of Orange County, New York; had worked as a cabin boy on a United States vessel in the Seminole War, and in 1850 had joined with Mifflin Kennedy in operating a line of twenty-six steamboats. During the Civil War, their little stern-wheelers, chugging along the Mexican bank of the Rio Grande and loading cotton into British ships at Matamoros, had made a mock of the Federal embargo.[25]

For twenty-six years, he had been a stockman. To circle the Santa Gertrudis Ranch of Captain King involved a ride of sixty miles. And this was only one of his properties. His herds of cattle, his horses, sheep, and goats, kept in employment three hundred Mexicans. For managers, outriders, and personal guards, he employed young Americans.

In the live oak thickets and chaparral of the Nueces country, great herds of cattle had sought shelter earlier from northers. Lack of branding during the Civil War had benefited Captain King, as it had many others, but even without such adventitious circumstances, his success would have been sure. Since 1865 he had not owned a vessel, but he thought of himself still as a captain. Orders at the home ranch were given by the ring-

[23] *Reports of Proceedings of West Texas Stock Association meeting called for purpose of perfecting plans for giving the assistance necessary to retaining the Special State Troops Company commanded by Lt. J. L. Hall in service.* This document contains the names of the Committee on Finance.

[24] See the portrait reproduced to illustrate "The World's Biggest Ranch," *Fortune,* December, 1933.

[25] Owen P. White, "Walled Kingdom," *Colliers,* May 11, 1935; Anna Cora Petz, "History of the Rio Grande Railroad," *Frontier Times,* December, 1936.

ing of bells. Lacking a crow's nest, his lookout was stationed on the roof of a blockhouse. The lookout was needed.[26]

The proximity of his land to the Rio Grande was a perpetual temptation to marauders. The Department of Agriculture's report for 1870 stated that in that year the ranch supported 65,-000 cattle, 10,000 horses, 7,000 sheep, and 8,000 goats. A thousand saddle horses were kept in use each year. The running W , most difficult to blotch,[27] was branded annually upon 12,000 calves. Each year, 10,000 steers were cut from the herds and shipped to market. Natural cattle increase was rated at 33⅓ per cent, but in 1877, the year of the Goliad meeting, the number of animals was less than shown in the census of 1870.[28] The reason was cattle theft by Mexicans.

Captain King's recorded claims against the neighboring country constituted a full-sized pamphlet. Reckoning not only cattle stolen, but loss of natural increase, in 1872 the claims amounted to $27,859,363.[29] They were a prime reason for the creation by Mexico of a commission. When the Commission reported the year following its creation, its findings resulted in counterclaims against the ranchman, his cowboys, and the private force that he employed. Every one in southwest Texas knew that, to the Captain, the only good Mexicans were the Mexicans in his employ. Against others he felt he had just reason for resentment. In turn, these others regarded his men as "gringados"—Mexicans diverted by personal advantage from loyalty to their country.

Captain King could be counted on to support a company so efficient and so needed as Hall's State Troops.

Another contributor, bluff Tom Coleman, was of the famous Chiltepec Ranch near San Patricio, where the Company had served in the hide and tallow war. One of Coleman's partners,

26 T. U. Taylor, "Honeymoon on the Old Cattle Trail," *Frontier Times,* October, 1936; Coleman McCampbell, *Saga of a Frontier Seaport* (Dallas, Southwest Press, 1934).
27 Charles Harrison, "Ranch Founded by Richard King Becomes an Empire," *Houston Chronicle,* quoted in *Frontier Times,* March, 1932. Mexicans called the brand "the little snake."
28 *Department of Agriculture Report for 1870,* quoted by W. MacL. Raine and W. C. Barnes, *Cattle* (New York, Doubleday, Doran & Co., 1930), 20, 21.
29 Owen P. White, *op. cit.;* Dobie, *Vaquero of the Brush Country,* 59.

J. M. Mathis, had built up an immense export business, shipping annually, first over the Morgan Steamship Line and then by freight, from forty to fifty thousand head of cattle.

For Cameron County, the solicitor was Colonel John S. Ford.[30] He was not outstanding as a ranchman. He was a promoter of the Rio Grande Railroad. He was a newspaperman. Sometimes he practiced medicine, sometimes he practiced law. Whatever his profession, he was best known as a militant and military politician. "Rip" Ford, he was called, and the name suggested the character of the dare-devil who had seen service in the war against Mexico; who, as a Captain of Rangers in 1858, had fought against Peta Nacona, chieftain of the Comanches, and in '59 and '60, against General Cortina and his *muchachos*. As Colonel of the Second Cavalry, he had commanded the Rio Grande district in the Civil War, and at Palmetto Road, near Brownsville, defeated Federal troops a full month after Lee's surrender.[31] One who knows the Southwest has pronounced "Rip" Ford "a Texian among Texians, aye, a Texican."[32]

But though the Colonel was a super-patriot, he believed that land across the Rio Grande also was good—so good that, perhaps, he wished to add it unto Texas. In 1852 he had been active in the Carvajal rebellion that had resulted in the formation of the *Zona Libre,* a state over which Mexico was able to exert only a wavering sovereignty. Her failure to prevent raids from that territory, and from other border states, gave the Colonel reason to claim that Texas would not be secure until she extended her frontiers past the Rio Grande and to the mountain range beyond, to Sierra Madre. In Brownsville, he actively supported Porfirio Diaz when Diaz, as a private citizen, sought aid for rebellion against President Tejado.[33] Most recently, the

[30] Colonel John Swisher, *The Swisher Memoirs* (San Antonio, Sigmund Press, 1932), Chapter vii; *House Misc. Doc. No. 64, 260.* For his service against the Comanches, see Arthur Curry, "Story of Cynthia Parker," quoted in *Frontier Times,* December, 1935.

[31] "Civil War Battle Fought after the War," *San Antonio Express,* June 9, 1936.

[32] J. Frank Dobie in *Coronado's Children* (New York, Literary Guild, 1930), 14.

[33] *House Misc. Doc. No. 64,* 253, 260 ff.

Colonel's service had been in fighting the battles of southwest Texas in Austin, in the Senate. He was a doughty opponent of solons from the east.[34] These, never trusting McNelly's Company, regretted that they could do no more than restrict its operations to land west of the Colorado. Kept in the field by the discretionary power of Governor Hubbard, financed by the West Texas Stock Association, and with "Rip" Ford as one of its sponsors, the Company was sure to be a target for criticism. However, the fire that it would draw from eastern solons might prove innocuous. Their aim was notoriously poor.

By correspondence with the Governor before the scheduled meeting, a plan had been arranged, so that when the stockmen assembled in Goliad matters were carried through with dispatch, in contrast to the delays of legislators. It was agreed that a sum would be collected from the twenty-four counties and advanced in two installments, for deposit with Runge and Company of Cuero. The fund would be disbursed on order of the Adjutant General.[35] The total amount was sufficient to reassure the Governor. To the jingling accompaniment of dollars, the men of broad hats and broad acres had spoken. The Lieutenant's troops were to remain in the field!

Lee Hall had no fear of any untoward obligation to the Association which had come to his support. His orders would still come from the Adjutant General. To the Adjutant General he would report. His men were not privately owned. They were Special State Troops of Texas.

[34] *House Report No. 701.*
[35] *Galveston Daily News*, August 2, 1877.

IX
A Matter of Extradition
(May-August, 1877)

"Oh, the dragoon bold, he scorns all care
As he goes around with his uncropped hair,
He spends no thought on the evil star
That sent him away to the border war."

—R. G. CARTER, *On the Border with*
Mackenzie, Eynon Printing Co.

IX

A Matter of Extradition

HALL paid off some outstanding accounts after the Goliad meeting of the Texas ranchmen, captured the bank robber, Bracken, who had occasioned his first scout, and arrested the Cavens, killers whose confessions implicated many others. He did not relax his guard over King Fisher and the men indicted for the Brazell murders. He trailed fresh scents and he kept a weather eye on war clouds gathering on the Rio Grande.

On his visit to Lieutenant Colonel Shafter at Fort Clark in May, 1877, he had found that officer indignant at the loss of two Mexican guides. Shafter told Hall that after the guides had aided him in pursuing Indians on American soil, they had been captured and imprisoned across the river from Eagle Pass at Piedras Negras. When Shafter had crossed to seize the jail and free them, they had been hurried away to the interior.[1] Nor had the Mexicans released them when the general commanding the Department of Texas notified authorities that, if harm was done the guides, it would be tantamount to a declaration that Mexico intended to coöperate with Indian marauders.[2] The Mexicans claimed that the guides were Mexican citizens and criminals, and that Shafter's entry into Piedras Negras constituted a hostile invasion.[3] The question of citizenship was im-

---

[1] Lieutenant Hall to Adjutant General Steele, May 16, 1877, *Hall Ms.;* General Ord's Testimony, *House Misc. Doc. No. 64,* 13-15.

[2] J. H. Taylor, Assistant Adjutant General U. S. A., to General Hipolito Charles, Governor of the State of Coahuila, Mexico, April 3, 1877, *Correspondencia Diplomatica.* This is a pamphlet of 94 pages on Mexico's relations with the United States, June to October, 1877.

[3] See statement of Mexican Minister of Foreign Affairs I. L. Vallarta, quoted in *House Misc. Doc. No. 64,* 310.

portant. The treaty of 1861 freed both governments from the necessity of surrendering any citizen who had committed crimes on the territory of the other. In this matter, even if the men who had seized the guides were criminals and had crossed to capture them, the United States could not claim extradition of the captors so long as they were Mexican citizens.

Shafter well knew that, unless the guides were released or avenged, others would fear to serve him. And guides he needed! He was eager to change the reputation of the army on the border—to show that there was a difference between his men and the men of the sixties, who chased Indians in mule-drawn wagons or astride grain-fed Missouri horses, lamed after a day in the chaparral. The Rangers, since the time of Governor Coke, had the privilege, with some restrictions, of crossing. Shafter suggested to his superior that his own troops be permitted to cross when marauders were in sight or when the trail was fresh. He told Hall that marauding Indians were aggravatingly close—only ten miles from the border. Hall relayed the information to Steele and informed him, also, that Shafter was eager for Rangers and soldiers to work together.[4] But later! The Colonel knew that his suggestion as to crossing would have to follow a devious line of red tape before it could be acted on.

The Commander of the Department of Texas was General Edward Otho Cresop Ord. Under him were all troops stationed in the chain of forts extending from Fort Concho south to Ringgold Barracks and westward to Fort Stockton. The chief part of the frontier that he attempted to protect was the 450 miles from the mouth of the Rio Grande to Fort Clark. General Ord was vigorous enough to ride the frontier with any corporal.[5] His courtesy and tact, men said, could be traced to his grandfather, that "first gentleman of Europe," who had married the beautiful Catholic, Mrs. Fitzherbert, before acceding to the throne as George IV.[6]

[4] Telegram of Lieutenant Hall to Adjutant General Steele, Eagle Pass, May 16, 1877, *Hall Ms.*

[5] This was General Sherman's opinion. For the disposition of U. S. troops in Texas, see *Misc. House Doc. No. 64,* 28, 29, 35.

[6] Bushick, *Glamorous Days,* 38, 39; Sweet and Knox, *On a Mexican Mustang,* 505-510.

All of his tact and all of his courtesy, he needed, for Texans were indignant that forts were not increased, nor were they adequately manned. The Ranger knew that in the summer of 1877 conditions were particularly bad. In one section alone— that between Corpus Christi and Laredo—Mexican bandits were plentiful and, as he reported to Steele, Indians raided as many as three times in a moon. The states of Tamaulipas, Coahuila, and Chihuahua were doing nothing to restrain them. Mexican towns vied with each other in showing their patriotism by purchasing stolen goods and stolen cattle.[7]

When General Ord received from Colonel Shafter the suggestion that United States troops, on occasion, be allowed to cross the border, he tugged at his white mustache and considered how best he could strengthen this into a recommendation. He knew very well that both American and Mexican officers, from time to time, had crossed without permission from officials of the "invaded" territory, and that Rangers did it frequently. With the hope of regulating the situation, General Ord relayed Colonel Shafter's suggestion to Washington.

The President, at this time, was Rutherford B. Hayes. He had in Texas a lifelong friend, Guy M. Bryan, on whom he depended for information.[8] Bryan had been frank in informing him of border dangers. President Hayes, after reading General Ord's dispatch, sent such instructions to his Secretary of War as he believed appropriate. The Secretary passed them on to General Sherman. Sherman embodied them in the famous order of June 1, 1877, which he transmitted to General Ord:

> "In case the lawless invasions continue, you will be at liberty . . . when in pursuit of marauders, and when your troops are in sight of them or upon a fresh trail, to follow them across the Rio Grande and to overtake and punish them as well as retake property stolen from the United States citizens on the other side of the line."[9]

[7] Colonel W. R. Shafter's report, dated March 9, 1877, *House Misc. Doc. No. 64*, 9, 10; General Ord's testimony, *ibid.*, 90.

[8] E. W. Winkler (ed.), "Hayes-Bryan Correspondence," *Southwestern Historical Quarterly*, April, October, 1924.

[9] J. Fred Rippy, *The United States and Mexico* (New York, Knopf, 1926); 299; *House Misc. Doc. No. 64*, 175, 176.

Accompanying the order was President Hayes's injunction that military forces observe the utmost vigilance for the suppression of all raids. If necessary, Ord should let the Mexicans know that depredations would make it necessary for his troops to cross the Rio Grande.

The neighboring President whom this remarkable order affected was Porfirio Diaz, newly possessed of power and determined to retain it. He had gained office, in part, by campaign speeches denouncing as illegal the concessions granted Americans by Lerdo de Tejado. How long Diaz could hold his rival's place was problematic. On January 19, 1877, Secretary Fish gave our minister, John Foster, discretional authority to recognize Diaz's provisional government.[10] With the change of administration in Washington, recognition receded into the background.[11]

News of the order of June 1, and news that an unprecedented number of troops were being massed on the Rio Grande under General Mackenzie, increased the difficulties of the President of Mexico. The size of the American force was large enough to convince its privates that soon they would be marching into Mexico. What they thought, they said. Border Mexicans listened and repeated.

The neighboring country seethed with indignation. Editorials referred to the fact that a Congressional committee in Washington, as early as February, 1876, had favored the practice of sending troops across the river at discretion. The Mexicans contended that the Americans were not really interested in recovering stolen goods, but wished to steal more territory. Our Minister to Mexico, John W. Foster, protested to a government we did not recognize that editorials carrying such imputations in official journals were reprehensible. Yet Foster himself was, and remained, doubtful of the honesty of the Washington administration. He was receiving visitors with dubious motives

[10] C. W. Hackett, "Recognition of the Diaz Government by the United States," *Southwestern Historical Quarterly*, July, 1924.

[11] John W. Foster, *Diplomatic Memoirs* (Boston, Houghton Mifflin, 1909), I, 92.

who were involved in a conspiracy to coerce Mexico into the sale of border states.[12]

Mexican citizens rejoiced when, instead of witnessing the sale of territory, they were given an opportunity to boast that government troops had entered Texas. The crossing of the River was the result of ardent pursuit of Lerdist bands that had raided from Texas and recrossed. In accordance with telegraphed instructions from General Ord, American forces did not pursue. On the contrary, when Lerdist colonels and their men sought refuge in Colonel Shafter's camp, the Colonel had them disarmed and temporarily detained.[13]

The United States protested violation of her territory. Diaz, to forestall the danger of another crossing, sent to the border General Geronimo Treviño, with orders to coöperate with Ord and to prevent raiding from either side. If Americans should attempt to put into effect the order of June 1, Treviño was to "repel force with force."[14] Diaz could not have done less than this to uphold the Extradition Treaty and maintain his place. The Mexican Secretary of Foreign Affairs, Señor Vallarta, proudly declared that not even his country's President had the power to permit invasion.[15] The United States, Vallarta claimed, was treating the Mexicans like "Kaffirs of Africa." He had information from Washington and from New York that convinced him war and annexation of territory were projected. The Mexican press continued bellicose in its denunciations. The officer whom Diaz had sent to the border was more reasonable than the Latin gentlemen of the Fourth Estate. Geronimo Treviño and Ord mutually communicated their orders, attempted to work in harmony, and formed satisfactory opinions of each other's honesty.[16]

Could Hall's Special State troopers and the Frontier Battalion be depended on for similar forbearance?

---

[12] *Ibid.*, 93.

[13] *House Misc. Doc. No. 64*, 15, 74.

[14] Foster's telegram to Acting Secretary of State Evarts, *House Report No. 701* (for complete citation see Note 4, Chapter iv), 1.

[15] Minister Vallarta's statements are quoted in *House Misc. Doc. No. 64*, 295; see also *Correspondencia Diplomatica* for Vallarta's protest of June 18, 1877.

[16] *House Report No. 701*, 247-50.

The temptation for a scrap was always present in the Nueces country and the *Zona Libre*.[17] In the former, the principal city was Brownsville. In the latter, the principal city was Matamoros. Who were Mexican citizens of the *Zona Libre* and who were American citizens of the Nueces Strip, officials found it difficult to tell. The treaty of Guadalupe Hidalgo stated that the boundary should be "where the Rio Grande now runs."[18] It was a fickle river, making cut-offs that left a thousand or so acres sometimes on the Texas side, sometimes on the Mexican. The cut-offs benefited neither country, but were highly prized by criminals of both. The problem of determining citizenship was increased by ignorance of Mexicans as to the land of their birth and willingness to change their ideas on the subject if political organizations—the "Reds" and "Blues" of Brownsville —would pay them for making marks on ballots.

The problem of ignorance in the *Zona Libre* was as nothing to the problem of criminality. Rangers were not expansionists. They did not read the *New York Herald,* nor exaggerate, as it did, the iniquities of their neighbors. But their interpretation of *Zona Libre* was "Catch as catch can within a mile of the River." Between Matamoros and Nuevo Laredo, they crossed when a man they wanted was on the other side. And they crossed frequently. The people of the *Zona Libre* were not versed in the Ten Commandments. Special State Troops and the Frontier Battalion were learned as to the contents of the Crime Book, but poor scholars of the Extradition Treaty; indifferent to Mexican politics; careless of the effect upon political *jefes* of excursions beyond the Rio Grande.[19]

The *muchachos* of Cortina, old enemies of the Rangers, kept the *Zona Libre* constantly astir. Their leader was imprisoned,[20] but they mingled with other bandits whose exploits had served to isolate Tamaulipas from Mexico and give excuse for the

[17] *House Misc. Doc. No. 64,* 145, 146.
[18] *Ibid.,* 225, 282.
[19] Testimony of H. C. Corbin, Twenty-fourth Infantry, *House Misc. Doc. No. 64,* 145-51.
[20] *House Misc. Doc. No. 64,* 81, 210. The Secretary of War in 1860 had directed Colonel Robert E. Lee of the Second Cavalry to push his efforts beyond the boundary of the United States to capture Cortina. *House Misc. Doc. No. 64,* 9.

creation of a free zone as necessary to preserve the state. A quota of soldier-adventurers had drifted in from the disbanded army of Maximilian. To them, were added contingents from more recent revolutionary forces. Some of the unsuccessful companies had been recruited on Texas soil. Americans were accustomed to making fat sums from sale to these of ammunition and provisions. For a certain group of citizens in Brownsville, Mexican revolutions were regarded as an industry. Some were willing to content themselves with gain from loans and contracts. Some hoped that northern influence might create a border state amenable to their wishes.[21]

Porfirio Diaz had more than once used Brownsville as a place of refuge. He had recruited on Texas soil. After becoming head of the provisional government, he changed his ideas on the rôle that Brownsville should play in Mexican affairs. He was alarmed at the activities there of Lerdo de Tejado. In Cortina's former stronghold, Tamaulipas of the *Zona Libre,* he knew that recruits against him were enlisted with vigor and dispatch. Across the river, in the Nueces Strip, the companies of his rival were enrolled with equal energy. Diaz feared a combination of Mexican political *jefes* with land-greedy Texans and renegade Americans from other states. Paymaster for the new recruits was General Escobedo,[22] ranchman and farmer, chief agent in the execution of Maximilian, Minister of War under Tejado, and three times a millionaire. His wish was to restore to Mexico the policies of Benito Juarez, and to that end he was lavish in the distribution of his wealth. Among his troops and those of Pedro Valdes, his lieutenant, were outlaws whose names Rangers had memorized as camp fires brought black print to light in well-thumbed Books of Crimes.

Mexican recruiting interested both state and United States troops. Five miles from Camargo, where in November, 1875,

[21] Sweet and Knox, *op. cit.,* 505-510. Thomas F. Wilson, U. S. Consul at Matamoros, testified:

"Since the Mexican War the frontier people of Texas have thought that an extension of the boundary to the Sierra Madre would be advantageous and they appear to desire it ... have at various times participated in revolutionary movements in Mexico, on the border sometimes with the object of setting up what is spoken of as the Sierra Madre Republic."

[22] Webb, *The Texas Rangers,* 285, 286.

McNelly had demanded the return of stolen cattle with success,[23] was situated Ringgold Barracks. At that post, from which in the fateful November Captain Randlett had come to McNelly's assistance, the Eighth Cavalry was stationed under command of Major Price. The Major watched with anxiety the rallying of outlaws to the Escobedo standard. He was uneasy that there should be such Mexican activity on Texas soil. When he heard that eight cases filled with Remington breechloaders and their ammunition were expected to arrive at Brownsville on the *S. S. Ackley* for use against Diaz, he notified headquarters in San Antonio. In accordance with Ord's subsequent orders, Price marched to the camp of the revolutionists and took as prisoners General Escobedo and two of his officers.[24] The *Ackley* docked, but its consignment of arms, lacking an address, remained unclaimed and was returned to the port of shipment. Escobedo and his officers gave bond to keep the peace, and pending trial were released.

Unfortunately, the army which the Mexican general was financing did not melt away. Since pay was not forthcoming, it disintegrated. The men who had expected to follow Escobedo, Valdes, and other revolutionists, reverted to civilian industries, most of them illicit. Lee Hall calculated that the disbanding of the army turned loose upon the border some three hundred cutthroats.[25] Twenty miles distant from Eagle Pass, one of their camps sent out frequent expeditions for cattle thieving.[26] Telegrams received by General Ord concerning this confirmed the information brought in by Rangers' spies. Officers and men, stationed at Fort Duncan, witnessed constantly the driving of stolen cattle across the River towards the outlaw camp.

Adjutant General Steele wrote Hall of a report that the border criminals were plotting his assassination and that of his Lieutenant, John Armstrong; that he had been warned they

---

[23] *House Misc. Doc. No. 64,* 89, 212, 263, 281, 282, 287; Webb, *op. cit.,* 248 ff. This raid doubled the price of beef on the border, according to the United States Commercial Agent at Camargo, *House Misc. Doc. No. 64,* 220.

[24] *Ibid.,* 75.

[25] Telegram of Lieutenant Hall to Adjutant General Steele, July 28, 1877, *Hall Ms.*

[26] Lieutenant Hall to Adjutant General Steele, Castroville, July 29, 1877, *ibid.*

would march then on Huntsville and Austin to empty the penitentiaries and add the convicts to their forces.[27] Lee Hall wasted none of his spies on the matter. Threats were not new to him, nor were assaults upon his life. He regarded this particular rumor as the meaningless sound and fury distilled from mescal and mendacity.

He received with far more interest a number of warrants for border arrests, for the news of raids and depredations had substance. The time for the "big round-up" had come. On July 30, with his pockets bulging with warrants, he rode out from Castroville with his Company.

The destination was Eagle Pass, but he broke the journey of 120 miles with a stop next day at the Ranger camp of Captain Neal Coldwell near Frio City. His men were joined there by a detachment of eighteen under Sergeant George Arrington, who himself was worth some eighteen more. When the Company reached Eagle Pass, the force divided to surround the town. What gaps there must have been between the sentinels! The capital city of the deposed King Fisher's domain submitted meekly when Lee Hall and his party entered, searched out its criminals, and lodged them in the jail.[28]

The arrests were too numerous to remain secret. Across the Rio Grande, the news of Hall's arrival produced "alarums and excursions." Certain wanted gentry developed a yearning for speedy visits to far distant points. When a detachment followed the River southward, news of their advance sped ahead and Mexicans delayed them by false directions. The largest group of outlaws struck camp and scattered. Not until August 6 were arrests made in any considerable number. On that day, Hall and his troopers rounded up forty of Valdes's men and cut out from the number four murderers and three horse thieves for whom the Lieutenant carried warrants.[29] James Beadsale, who had evaded an engagement with the hangman for a matter of seventeen years, was rated first among the captives.[30] Those

[27] Webb, *The Texas Rangers*, 339.

[28] Lieutenant Hall's report to Adjutant General Steele, Eagle Pass, August 15, 1877, *Hall Ms.*

[29] Telegram of Lieutenant Hall to Adjutant General Steele, Eagle Pass, August 6, 1877, *ibid.*

[30] *Daily Democratic Statesman*, August 18, 1877.

released made off with alacrity. Two Mexican officers and forty-four men, in flight towards Eagle Pass, were promptly re-arrested by another detachment of the Company, scouting with troops from Ringgold Barracks.[31] Since Hall's men had the power of sheriffs, the cavalrymen could witness arrests that would not bring evil consequences. Pettifogging lawyers would have no chance of gaining fees by plaguing Uncle Sam for detention of unsavory clients.

On August 10, the sheriff of Webb County added to the quota by the arrest of two Mexican captains and Pedro Valdes,[32] second only to Escobedo among the enemies of Diaz.

By the middle of August, Hall and his men had filled the jail at Eagle Pass to capacity. There seemed small chance of taking more, for the element of surprise had been eliminated. The American side of the border had become scrupulously obedient to the law. The Ranger yearned for a return to DeWitt and a scout into Nueces—counties where unfinished business made a clamorous call.

Adjutant General Steele was right in keeping him at Eagle Pass. On the Mexican side, men felt the pinch of enforced and unaccustomed honesty. The anti-Diaz faction still was strong. Anger at arrest of their leaders made its members denounce Americans with oaths so ardent as to seem superbly patriotic. They longed for the return of Cortina, prisoner of Diaz in San Juan de Ulloa. They fanned their wrath by recounting the raids of Captain McNelly and Captain Randlett at Camargo in '75. In *tiendas* and *tabernas,* men boasted that the Captains had been compelled to retire. No Mexican was so disloyal as to mention that the episode had not been ended till McNelly's demands were met and stolen cattle delivered to the Rangers in Rio Grande City. But Mexicans remembered this privately, and it was for this they wished revenge. With each new man the Rangers jailed, the wish increased. And yet Lee Hall kept peace. Respect for the red headed Lieutenant and fear of him were so great that the inevitable border incident, when it took place, occurred not at Eagle Pass but at Rio Grande City.

[31] *House Misc. Doc. No. 64,* 15.
[32] *Denison Daily News,* August 10, 1877.

x
Fandango Across the Rio Grande

"He never made parade of tooth or claw,
He was plain as us that nursed the bawlin' herds,
Though he had a rather meanin' lookin' jaw,
He was shy of exercisin' it with words.

.   .   .   .

"For he stood for peace and order on the lonely,
      sunny border
And his business was to hunt for sinful man."

— BADGER CLARK, *Sun and Saddle Leather.*

Fandango Across the Rio Grande

In August, 1877, the small jail in Rio Grande City, like the large one at Eagle Pass, was crowded. In Camargo, men complained that there were held in durance *gente de honor*—men of Mexican blood who had killed Americans, the ravishers of their *patria;* fellow-citizens who recovered cattle from Americans who had driven them across the river and sold them to other "gringos." Americans listed these patriots as three murderers and sundry horse and cattle thieves. One, only, was sufficiently important to be kept in irons. This was Segundo Garza.[1] Formerly a captain under Lerdo de Tejado, he headed a political party that kept alive the hatred and methods of Cortina and was leader of the remnant of his *muchachos.* Segundo Garza boasted that he had killed seventeen Americans. For such prowess and discrimination, he was rated a hero. That he should be in jail at Rio Grande City was as great a humiliation to his compatriots as had been the return of Las Cuevas cattle in 1875.

On the night of August 12, Segundo's brother, Rafael, with a group of his *compadres* crossed the river from Camargo. Rafael stationed some of the men around the jail as lookouts. Then he attacked. The jailer, three guards, and the county attorney were wounded while attempting a defense. As they lay helpless, Rafael's party broke in, found Garza stretched out on a rawhide, struck the handcuffs from him, and carried him out. The other prisoners followed. All ran for the river pursued by Major William Price, Lieutenant Fountain, and a detachment

---

[1] Major Price's testimony, January 26, 1878, *House Report No. 701* (for complete citation see Note 4, Chapter iv).

of cavalry. The Mexicans crossed. The American officers did not follow.[2] The Order of June 1 had been weakened by instructions not to go over unless there was no Mexican force ready to suppress and punish marauders.[3] The order's application to the present case was doubtful. It did not refer specifically to jail deliveries, and only by an interpretation as wide as a church door could the prisoners be regarded as "property stolen from the United States." The cavalry officers watered their horses in the muddy Rio Grande, swore, and returned to barracks.[4]

Since the United States still extended recognition to Lerdo de Tejado, and since Escobedo, his official, had given Major Price his oath that he and his men would keep the peace, the American commander, on returning to Camp Ringgold, telegraphed to Escobedo at Mier. He reminded him of his pledge and demanded assistance. If this was not forthcoming, the Major threatened to cross the river and take Garza and his rescuers wherever he could. Also, the officer telegraphed an account of the jail delivery to General Ord.

Jail breakers and jailbirds breakfasted together before an audience of admirers that converted the meal of *café, con huevos rancheros,* into a public celebration.

A few hours later, the Sheriff and Major Price crossed to demand surrender of the prisoners and punishment of their deliverers. Though it was not the time of the *siesta,* 'dobe houses were shut and silent. Dust lay in heavy quiet in the streets. On

---

[2] Dan Roberts, *Rangers and Sovereignty,* 95; Reports of Commanding General, Department of Texas [E. O. C. Ord.], *House Misc. Doc. 64,* (for complete citation see Note 3, Chapter IV), 76; October 1, 1877, *ibid.,* 12; Governor Hubbard to President Hayes, August 13, 1877, *House Report No. 701,* 331; Major Price's testimony, January 26, 1878, *House Report No. 701.*

[3] Colonel Shafter's testimony, *House Misc. Doc. No. 64,* 163, 164.

[4] By the treaty of 1861 the governments of the two signatory powers were mutually exempt from the obligation of surrendering their respective citizens. In the matter of the Rio Grande jail delivery, the Mexicans later made an exception, ordering the delivery of two or more raiders that they acknowledged were Mexican citizens. This, the Mexican government held, was not to be considered as forming a precedent, *(House Report No. 701,* 334). Major Price acknowledged that under the treaty there was no remedy for the sufferers from this Rio Grande raid, and added:

"Under such a treaty I do not see how anyone is safe on that border." *(House Misc. Doc. No. 64,* 120).

the shady side of corners, where men usually squatted to exchange the gossip of the day, there was no animation. Outside the butcher shops, meat hung in the dry hot air. No black-shawled women, with children tugging at their skirts, came by to purchase. A few dogs dozed in the shadows of high walls. Gamecocks in wooden coops stared obliquely at the officers and then resumed their pecking. An old negro, alone in the somnolent plaza, explained the unaccustomed quiet: the men were meeting in the Court House.

There the Americans followed with their demands.[5] If citizens had entertained the idea of inducing the visit of the officers and detaining them, they gave up their plan. Mexican troops had not yet arrived and American cavalry might cross to investigate. The leaders in the Court House pretended to be submissive. They lied and were evasive and rejoiced that their accusers realized the deception was not intended really to deceive. The officers returned to their side of the river and the Major sent a telegram to General Ord which ended: "Am ready with one hundred men and two Gatling guns."[6]

Ord's telegram to Governor Hubbard quoted this and added: "This is a matter for you to act on."

The Governor acted. He telegraphed, in the General's care, a demand[7] to be conveyed to Tamaulipas authorities by wire "or otherwise," as Ord desired. He offered to call out the militia, and asked that General Ord take over the command of all State troops on the border.

That night, the thirteenth, thirty Mexican cavalrymen clattered into Camargo from Mier—the first of the men sent by Escobedo, ostensibly to give assistance to Major Price, but really to prevent Americans from crossing, or to give them a warm welcome. Escobedo, with a battalion of 250, and Major Regino, with a troop of cavalry, began a forced march the same

[5] Extract from dispatch of Lieutenant Hall to Governor Hubbard, *Daily Democratic Statesman*, August 25, 1877.

[6] Major Price's testimony, January 26, 1878, and papers relative to raid, *House Report No. 701.*

[7] Vallarta's reaction to the Governor's demand is recounted in his reply to Foster's inquiries as to what Mexican authorities were doing to apprehend and punish the jail breakers. *(House Report No. 701, 458).*

[113]

day. They set out with jubilation to kill "gringos." The distance from Mier to Camargo was only about twenty-eight miles, but tumultuous enthusiasm and the August heat caused fourteen men to die of sunstroke. The dead were eulogized in the *Mier Whip* as "victims of gringo politics."[8]

Garza and his party were never more than ten miles distant from Camargo.[9] They entered frequently to bask in the admiration of its inhabitants. Wherever they went, they engendered enthusiasm. Passion was so aroused that Escobedo's men in Camargo could have been increased by from two to three thousand in forty-eight hours.[10]

On August 13, the Governor wrote President Hayes of the jail delivery, stating that under the Extradition Treaty he had authority to demand extradition of criminals from Mexico, which he proposed to do, and he solicited, moreover, the co-operation of a simultaneous demand from the President. He intended to ask, also, reparation for the raid and punishment of the raiders. The Governor addressed a similar letter to General Ord.[11] Both dispatches, as well as the Governor's demands on Mexico, were published. Indignant citizens in Austin, San Antonio, and Brownsville, held meetings. Young hotbloods talked of recruiting. Old war horses, like Rip Ford, smelled battle and calculated the time they had to wait.

The Acting Secretary of State, F. W. Seward, telegraphed assurance that the Governor's demand was in accordance with treaty stipulations and that appropriate measures would immediately be taken. The measures consisted of instructions to United States Minister to Mexico, John W. Foster, to supplement the demands, if necessary, with Federal demands for extradition. This was done. Much courtesy was shown our Min-

---

[8] Major Price's testimony, January 26, 1878, *ibid.*; Webb, *The Texas Rangers*, 294.

[9] Major Price's testimony of January 26, 1878:
"They were all for a week or ten days within a radius of ten miles."
Lieutenant Hall to Governor Hubbard, Rio Grande City, *Daily Democratic Statesman*, August 25, 1877: "I was reliably informed they were within five miles of this place." General Ord's testimony, *House Report No. 701:* "It was reported to me time and again by Captain Hall of the State Forces ... that the principal man of the party and several others of the party were living but four miles from our side of the river near the city of Camargo."

[10] Major Price's testimony, January 26, 1878, *House Report No. 701.*
[11] *Ibid.*, 331.

ister. There was no action. Nor did appeal to the military authorities of President Diaz bring results. General Ord, when he asked the assistance of General Treviño, found him unwilling to coöperate.

"I have told you," wrote Treviño, "that the government of my country will use such means as she has at hand to give protection to the residents in Mexican territory,"[12] [troops massed on the border, instructions to 'repel force by force,' Ord must have commented!] "but it will not be able to take care also to insure the same security to the towns of foreign territory."

Let American citizens look after themselves, guard well their jails and county attorneys!

So much for the attempts of Major Price, General Ord, and our diplomat! Affairs had been twisted into a knot so complicated that it appeared it could be loosened by no other methods than those used by Rangers—forceful, direct demands, followed, if need be, by forceful, direct impacts of bullets. General Ord had not accepted the Governor's offer to take over command of state troops. Adjutant General Steele ordered to the border two companies of the Frontier Battalion and Special State Troops under Lieutenant Hall.

A detachment of nine men was in Eagle Pass with Hall. Sergeant Watson had neglected to report and his exact location was not known. Lieutenant Armstrong, because of his self-inflicted wound, was still unable to serve. Hall was encumbered with as many prisoners as he had men—the result of scouting in the district. He and some of the others had been ill. Several remained on the sick list. Many of the mounts, due to hard riding, were not fit for immediate service.[13] On receipt of the order to go to Rio Grande City, Hall telegraphed Steele that he would set out next morning. The absent men were ordered to join him on the border. The distance from Eagle Pass to Rio Grande City was 225 miles. Fevered with heat, gaunt from lack of food, tongues swollen under their bits from lack of water, many horses died before the journey's end.

---

[12] *Ibid.*, xviii.
[13] Lieutenant Hall to Adjutant General Steele, Eagle Pass, August 15, 1877, *Hall Ms.*

While the detachment put the miles behind them, President Diaz took action. His wish was that the matter of extradition be disposed of pacifically. When some of the prisoners delivered from the jail of Rio Grande City fled to Matamoros, he sent General Benavidez there as special commissioner, empowering him to offer $2,000 for their capture. On August 17, Benavidez telegraphed General Ord that one of the prisoners had been captured at Guerrero.[14] Other arrests followed. The criminals were held by the Commander at Matamoros, who hesitated to surrender them to General Benavidez, even on the express orders of President Diaz. Resentment at the interference of the central government was so acute that Benavidez had to disguise himself and flee by night to Brownsville. He traveled light and swiftly, leaving behind the gold-braided uniforms and such other habiliments and appurtenances as were proper for a Mexican general representing *el Presidente*. His flight and the resistance of Matamoros to the government's commands strengthened the opposition to Porfirio Diaz.[15] It was claimed he was not able to make himself even a president *de facto*. Thus matters stood when Hall and his detachment reached Rio Grande City on August 21, just four and a half days from the date they started. Two years before, McNelly's Company had received there the Las Cuevas cattle. Men of the Company remembered Camargo—and Camargo remembered the Company.

Major Price came at once to consult with its commander. The cavalry officer was quick to like the Ranger who could bring his men 225 miles in four days and a half, and use the other half day to confer as to what was to be done next day. Equally, Lieutenant Hall liked the Major. The "Benzine Board" had cleansed the border of officers who, during the Civil War, had become too much addicted to alcohol. The Major was of the new order—alert, clear-eyed, and daring. He and the Ranger spoke the same language. Had they been able to act together in the beginning as they wished, results would

---

[14] This was Rudolpho Esproncedo, *House Report No. 701.*

[15] Testimony of Julius G. Tucker, ranchman and contractor for military supplies and provisions, *House Misc. Doc. No. 64,* 231. General Ord testified that General Benavidez fled in fear of his life.

have been speedy. As it was, the Major was constrained to say that he had been ordered not to cross, that the matter was to be settled only by the civil authorities of Texas.[16] According to his testimony given later before a committee of the House, his instructions were to place the matter in the hands of extradition agents. However, Hall reported that, to him, Price used the term, "civil authorities of Texas."[17] The wording is important, since the Lieutenant and his ununiformed men had the power of sheriffs and regarded themselves in such capacity as civil officers.

On August 22, Major Price and Lieutenant Hall rode the five miles to Camargo to confer with the *Commandante,* Colonel Gomez. They found him suavely courteous. He assured them that Mexican officials were doing everything possible to cooperate. And yet, according to the information of the American officers, some of the wanted men were at that time no more than four miles distant from the *Commandante's* headquarters, and under surveillance, so that, if necessary, they could be given up. Lieutenant Hall referred him to a copy of the *San Antonio Express,*[18] in which was prominently displayed

"THE GOVERNOR'S DEMANDS[19]

"Austin, August 13—To the Governor or Chief Civil Authority of the Republic of Mexico: I am officially advised through Brig. Gen. Ord, commanding the Department of Texas, that on the 12th inst. a number of men crossed the Rio Grande to Rio Grande City, in Starr County, in the State of Texas, and did unlawfully break open the county jail thereof, release two murderers and desperadoes confined therein, and wound the County Attorney, Noah Cox, and three jailers severely.

"If any of these jail breakers be not citizens of Mexico, I demand under the extradition treaty, on proper proof, that they be delivered to the authorities of Starr County, to the sheriff or other

---

[16] "Colonel Price . . . told me that he had instructions to turn over the whole matter to the civil authorities of this state."—Lieutenant Hall's dispatch to Governor Hubbard, Rio Grande City, August 25, 1877, *Daily Democratic Statesman,* August 27, 1877.

[17] Major Price's testimony, January 26, 1878, *House Report No. 701.*

[18] The visit is recounted in the dispatch of Lieutenant Hall to Governor Hubbard, noted *supra.*

[19] *San Antonio Express,* August 15, 1877.

legal officer for trial. Also that the rescued prisoners be returned. The demand will be forwarded through General Ord, who will, at my request, see to its execution through the proper official channel."

—R. B. HUBBARD, Governor.

The Mexican *Commandante* noted the understatement as to the number of men released and that the demands were addressed to "the Governor or Chief Civil Authority of the Republic of Mexico." In the same paper was a copy of Hubbard's message to Ord, offering to subject State troops to the commands of the United States officer and to call out the militia.

Rolling his brown cigarette, the Lieutenant gave the *Commandante* exactly four days in which to deliver the jail breakers and the men they had released.

It is not surprising that uneasiness led to confusion. The angry presence of Major Price and the Lieutenant was alarming, and the *Commandante*, when he reported the interview, claimed that Hall threatened invasion and stated that, in Texas, a force of 25,000 men was being organized.[20] Hall's telegram next day to the Adjutant General, told of nothing more belligerent than the demand for the surrender of the wanted men.[21]

A certain Brownsville citizen, Julius Tucker, heard of the interview from General Benavidez. Tucker was a ranchman and contractor, with a habit of provisioning Mexican revolutionists. His own politics, he said, stopped with his pocketbook. He had sold arms to Diaz, via Colonel Ford, and later furnished them to Escobedo, when that General was trying to oust Diaz from Matamoros. According to Tucker's somewhat unsavory testimony, the *Commandante's* account of the interview caused Benavidez to renew his efforts to carry out the pacific mission of his President. Probably, also, Benavidez's alarm was occasioned by the fact that, on the twenty-third, a formal requisition for extradition was presented to General Canales, Governor of Tamaulipas. Three of the men, Canales held in Mata-

[20] The *Commandante,* Colonel Gomez, reported this to the sympathetic *Commandante* at Matamoros, General Canales, who was delaying the surrender of prisoners whom President Diaz had ordered to be given up.
[21] Lieutenant Hall to Adjutant General Steele, Rio Grande City, August 23, 1877, *Hall Ms.*

moros under guard. He claimed that, since they were Mexican citizens, he was not bound to surrender them, that he would not be known as Diaz's cat's-paw—he preferred popularity and re-election to his office. The position of Benavidez, a refugee in Brownsville under American protection, was not one that he envied. The Federal troops, sent to support the demands of Benavidez, were fraternizing with the rebellious forces of Tamaulipas. General Canales felt secure in his defiance.

The Mexican General on the Texas side of the Rio Grande felt otherwise. He could not return to Diaz and report his mission a failure, and he was so hated by the anti-Diaz faction that his life was in danger. In extremity, he appealed to the ammunition contractor, Julius Tucker, to go to Camargo and urge compliance on the *Commandante*. Tucker undertook the mission, but first informed the United States Commander at Fort Brown of Lieutenant Hall's threat of invasion. While telegrams were flying, Tucker had himself driven one hundred miles to Camargo, arriving August 24.

The streets were crowded. *Rancheros* from Las Cuevas and Bolsa, strongholds of the "wet stock" industry, mingled with the varied smugglers of the *Zona Libre*. The Mexicans carried their guns and *machetes* with bravado. Shuck cigarettes no longer drooped from loosened lips. Knife-straight, they looked belligerent. The *alcalde*, pointing to the bravos, suggested to Tucker that, in Camargo, it would be difficult to follow the instructions of General Benavidez. The contractor found Major Price and Lieutenant Hall standing at ease in the store of the American commercial agent. Major Price told Tucker that, if permitted, he could himself arrest the outlaw, and arrest him quickly. Afterwards, in testimony given before a commission of the House, Tucker claimed the two officers had been drinking.[22] In testimony of a later date, he expressed no such opinion.[23]

Meanwhile, General Ord was alarmed by a telegram from the commander at Fort Brown which gave Tucker's version of Hall's threat of an invasion. The General communicated the in-

---

[22] *House Misc. Doc. No. 64*, 230-33.
[23] Testimony of Julius Tucker, January 24, 1878, *House Report No. 701*, 109. At this time the contractor referred to "Lt. Hall." In his earlier testimony he spoke of him as "this man Hall."

formation to the Governor. Hubbard, thereupon, telegraphed the Ranger that *he had not been sent to invade Mexico, but to assist the civil authorities to keep the peace.*[24]

In view of Hubbard's statements published in the *San Antonio Express* of August 15, it is difficult to blame Hall for thinking that he had been sent to the border to catch the jail deliverers and regain the released prisoners. The Governor then had recommended that the "outrage" be followed up "sharply and vigorously." The Lieutenant at once told Tucker of the receipt and contents of the Governor's telegram. Next day, Hall answered it by giving a very clear account of his actions. He reminded the Governor that Major Price had stated that the matter of the released prisoners and jail breakers had been entrusted to the civil authorities of Texas. Hall denied that he had spoken to the *Commandante* either of an invasion or of the organization of a force of 25,000 men.

Extracts from his dispatch were given to the press by the executive. When the *Galveston News*[25] and other state papers published Governor Hubbard's explanation of the incident, it was seen that Hall had not been censured: his demand that the men be turned over in four days was "not strictly pursuant to executive orders," but the Lieutenant had evidently been misled by what Price had told him, and thought that he, as a civil authority, was privileged to make the demand. All Rangers had civil powers to make arrests. The Governor did not doubt that Hall had supposed himself to be acting "properly and legally."

It is illuminating that it was Lee Hall's demand, rather than the Governor's, that occasioned the strongest reaction at Camargo. The indiscretion did not damage the Ranger's reputation. The *San Antonio Express,* before the month was over, recommended him for the command of all state troops.[26]

During the summer, newspapers throughout the country,

[24] Directions of the Governor to Lieutenant Hall communicated to Commanding General of the Department of Texas, August 25, 1877, *House Misc. Doc. No. 64,* 76.

[25] Hall's dispatch to Governor Hubbard, dated Rio Grande City, August 25, 1877, and published in *The Daily Democratic Statesman,* August 27, 1877; *Galveston Daily News,* September 2, 1877.

[26] *San Antonio Express,* August 28, 1877, quoted in *Austin Statesman,* August 28, 1877.

with such a notable exception as the *New York Herald*,[27] reflected definitely a disinclination for war with Mexico. In Texas, Rip Ford's handbills for recruiting met with slight response. There were more officers than privates in his paper company. And yet not a single border problem had been settled. The American Minister was still making calls on Señor Vallarta and could not report progress regarding the extradition of the jail breakers. Success had not attended the efforts of the Texas Governor nor of General Ord. The explanation of the changed attitude towards Mexico was that from the ranks of strutting, gold-laced generals and beribboned statesmen across the River, there had stepped forth a man. Adventurer he was, but Porfirio Diaz was a creator and builder as well. In 1877, he was not strong enough to play the dictator among his own people, but he was strong enough to end the temptation engendered by a rich country's being weakly held. He had still to humor the prejudices and passions of his people, but his aim was to control, not pander.

Early in September, he ordered 1,500 men to embark on the *Independencia* at Vera Cruz for Matamoros. This meant that commands would be enforced. An epidemic of resignations took place among the civil officials. On September 11, Canales submitted to the extent of delivering three of the men connected with the Rio Grande jail delivery. One was a murderer, two were friendless, homeless vagabonds, who had been accomplices of the leaders. All three were followers of Lerdo. To show that he had been coerced, Canales made the surrender to military, rather than civil authorities, and he tried to do it inconspicuously at midnight. When the Mexican officers turned the men over to an official from Brownsville, crowds gathered and followed to the ferry to watch the passage to the other side. Perhaps this time it was the River that prevented bloodshed. The Mexicans on the banks were mutinous.

Across the Rio Grande, Americans heard them shouting "Down with Canales!"

[27] This is the opinion of J. Fred Rippy, *The United States and Mexico*. In July, 1877, *The New York Herald* published a detailed project for the cession of the northern states of Mexico. The paper was loath to give up its project (Callahan, *American Foreign Relations,* 381).

Then shouts resounded for the imprisoned leader, who in the past had hauled down the stars and stripes and flown his own flag over Brownsville—"Up with Cortina!"

The once popular Governor of Tamaulipas resigned.

Soldiers from Fort Brown escorted the prisoners to Webb County, where a detachment of Hall's men met and returned them to the fateful jail in Rio Grande City.

The Ranger Lieutenant remained behind in Matamoros and attempted to gain the extradition of murderers wanted in Duval and Hidalgo counties.[28] Since excitement was high and a revolution imminent, his demands were denied. Mexican officials had evolved a new doctrine, quite without the sanction of a treaty: American citizens of Mexican race or Mexican origin were not to be surrendered.

In Rio Grande City, Hall's men stood guard each night and at all times went under arms. They kept themselves in prime condition. They had received no pay while there and were hard pressed for money. Those who had served under Captain McNelly—and most of them had—were saddened in September by the news of his death. They believed that his fatal disease had been due to the gruelling service against the Mexicans in the very section where the Company was on duty. And it was a part of Ranger belief to avenge a comrade. Perhaps, because Lieutenant Hall did not impose a rigorous discipline, his men found it possible to act in conformity with his pacific wishes. They kept themselves in hand. Equipped always for instant action, they took part in whatever recreations were available— raced horses, played marbles with small boys, laid bets on cockfights, dealt monte, and lost and won their hypothetical pay a dozen times a day. Inwardly, they swore at their inaction with all the fervent "cuss words" that enlivened their vocabularies. It is to their credit and their leader's that no border "incidents" took place near Rio Grande City.

Late in September, Rangers and townsmen attended the trial of the three men whom General Benavidez had forced the Governor of Tamaulipas to surrender. Excitement was intense, for

---

[28] Lieutenant Hall's telegram to Adjutant General Steele, September 10, 1877, followed by report of September 15, 1877, *Hall Ms.*

many citizens of Camargo were in the court room and it was believed they would attempt a rescue.[29] Each of the accused was sentenced to five years[30]—a light sentence considering the efforts of army, Federal, and State officials, and Rangers to bring the men to justice.[31]

After the trial, Hall was ordered to break camp. And then "the lid blew off." The Rangers' whoops and yells could be heard two miles away. Rio Grande City feared the camp had news of an impending war. The orders were nothing more than directions to deliver prisoners at various points and proceed to Cuero. As far as Los Olmos, the Company served as escort for the sheriff of Starr County, who was taking the two prisoners just convicted to the penitentiary at Huntsville. At Corpus Christi, the Rangers deposited a third.[32]

The Lieutenant received disconcerting news: authorities at Matamoros, in retaliation for the Rio Grande City convictions, had released the five murderers wanted in Duval and Hidalgo Counties. They had done this under the guns of the fort, and in the presence, it was said, of over a thousand regulars from the Central Government. It was a public act in utter defiance of the extradition treaty. The men had been indicted in the district courts of Texas and formally demanded by our extradition agent. Lieutenant Hall had made two trips and Sergeant Watson, one, in the hope of receiving them. No question of their citizenship had been raised.

Governor Hubbard again went into action. He instructed the extradition agent to make no more demands until further orders, but to inform the Mexican authorities that the release showed "either inability to observe the treaty or hostility to all Texans and Americans, or perhaps both." The Governor appealed to the United States Government. He sent to Secretary

[29] Hall discredited the rumor. Telegram to Adjutant General Steele, Rio Grande City, September 27, 1877, *Hall Ms.;* General Ord's report to General Sheridan, *House Misc. Doc. No. 64,* 76.

[30] Lieutenant Hall's telegram to Adjutant General Steele, Rio Grande City, September 29, 1877, *Hall Ms.;* report of the extradition agent, Judge Russell, to Governor Hubbard, Brownsville, September 26, 1877, *House Report No. 701.*

[31] Major Price's testimony, January 26, 1878, *House Report No. 701,* 120.

[32] Letter of a Ranger in Lieutenant Hall's Company, dated Corpus Christi, October 29, 1877, printed in *Galveston Daily News,* November 10, 1877.

Evarts all correspondence between State and Mexican authorities. He urged the need of better protection, reminding the Secretary that this had been asked for by every Texas legislature since 1846, that lack of it had forced the State to place special militia in the field for border service at an expense of two million dollars.[33]

Certainly, not much of this amount had found its way into the vest pockets of Lieutenant Hall's men. After a week's court duty in Cuero, they reached Corpus Christi on October 21, and one of them wrote jubilantly that they had their first square meal since July. He boasted that the detachment consumed 400 oysters at a sitting and felt as grandly corpulent as Governor Hubbard or any New York alderman. They guarded prisoners on an upper floor of the new Court House and flirted with pretty girls who walked through Court House Square. Whatever chagrin their leader felt at the defiant release in Matamoros, the men themselves were not concerned. "Hall's bold troopers" took things as they came, and for the present found life good.[34]

Recently one of the men, George Talley, has described the jail delivery in this wise:

"The Company went to Rio Grande City where some Mexican bandits had come across the river and taken some prisoners out of jail. Nothing come of it."[35]

Perhaps not. None of the questions at issue had been really settled. Both countries continued to maintain large forces on the border. And yet the dignity of the Governor of Texas had been preserved; Hall's "indiscretion" at Camargo, more than any one factor, had gained the delivery of a sufficient number of prisoners to prevent loss of prestige on the Rio Grande; officials of Tejado's faction, who had shown themselves anti-American, had been forced from high positions; and Americans of many classes and for many reasons had been shown the strength of Mexico's new President. Porfirio Diaz was a neigh-

---

[33] Governor Hubbard to Mr. Evarts, *House Report No. 701.*

[34] Ranger's letter, dated Corpus Christi, October 29, 1877, *Galveston News,* November 10, 1877.

[35] G. W. Talley's conversation with Mr. Kleber Miller at Falfurrias, April, 1935.

bor who was approachable and amenable, but one whose intention was to remove border grievances, strengthen his army and his Rurales and be prepared to repel force with force.

Ranger Captain Dan Roberts, who realized that the political atmosphere was highly charged by clouds that shadowed the devious Rio Grande, has cast a long look backward through the years and described the disturbance as only "a chinook wind." After a little ruffling of international passions at Matamoros and Brownsville, Rio Grande City, and Camargo, it died away. It might have blown into a border hurricane.

XI

Captain Commanding Special State Troops

(December, 1877-May, 1878)

"*I have a word to speak, boys, only another to say,
Don't never be no cow thief, don't never ride no stray,
Be careful of your rope, boys, and keep it on a tree,
Just suit yourself about it, for it's nothing at all to me.*"

—CHARLES FINGER, *Frontier Ballads.*

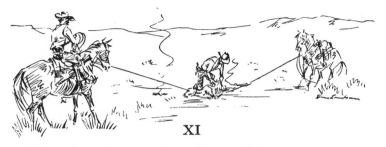

XI

Captain Commanding Special State Troops

It was in December, 1877, that Hall received his commission as Captain of Special State Troops,[1] although he had been in command since the reorganization six months earlier. Rangers are born, and Ranger officers in the seventies evolved from their companies. Armstrong's commission as a first lieutenant arrived at the same time as Hall's. Both promotions were recognitions of service, not badges of seniority, not routine advances due to order of succession. The Captain deserved promotion both for what he had done and what he had not done on the Rio Grande. Armstrong had demonstrated merit in a different fashion. While Hall and his men scouted on the border and chafed under the prohibition of matching the raid on a Texas jail with a raid to arrest the jail breakers; while consuls, ministers, Governor Hubbard and the Governors of Tamaulipas and Coahuila were variously considering the activities of the Company; while swirls of red tape were almost reducing it to inaction; John Armstrong added to its glory by taking a leading part in the capture of John Wesley Hardin.

Almost twenty years after the event, Hall allowed publication of a statement showing his own connection with the matter. According to the account in the *San Antonio Semi-Weekly Express*, of September 13, 1895, Adjutant General Steele told Hall that he wished him to attempt the arrest not so much because of the reward on Hardin, as because the State wanted to

---

[1] His first report to Adjutant General Steele signed as Captain is dated December 26, 1877. His commission and Lieutenant Armstrong's were enclosed in a letter from Captain Beall. Captain Hall's acknowledgment was dated January, 1878, *Hall Ms.*

[129]

bring to justice leaders of the Taylor and Sutton factions. Hall's first selection of a detective proved a failure. Then Dick Hudson of DeWitt County, a member of the Sutton group, told Hall that Hardin was in Florida under the alias, "John Swayne." Hudson could not state his location. After this, Hall went to Dallas and secured as detective, Ranger Jack Duncan.[2]

Duncan followed Hall's plan of working through Neal Bowen, Hardin's father-in-law. For a year and a half, the detective labored on the case, and convinced Bowen finally of his friendship. One day at Neal Bowen's place in DeWitt County, he offered to buy a wagon that was no longer in use. This, the father-in-law could not sell, since it belonged to Hardin. Duncan asked Bowen to write to find out the price. They went together to Cuero, where Bowen was induced to do some heavy drinking. Then the detective reminded him of the letter he had promised to send, at the same time handing him a marked envelope in which to send it. After Bowen wrote and mailed the letter, Duncan went to the post office and told a story about having misdirected some mail. The postmaster obligingly sorted the letters, Duncan caught sight of the marked envelope and noted the address.

Hall's detective, by determining Wes Hardin's location, laid the groundwork for the outlaw's capture, but his services did not end there. Wes Hardin, in his autobiography,[3] tells how Jack Duncan came ahead of Armstrong to Pensacola Junction in August, 1877; how, after a scuffle on the train, Duncan deprived Hardin of his Colt .44 six-shooter, when others thought that the outlaw was disarmed; how, at Memphis, Duncan saved Armstrong from attack when Hardin's handcuffs had been removed at the dining table. He tells how Hall's detective, instead of entraining at Montgomery, where Hardin's friends were waiting for a rescue, took the outlaw in a hack to a station

2 John Duncan's part in the affair is recounted also by N. A. Jennings, *A Texas Ranger*, 301-305; and in the chapter on Wes Hardin in Eugene Cunningham's *Triggernometry* (New York, Press of the Pioneers, 1934); J. B. Gillett's *Six Years with the Texas Rangers* (New Haven, Yale University Press, 1925); Owen White, *Trigger Fingers*; Thomas Ripley, *They Died with their Boots On* (Garden City, Doubleday, Doran, 1935).

3 J. W. Hardin, *Life of John Wesley Hardin* (Seguin, Texas, Smith & Moore), portion reprinted by *Frontier Times*, December, 1925.

several miles back from Montgomery and boarded the train there. In an interview published in the *Austin Statesman* of August 29, 1877, Armstrong generously stated that all the credit of working up the case was due to Duncan.

Hardin's connection with the Taylor-Sutton feud made news of his arrest doubly welcome to Captain Hall. It was Hardin who had killed Sheriff Helms; Hardin who, with his cousins, Jim, Scrap, and Tom Taylor, had planned the assassination of Sutton and Slaughter at Indianola;[4] Hardin who had killed Deputy Sheriff Webb of DeWitt County. Had Hardin not been captured and brought home in irons, he would, in time, have returned to avenge more thoroughly the lynching of his brother and the crimes of the Suttons against his cousins. It was a big step towards law and order when the outlaw was safely lodged in Travis County Jail. The pig-like eyes with their rattlesnake glitter and rapid motion, left to right and back again, the nimble fingers that could wheel two heavy Colts in the deadly 'border roll,"[5] were now no more than the innocuous eyes and fingers of a guarded prisoner.

Hall's men, lacklands and emptypockets that they were, speculated in Rio Grande City on the good fortune of their comrade whose wound had rendered him unfit for border service. They wondered what share he would have of the four thousand dollars offered as reward. As for Hall, he wrote to Steele of his pleasure at Armstrong's success. Duncan had worked the case up earlier than the Captain expected, and while border service for the commander still was necessary.[6]

The *Galveston News* of August 25, 1877, recorded that Hardin had been eager to return, but was warned by a letter that he could not expect peace in Texas because Hall's Company, the Frontier Battalion, and the State government had no regard for Magna Carta. The outlaw's entry into the Travis County jail showed him that Ranger activities were effective: as fellow-guests, he found notorious criminals, several of them as desper-

4 White, *Trigger Fingers*, (New York, Putnam's, 1926).
5 C. L. Douglas, *The Texas Rangers, or Gentlemen in the White Hats* (Dallas, Texas, Southwest Press, 1934).
6 Lieutenant Hall to Adjutant General Steele, Rio Grande City, September 1, 1877, *Hall Ms.*

ate as himself—Bill Taylor, Brown Bowen (Hardin's brother-in-law), Manning Clements, John Collins, Jeff Ake, John Ringo, and two members of a gang then terrorizing North Texas under the leadership of one Sam Bass.

The Captain, on silently contemplating Wes Hardin in the jail, regretted that he had been deprived of settling a personal score, for Hardin was the one man who had witnessed the Ranger's retreat.

It had taken place near Rancho, in Gonzales County, on a cold day in the last December. Hall knew Bill Taylor was in Rancho, and surmised the Goliad robbers and Hardin too might be there. With a posse of six, the Ranger found the location of Hardin's camp, rode to a lake nearby, and dismounted. He made a low-voiced, fighting talk, to work the men up to a running charge. John Wesley Hardin's reputation proved more eloquent. When the outlaw and his band sighted the detachment and fired, the only answering carbine was Lee Hall's. The Ranger glanced behind, saw that his men had fled, then ran himself—ran for his life. By the time he reached his horse, he had one bullet hole in his hat and three in his clothing. A singed smell accompanied him for days. It took him twelve hours to hunt down his posse, and he gave them a tongue lashing they remembered.[7] Because of this, when he posted lookouts before the arrest of the Brazell murderers, he made a second trip to see that they remained in place.

It was one of Hall's unpleasant duties in May, 1878, to make sure that the hanging of Wes Hardin's brother-in-law, Brown Bowen, was carried through in accordance with the law. Aleck Sweet, the Texas humorist, who was present, has left a description.[8] In front of the outside stairway of the stone jail in Gonzales, a gallows was erected on a platform level with the cells on the second story. At the touch of a lever, a trap-door was arranged to fall so that the man suspended above would be precipitated a distance of twenty feet, thus ignominiously connecting with eternity. Bowen was to be the man. He heard the

---

[7] Jennings, *A Texas Ranger*, 305; Jennings, "Lee Hall Fighting Man," *Saturday Evening Post, January, 1900.*
[8] Sweet and Knox, *On a Mexican Mustang through Texas*, 424-28.

scraping of saws and blows of hammers while the contraption was being built. One morning he saw a sprightly cavalcade of Rangers riding toward the jail, and recognized Captain Hall by his red head. The detachment took up quarters in a frame building on the other side of the gallows. Bowen felt proud that the State had sent so valuable an officer to give him the protection that would ensure an orderly hanging.

These final preparations were sobering, but, the condemned man hoped, unnecessary. He claimed that the murder for which he was sentenced had been committed by his brother-in-law, Wes Hardin. Frantic appeals were being made by the family to induce the noted outlaw to confess and save Brown Bowen. The man in jail at Austin, with more murders to his discredit than there were years of his life, was as unresponsive as the walls that shut him in.

"Let every tub stand on its own bottom," said Wes Hardin.[9]

Hall and his men could have foretold this answer. They understood Bowen's psychology too, and were amused at the pompous efforts of his lawyer to arrange a private hanging. Such privacy, they knew, would not be to Brown Bowen's liking. The criminal preferred an audience, and sent a message to his lawyer's children to come along with the rest to see the ceremony. Meantime, he wanted a brandied peach—"wanted it bad"—and the good-natured sheriff had one brought.

Next day, the brown eyes of the prisoner looked down with some satisfaction at the audience of forty-five hundred[10] which had gathered to see his gallows bow. His little hour had come, and during it he was to be more noted than his brother-in-law, Hardin, the killer. Men, women, and children surged against the picket fence surrounding the jail yard. Inside, a favored group pushed their way toward the platform. Lee Hall and Ranger Ben Riely kept them back by ropes. The ropes failed to make the circuit, so the two dug a furrow with their boot heels and threatened to kill the first man that attempted to cross.[11]

9 Hardin, *op. cit.*, 136-38.
10 *Dallas Weekly News*, May 25, 1878.
11 This was related to Captain Hall's daughter, Mrs. Isham Keith, many

Three clergymen, for whom Brown Bowen had not sent, tried to induce him to confess. They found his conscience geographical. He showed concern for those crimes he was accused of having committed in Texas; those committed beyond its borders worried him not at all. With one clergyman still in attendance, he stepped upon the platform. At Bowen's side walked, also, the sheriff and his deputies. It was difficult to hear the reading of the death warrant. Donkeys were braying, and children, alarmed at the unaccustomed crowd and the nervous tension of their elders, added shrill crying to the din.

Relief came for a time through a swift gale of laughter. The clergyman had carelessly placed his hand on the lever, and the sheriff, standing on the trap-door, would have been plunged downwards had he not clung to the railing. Even the man awaiting death grinned at the wry face the officer made at this brief taste of law's bitter medicine. Then Bowen's face grew stern as he listened to the reading of his statement as to Wes Hardin's guilt. After that, there was a prayer, and when the preacher's voice wavered in the plea for mercy, the crowd realized the jig of death was near. Bowen himself adjusted the noose, and let them draw the black cap to his neck. A sharp noise of the trap-door's falling, a thud, and the center of the picture ceased to be.

The crowd broke into groups, silent, white-faced, walking off quickly—leaving behind an incongruous litter of pasteboard, scraps of lunches, and a huddle of awkward clothing over a poor, young body only fit for burial. What the crowd had come to see was quickly over; the mental vision long remained.

Hall's own life was so full that he had little time to notice after images. Yet these remained: things that had been all life and movement, suddenly still; frayed shirts and dusty boots rotting on flesh that once had worn them jauntily; circling of buzzards slowly downward over human cadavers. And in his mind's eye, there were many eyes—eyes venomous with hatred, pleading eyes, agonized eyes, furtive eyes, eyes that stared

---

years later by Mr. Ben Riely. Second in command of the twelve men in Captain Hall's detachment was Lieutenant Armstrong, *(Galveston Weekly News,* May 18, 1878).

starkly upward and did not know that they were staring. What these things meant, Hall did not question. His life was one of deeds and held no time for introspection. In an age of action, his career is still noteworthy as presenting a sort of kinematic anachronism of twentieth century speed. Travel was usually on horseback, and high water and scarcity of forage in the winter of '77 and '78 caused difficulty. Nevertheless, from February 23 to April 15,[12] the Captain was in no single place longer than three days. In March alone, he arrested more than twenty men.

The *Austin Statesman*[13] told its readers that Captain Lee Hall would keep his headquarters for the winter in Corpus Christi. "His headquarters will be mostly in the saddle."

Another paper said that he was like the little joker, "Now you see him and now you don't." Because of this, he was a terror to evildoers. None knew when he would pounce upon them, "like a duck on a June bug."

The *Corpus Free Press* said there was no one like him for turning up in one place when he was supposed to be in another. He had been visible in Corpus, "but he's gone again, the Lord knows where."

During one short stay, he put into force a novel piece of legislation. The most disreputable of the riffraff, the "dog-towners," had used their weapons too freely. An ordinance was passed in Corpus against "gun totin'." When it was rumored that Hall took the matter seriously, bets were placed on just how long he had to live. In spite of the public's forebodings, he accomplished his purpose. One evening, unarmed, the Ranger appeared in the saloon where he knew he would find the largest number of men with the largest number of arms.

"Boys," he said, "I want your pistols."

He laughed—a good laugh, an infectious laugh—and held out his hands.

"You won't mind. I'll get two bits for every one I turn in."

The men laughed, too, and somehow, as though hypnotized, gave up their firearms.[14]

---

[12] Captain Hall's report to Adjutant General Steele on this date, *Hall Ms.*
[13] Issue of December 11, 1877.
[14] An undated letter by Sarah Halter to Captain Hall's daughter, Mrs. Isham Keith, tells of the Dog Town incident.

A more difficult problem was the suppression of a well-contrived organization for wholesale cattle theft. Its members passed their herds north, through relay stations, to Indian territory. There other thieves disposed of them, disbursing the profits down the line. The Captain received daily appeals from Victoria, Nueces, Lavaca, and Live Oak Counties. His scattered arrests proved ineffective, and he determined to discover the brains of the system and scotch its chiefs. The ringleaders, he suspected, lived near San Antonio, a location convenient to cattle trails. The men of the relay system believed in varying their routes. The Captain employed W. T. Cavin and J. E. Lucy to work as cowboys and report as spies.

Hall with his detachment encamped twelve miles above the city, on the San Antonio River. Stockmen from the coast assisted in regaining stolen cattle, chiefly steers that had been driven up the San Antonio River from Calhoun and other counties on the Gulf. The first destination of the herds was the ranch of Warren Goodin, chief of the relay system. From there they were driven north. At Ligartoville, in Live Oak County, the Rangers cut 700 from herds,[15] as being stolen or purchased from those who had no right to sell. Only one hundred of these were claimed. Mexican owners of the rest too greatly feared the cattle thieves to acknowledge ownership. Hall's men could do no more than the camp cook, when he had slung together a batch of biscuits; they could only sing out, "They're here, they're yours. Come and get 'em!"

The Rangers caught some of the thieves in San Antonio. At Ligartoville, they arrested the Cook brothers and plastered them with indictments. On the way back, the detachment halted eleven herds of cattle and cut out an even hundred steers. Pastures near San Antonio were well combed; stolen cattle were headed off in a herd on the way to Fort Ewell, but the chiefs of the system were at large and thefts continued.

The story is told that one of the leaders, who owned a small ranch near Hall's camp, decided to forestall capture by setting

---

[15] Captain Hall's report to Adjutant General Steele, April 15, 1878, *Hall Ms.* Sheriff R. C. Houston of Wilson County forwarded a capias for Goodin, May 28, 1878. The reward for his capture was $850, Captain Hall to Adjutant General Steele, March 18, 1878, *Hall Ms.*

a trap for the Captain.[16] He baited it with his two daughters. The young Ranger suspected trouble when the girls told him they were planning a party in his honor. It was a murder that was planned. On the appointed night the Captain attended, taking one man with him. His suspicions were strengthened when, as he entered, all of the women ran from the room. Ignoring the exodus of his dance partners, he walked to the father, disarmed him, and with the help of the other Ranger disarmed eight men who were accomplices. With their hands tied behind them, he delivered them to the San Antonio jail on Market Street—the old Bat Cave.

On every visit to the city, Hall searched for the man he believed was their chief, the elusive Warren Goodin.[17] He had, also, to consult there with the officials of the Sunset Route and with the banker, George Brackenridge, because of the financial needs of his Company. The Southwest Texas Stock Association, by February, 1878, had paid only $1,500 of their Goliad subscription.[18] The Governor sought funds from the railroads. In 1877, the Galveston, Houston & San Antonio had entered San Antonio. Its officials were eager for peace in the Southwest. The vice president and general manager, Colonel H. B. Andrews of San Antonio, responded favorably to Hall's request in behalf of the Rangers.[19] Roads in north Texas furnished transportation for detachments that trailed stage robbers outside of the Ranger Company's territory. The *Southern and Western Guide,* for 1878,[20] said that it would be "folly to deny" that rampant lawlessness existed in the sparsely settled counties of the bor-

16 This is Sheriff Ben E. Cabell's story of Lee Hall, contained in a newspaper clipping in the collection of Captain Hall's mother. In the issue of the *New York Times,* March 15, 1914, it is related under the title, "Arrest of the Chief of the Relay System."

17 "They don't let Warren Goodin rest in peace. Lee Hall pursued him and he fled for Corpus Christi. Then he went to Lee County and was arrested for some offence and escaped, and now they have him in custody in Montgomery County for murder done long ago in Jefferson."—*The Daily Democratic Statesman,* July 4, 1879.

18 Captain Hall to Adjutant General Steele, February 11, 1878, *Hall Ms.; Galveston Daily News,* January 21, 1878.

19 *The Daily Democratic Statesman,* January 13, 1878. Governor Hubbard announced the news in an address at the Victoria Fair.

20 Rock and Smith, *Southern and Western Guide for 1878,* (St. Louis, A. H. Granger, 1878), 24.

der. Steel of rails and steel of Rangers' pistols both were necessary for the taming of Texas.

A new type of bad man had made his appearance, the fencecutter. His detection and punishment for long increased the work of the Rangers. By 1877, about seven thousand tons of barbed wire had been put into use.[21] Introduced into Texas six years earlier by John W. Gates, a hardware merchant, later called "Bet-a-Million Gates,"[22] it had few buyers. The cattlemen's preference was a stockade fence like Captain King's. Invention of the "S" barb came in 1873.[23] In 1875, Henry B. Sanborn sold ten miles of the newfangled fencing at Gainesville.[24] When it was strung, the glories and perils of the open range began receding. Cattle thieves and jobless cowboys recognized the disadvantage of these fences and were quick to cut them down. Men of Hall's Company, on scattered secret missions, continuously brought news that the man with the pliers had become a greater menace to property rights than the man with a rope and pistol.[25]

In addition to the relay men and fence-cutters, there remained the border criminals: men of the United States, Mexicans and Indians. Scouts were made from Corpus Christi, San Diego, and from Banquette,[26] terminus of the narrow gauge railroad. There Mexican trains often loaded and unloaded under the fire of Americans. Frontier depredations continued, and Hall regretted that the Adjutant General did not send him to the Rio Grande. Governor Hubbard's enemies east of the Colorado were making political capital of the fact that the Company had been financed for a time from funds appropriated for frontier defense.[27] The matter was awkward, for the Governor was standing for reëlection. In spite of opposition, he determined to keep the men in the field. If he incurred the anger of eastern

[21] Osgood, *The Day of the Cattleman*, quoted in Raine, *Cattle.*
[22] "Muzzle Loadings," *Frontier Times*, November, 1926.
[23] Reprint of Arthur G. Warren's *The Iron Age*, June 24, 1926.
[24] *San Antonio Express*, June 9, 1936; "Introducing Barbed Wire in Texas," *Frontier Times*, November, 1931; Dobie, *Vaquero of the Brush Country*, 117, 118.
[25] Captain Hall's report to Adjutant General Steele, December 26, 1877, *Hall Ms.*
[26] "A Ranger's Experience," by one of Hall's Rangers stationed at Banquette, *The Galveston Daily News*, December 26, 1877.
[27] "Hall's Command," *Galveston Daily News*, February 1, 1878.

politicians, he balanced this by support of the western press. Not only in frontier counties was the claim made that economy urged increase, rather than reduction, of Hall's forces:

"The State of Texas is a big place and thirty men are a small squad."

"Give Captain Hall 200 men," one paper advised, "and take away all the stylish soldiers, and the country will be at less expense and ten thieves and murderers brought to justice where there is one now."

The Captain was called "the finest military officer in the State." It was said that the coming of his "gentlemanly-looking boys" ended crime wherever they were stationed.[28]

Runge and Company, the Goliad firm that had subscribed more than any of the stockmen, continued to furnish provisions. They had to protest again and again over the State's reluctance to honor their vouchers.[29] Fear of a forced disbandment quickened the dilatory trickle of subscriptions from the stockmen. One detachment, working near Santa Gertrudis, was given the benefit of free forage by Captain King when others were paying forty dollars a ton for hay. The Rabb crowd, who had been making life unsafe in Nueces County, were encamped near the King Ranch.[30] Forage was spared with good reason.

With pay, or without, the Captain and his men worked on. Cattle thieves were trailed to Calhoun County. The new scout and detective, Cavin, worked up the case there by pretending to be one of the gang. When the outlaws made an excursion into store robbing at Fulton, they placed him outside as guard. Corporal Rudd had been notified to be on hand with his detachment. The plot did not work perfectly. The robbers, surprisingly, showed fight. About thirty shots were fired. Only one of the gang was captured, one wounded.[31] A few days later, Frank

---

[28] The preceding four quotations are extracts from clippings in the collection of Captain Hall's mother. Unfortunately, the names and dates of the papers do not appear.

[29] For the difficulties involved in this support, see letter from Hall to Adjutant General Steele, February 11, 1878, *Hall Ms.*

[30] Captain Hall to Adjutant General Steele, February 1, 11, 1878, *Hall Ms.*

[31] Cavin's letter to Mrs. Isham Keith, dated Ballinger, Texas, March 28, 1928; dispatch dated February 25, 1878, newspaper clipping in collection of Captain Hall's mother.

Hartman, the leader, was arrested at Indianola.[32] After a skirmish on an island in the Gulf, four more surrendered. In all, a full month elapsed before the job was finished.[33]

The persistence and courage of the Company was notable, but Lee Hall could not prevent deterioration of equipment. By December, 1878, most of the wagons and tents were worn out. Packsaddles, the bookkeeper's desk, one wagon sheet, and one spade, were rated as worthless. The monthly return showed, however, that thirty-three Winchester carbines, four double-barrel shotguns, two Sharps carbines, thirty-seven Colt revolvers, and eight hundred rounds each of Winchester cartridges and pistol cartridges were in good condition. Hall stood security for his men wherever they were stationed. The bookkeeper broke down as completely as the Company's desk. When he died of brain fever, a burying squad went seven miles before they could find an old house with lumber that would serve for his coffin. He was the first man to be buried in the little village at Fort Ewell[34]—the village that was beginning to call itself Cotulla.

In addition to his normal duties, the Captain continued visiting San Antonio in behalf of the Company's support. He did not find this irksome, for the doors of many homes were opened to him, and friendships formed then endured throughout his life.

The stories told of him and his magnetic personality combined to make him a rival in popularity with Elizabeth Thompson, the reigning belle. He weighted the scales in her favor by the frankness of his homage. At San Pedro Springs, he waltzed with her, and on Bowen's Island and at the Menger Hotel where Robert E. Lee and many others of the illustrious had been entertained. She was tall and straight and dark, a match for Hall himself in valor and high spirits. Once when he was dancing attendance at the Menger, a summons came from the Adjutant General, and with scant adieux the Captain turned to run down the stairway. There are old ladies still alive who shake

[32] Telegram of A. S. Mackay of Hall's Company, March 1, 1878, *Hall Ms.*
[33] Cavin's letter to Mrs. Isham Keith, March 28, 1928.
[34] *Ibid.*

their heads and say his departure made the evening desolate. Perhaps, the hasty exit was caused by news of Indian raids. Depredations were frequent that year. During one foray that lasted six long April days, the Indians traversed 270 miles in Webb County and LaSalle. Many lives were lost.[35] Citizens of the thorny land of woe between the Nueces and the Rio Grande suffered because a drunken governor in Coahuila was giving protection and encouragement to the Indians. From Coahuila, and from Tamaulipas in the *Zona Libre*, the Red Men came on foot, wearing soft moccasins that left no tracks. They worked east from the Rio Grande, through cedar brakes and spiny bush. During the day, for the most part, they lay concealed. It was the light of the moon that revealed the blackest of their deeds. Of the million and more inhabitants of Texas in 1878, Lieutenant John L. Bullis has testified not one would live within a hundred miles of the mouth of Devil's River. The Frio and Sabinal valleys, though potentially valuable, were abandoned through fear of Indians.[36] But Webb and LaSalle were white man's country, and the Texans were determined to keep them so.

Petitions were sent to Washington. The Secretary of State was abundantly informed of the anger of the citizens and of their impatience with the army.[37] At a meeting in Corpus Christi, one petitioner, Captain John J. Dix, asserted that against Indian marauders a single company like Hall's would be more effective than a regiment of regular troops.[38] There were many districts in which the Company was not supposed to operate, so at times the Captain scouted after Indians without formally reporting his activities. Colonel Mason, U.S.A., has testified that though "McNelly's old Company" was chiefly occupied in arresting criminals, when an Indian raid was heard of officers notified the Company at once and the Rangers took up the pursuit.[39]

[35] Colonel M. L. Crimmins, "An Indian Border Raid near Laredo," *Frontier Times*, August, 1933.
[36] *House Misc. Doc. No. 64*, 197-99.
[37] *An Appeal by the People, etc., sent to the Hon. William Evarts, Secretary of State to the United States*, (Corpus Christi, Free Press Print, 1878).
[38] Ben C. Stuart, *Texas Indian Fighters and Frontier Rangers*, 208, 209.
[39] Lieutenant Colonel Mason, December 7, 1877, testified as to the Company's activities in pursuing raiders, *House Misc. Doc. No. 64*, 119, 120.

Such a raid as that of April 14–19, 1878, revealed that a salutary lesson was much needed. Recognition of the Diaz government had been accorded exactly three days before the raid began. However, the report on the border was being drafted by the subcommittee on foreign affairs. The report was stiffened, and when submitted by its chairman, Gustave Schleicher, the Texan, it was accompanied by demands that imperiled the peace,[40] for Mexico was restive. Hall reported that the wish of its war party was to push the frontier back to the Nueces.[41] Only a few citizens of either country, however, desired expansion and destruction, and a very small number of these were Texans. Guy M. Bryan correctly gauged state sentiment when he wrote to his friend, the President, that Texans did not want war,[42] but they did want Ord kept on the border—"the right man in the right place."[43] They did want protection.

They were hopeful of future security when state papers reported that, on May 10, General Ord and Captain Hall had gone to Austin together on a special train.

"It is whispered they go to see the Governor in reference to continuing the Rangers in the field, and possibly about the cooperation of the United States troops."[44]

Four days later, the Austin correspondent of the *Galveston News* reported that "Arrangements for keeping Hall's force in the field and paying expenses are again satisfactory."

During the same month, the United States adopted measures both punitive and precautionary against Mexicans and Indians. General Ranald S. Mackenzie with eleven troops of cavalry crossed the River near Del Rio, penetrating 150 miles into the interior. Here Colonel Shafter, with infantry, artillery, and cavalry, established a supply camp, bringing in such stores of provisions as indicated willingness to maintain as long an occupation as necessary. Mexico submitted.

[40] Matias Romero, *Mexico and the United States*, (New York, G. P. Putnam's Sons, 1898), I.
[41] From an interview with Captain Hall at the Laclede Hotel, San Antonio, contained in a newspaper clipping in his mother's collection.
[42] "Bryan-Hayes Correspondence," (Winkler, ed.), *Southwestern Historical Quarterly*, April, 1924.
[43] *Ibid.*, October, 1924, letter dated April 27, 1880.
[44] *Galveston Daily News*, May 10, 1878.

One reason for keeping Hall and his men in the field was eliminated. There remained the pursuit of desperadoes. By a quirk of fate, a hunt for one of these led detachments of the Company into the country of its bitterest opponents. The object of their search had learned something of the state's geography by his connection with the relay system, but he had never stooped to fence-cutting, and he scorned the hospitality that Mexico extended renegades. He did not represent all problems of the Rangers, but he was himself sufficiently a problem to make them sometimes careless of the rest. Out of the north, he gaily rode to take his place in Texas folk-lore.

The object of the Ranger search was young Sam Bass.

XII
Enter Sam Bass—Exit!
(1874-July, 1878)

"Sam Bass was born in Indiana;
It was his native home;
And at the age of seventeen
Young Sam began to roam.

"He used to deal in race-stock—
One called the Denton mare.
He matched her in scrub races
And he taken her to the fair."

—JOHN A. LOMAX, *American
Ballads and Folk Songs.*

XII
Enter Sam Bass—Exit!

It was at the age of twenty-three, while Lee Hall was making his reputation in Grayson County, that Sam Bass became possessor of the little sorrel that races through the ballad[1] as the "Denton mare." The young City Marshal of Denison perhaps saw some of her victories and observed her owner. Four years later, Hall said that he could identify Sam Bass on inspection, and that Bass would know him at sight.[2] Much had happened since a rowdy evening in 1874 when young Sam aligned himself with Deputy Sheriff Tom Gerren, prevented bloodshed in a Denton dance hall, and saved Gerren's life.[3] By 1878, Hall was in the vanguard of the forces that made for law and order. Bass was the most wanted criminal in the State. The reward for his capture was the largest, his description the most besmudged, of all the 4,402 criminals on the Adjutant General's Fugitive List:

"25 to 26 years old, 5 ft. 7 inches high, black hair, dark

[1] This has more than one hundred verses and as many variations. It is included in John A. Lomax's *American Ballads and Folk Songs* (New York, Macmillan, 1934), and Charles J. Finger's *Frontier Ballads* (New York, Doubleday, Page & Co., 1927).

[2] Wayne Gard narrates this incident in *Sam Bass* (Boston, Houghton-Mifflin, 1936). This book is the most authoritative and complete of the many dealing with the outlaw. Among other interesting accounts are those in Eugene Cunningham's *Triggernometry*, and Owen P. White's *Them Was the Days* and *Trigger Fingers*. These are based on conversations with old-timers, newspaper accounts, etc. The best early biography is by "A Citizen of Denton:" *Authentic History of Sam Bass and his Gang* (Denton, 1878), reprinted by *Frontier Times*, 1932. The author probably was Judge Hogg, a brother of Governor James Hogg. The excellent account in Roberts' *Rangers and Sovereignty* is based on very direct evidence of Rangers who participated in the chase.

[3] Captain Hall's account of the incident appeared in *The San Antonio Semi-Weekly Express*, September 13, 1895. A clipping containing this was kindly furnished me by Mr. Marvin Hunter, editor of *The Frontier Times*.

brown eyes, brown mustaches, large white teeth, shows them when talking; has very little to say."[4]

In addition, Hall has described him as having a Roman nose and "a Jewish cast of countenance," a stoop that came from hard work on a farm, and a voice that was thin and high.[5]

In collecting the herd that he drove from southwest Texas in 1876, Bass and his partner in the venture had not been scrupulous.

> *"Sam left Joe Collin's ranch*
> *In the merry month of May*
> *With a herd of Texas cattle,*
> *The Black Hills for to see.*
>
> *"Sold out at Custer City*
> *And then got on a spree*
> *A harder set of cowboys*
> *You seldom ever see."*

It was in 1877, and outside of Texas, that Sam expanded his activities of card and race track sharper into those of a number one bad man. Seven stagecoach robberies, while not lucrative, contributed experience. Then came the big haul! On September 18, 1877, his band robbed the Union Pacific Express at Big Springs, Nebraska, relieving passengers of jewelry and money amounting to $1,300. The real prizes were consignments to New York: two to Wells Fargo and Company, and one to the National Bank of Commerce—gleaming twenty-dollar gold pieces of San Francisco mintage. They totalled $60,000. Wells Fargo promptly offered $10,000 for capture of the robbers and return of its consignment—the amount to be prorated, should a portion of the money be regained or any member of the band apprehended.

When the offer was made, Bass was on his way to Denton to pay off old debts, to make new friends, and to plan fresh adventures. Once, when he thought himself the owner of a mine

[4] Quoted in Gillett, *Six Years with the Texas Rangers,* 111, 112.
[5] Captain Hall's account, *The San Antonio Semi-Weekly Express,* September 13, 1895.

[148]

rich in quartz, he boasted that he "had the world by the tail with a down hill pull."

He had been deceived, for the mine was worthless. This time his fortune seemed secure. Across the plains of Kansas he traveled with one companion, and when they slept, their ponies were staked with bags of minted gold. To be sure, United States troops were after them. Bass knew, for cavalrymen told him when they lent him pots and pans to cook his grub. He looked them in the eyes and laughed with them, for luck was his. No man had lost his life at Big Springs, and memory of early hardships and injustice kept dishonesty from burdening his conscience. He and his companion, Jack Davis, bought a work horse and an old buggy,[6] concealed their wealth, and at Red River Station crossed to Texas.

> "Sam made it back to Texas,
> All right side up with care—
> Rode into the town of Denton,
> With all his friends to share."

It was on the first of November that the two men reached Denton, drove on to Fort Worth, and then separated. Bass was glad to get rid of the buggy, glad to bestride a horse, glad to turn his head toward Denton. He made his camp at a considerable distance from the town, in Cove Hollow, a six-mile ravine bordered with limestone caves large enough for hideouts. The Hollow was dense with undergrowth and darkened by the shade of oak and walnut trees. Old friends were close at hand. One of these, Jim Murphy, agreed to keep for Sam a store of the twenty-dollar pieces, and did not question the story that they were profit from pay dust in the Black Hills. Other friends, Sam found at Denton in the night. None connected him with the robbery at Big Springs. Gold eagles flashed under the swinging lamps of barrooms. A good time was had by all.

> "Sam used to coin the money
> And spent it just as free . . ."

[6] Gillett, *op. cit.*, Chapter ix.

[149]

On November 23, 1877, Lee Hall, also, returned to a former home. He was in Sherman, Grayson County, and Grayson adjoined Cooke, where Cove Hollow was located. On that date he telegraphed the Adjutant General that he was "unable to do anything." The country was full of Chicago detectives.[7]

Meantime, the San Francisco gold and the high spirits of the train robber had joined to the fortunes of Sam Bass those of his old pals, Henry Underwood and Frank ("Blockey") Jackson. In late November the three started to San Antonio for such a spree as would erase the memory of Sam's having sold there, earlier, his Denton mare.

Hot on their trail followed Tooney Waits, Pinkerton detective from the North; Tom Gerren, Deputy Sheriff of Denton, and William C. Everheart, Sheriff of Grayson. On the request of the Governor of Nebraska, Governor Hubbard issued a warrant for Bass, entrusting Everheart with its execution. Gerren, it developed, was in the city with a double purpose—he wished to arrest Underwood for an old crime, and he wished to save Sam Bass. San Antonio was as well prepared for a chase and a street battle as for less fatal entertainment.[8] For the first, there were winding streets with many bridges spanning a sinuous river. For the rest, gold eagles could be broken and spent for fine cigars at the tobacco shop of Rafael Diaz. On Commerce Street, the Duerler and Baer confectioneries sent out rival aromas, and Sam Bass was a boy for candy. At Grandpa Sartor's, one could buy a gold watch, fine and thick, and excellent bowie knives were on sale at Samuel Bell's. Good food was tempting at the restaurant of Antonio Manchacas. Captain Tobin's hotel, Ford's, and the Central, were open for those who did not feel at home in the more elegant atmosphere of the Menger.

On Losoya Street and Paseo Hondo (Houston), were the headquarters of the United States Cavalry, where Bass might match his acquaintance with that other cavalrymen who, in Kansas, had given him his name and address, so that if he heard news of Sam Bass, he could let him know. The city was

[7] Captain Hall to Adjutant General Steele, November 23, 1877, *Hall Ms.*
[8] Vinton L. James, "Old Times in San Antonio," a series in *Frontier Times*, July-September, 1929; King, *The Great South*, 167; Rock and Smith, *Southern and Western Guide.*

the outfitting and supply point for all lands south and west to the Rio Grande, capital of the cattle country. Sam Bass, from earlier visits, would know his way about—know how to find the most flavorous of the saloons where whiskey was uncut, talk racy, and play high—the Bull Head, the White Elephant, Jack Harris's saloon, or George Horner's, where liquor was still better, and Sam

> *"Always drank good whiskey,*
> *Wherever he might be."*

It was good to be in San 'Tone after the Kansas plains and the hideaway coves and ravines of Cook County. The city was tumultuous with abounding life; the profanity of ox drivers contended with the popping of whips by those who walked beside the burros that drew the "Mexican Railroad;" on Market Street, one could watch the unloading of the railroad's man-high carts. North of Alamo Plaza, in the Irish Flats, some kind of a shindig could be counted on. At Sappington's Livery Stable, there was chance of a good trade for men who could judge horseflesh, and Sam could. There were dingle-dangle theatres and there were chili stands. There were wrinkled Mexican women selling drawn work and caged mocking birds, and there were comely young ones who offered boutonnières from flowery trays and baskets.

Cobbled sidewalks were noisy with the jingling spurs of jostling cowboys; dusty streets resounded with the thud of dry hooves of longhorns being driven to Kansas City and Abilene. On South Flores, were trading yards that offered gambling as risky as that at the Green Front or the Silver King saloons. In front of the Alamo was "Sweeney's mudhole," and there, or under drain spouts jutting from concrete roofs, a well directed shove could make a laughingstock of a companion—perhaps could cause a fight. "Pistol totin' " added the spice of danger to the joker, for against this, Mayor French had suspended the law. The "Fence Cutters' War" made firearms necessary. On Military Plaza, the peril of disorder was preached by an old jail, "Bat Cave," most sinister of the flat-roofed, close-shut 'dobe buildings.

Hunters and hunted took their fill of entertainment. Everheart complained that Gerren "leaked"—revealed their purpose to some Delilah of the streets, who tipped off Bass and his companions in time for them to cut short debauchery and, on the third of December, take their leave.

Everheart, in a newspaper interview the following April,[9] said that he came to distrust Gerren and telegraphed Captain Lee Hall for aid, and that in Sherman after the San Antonio visit, Gerren showed to a deputy United States Marshal a roll of fifty and one-hundred dollar bills, a present from Sam for having been his friend.

However this may have been, Lee Hall's visit to San Antonio on December 5 was not made at the summoning of Everheart, but because Governor Hubbard instructed him to assist in every way Detective Gaines, the Union Pacific agent, in accomplishing the arrest of Bass. Neither Gaines nor the sheriffs could tell which way Sam and his friends had gone, and Hall had to remain one day to gather information. Then with Sergeant Parrott, two other Rangers, Everheart, and the detective, he set off on the trail for Castroville. There they heard that their men had gone on to Uvalde to buy cattle. Hall and his group were near Uvalde on the eighth, but, due to misinformation, followed a false scent to Fort Clark. Doubling back, they again picked up the trail. Bass and his companions were off to Frio City.

Hall left the hunt to Parrott and the others, for the trial of the Brazell murderers at Cuero required his presence.[10] And there duties held him until after Christmas. Parrott, the detective, and one other Ranger followed north, hoping to intercept Bass before the twenty-seventh, when, they believed, he had arranged to be in Denton County.

In Fort Worth, Bass and his party had another taste of the fleshpots before retreating to Cove Hollow. When life grew monotonous, Bass instructed his men in stage robbery. Their first attempt they carried through at Mary's Creek, west of Fort Worth. It netted less than $50. On Christmas Day, the

[9] His statement is dated Sherman, Texas, April 23, 1878, and is contained in the collection of clippings made by Captain Hall's mother.
[10] Captain Hall's report to Adjutant General Steele, December 26, 1877, *Hall Ms.*

small band was depleted by Everheart's arrest of Underwood. The man had left the others to spend the day with his family. Bass and Jackson remained hidden in the brakes of Hickory Creek, south of Denton. Late in January, between Fort Worth and Weatherford, they levied on the passengers of another stage, relieving them of gold watches and $400. After that, in lonely hideouts near Hickory Creek and in Cove Hollow, Bass talked to Jackson of the greater gains and greater thrills that came when an "iron horse" was stopped for raids on express and passenger coaches. But for this, more than two men were needed. Bass and Jackson decided to recruit.

When young Seaborn Barnes ("Nubbin's Colt") and be-whiskered Tom Spotswood elected to join them, Bass believed that he was strong enough to organize a train crew—a shadow crew: engineer for engineer, mail clerk for mail clerk, conductor for conductor, express agent for express agent. The date selected for his exploit was February 22; the place, Allen, on the prairies of Collin County, twenty-four miles north of Dallas; the train, Number 4 of the Houston and Texas Central. Since officials of several railways were in its St. Louis sleeper, the robbers, incidentally, afforded to those gentlemen a personal experience of the helplessness of travelers. The only pistol among the passengers was a toy one filled with candy. No one offered resistance and no lives were lost. Division of $1,280 among the robbers was convincing proof of the advantages of their latest enterprise.

Governor Hubbard immediately offered $500 for each man captured. Next day, the Texas Express Company and the H. & T. C. matched this, so that for any capture the reward was raised to $1,500. Captain Hall was in Austin the day of the robbery. Next morning he went to Houston and arranged with the H. & T. C. for the transportation of Sergeant Parrott, J. E. Lucy, and three others. On February 25, his detachment met him in Houston and went on to Allen to inspect the scene of the crime. Afterwards the Rangers went to McKinney,[11] ten

[11] Captain Hall's telegram to Adjutant General Steele, Houston, February 26, 1878, *ibid.*; letter to same, March 4, 1878; report to same, San Antonio, April 15, 1878, *ibid.*

miles away, where the Express Company furnished horses for scouting. On February 27, Lucy contributed, at Pilot Point, to the arrest of Spotswood.[12] Hall himself had to go to San Antonio to see officials of the G. H. & S. A., about payment of his men. Early in March, he arranged with Sergeant Parrott for a meeting with the scout, Cavin, who had just finished with the Fulton robbery case. The detachment was to remain in north Texas as long as the Express Company furnished horses and there was any chance of success.

Hall was less able than the rest to undertake the scout. He was known at sight to Barnes, Bass, and Jackson; he had to divide his time in order to carry through work already begun, such as assistance at the trials of those accused of the Brazell murders; again, because of his office, he had to undertake the increasingly difficult job of raising money for the Company's pay; the Act by which his Company functioned restricted their activities to the district west of the Colorado. Perhaps, because of this, he did not leave for permanent record in the Adjutant General's office an account of all that befell him in north Texas. The *Denison News* of April 4, 1878, records that at Pilot Point, in the northeastern part of Denton County, he was attacked, "sometime ago," by Jim Whitney, an assailant later arrested in the Indian Territory. Pilot Point was so near to Bass's hideaway, and there were so many friends and harborers of the bandit, that the newspaper item provokes speculation.

The chance for arrests diminished when the country became overrun with sheriffs, deputies, marshals, and their posses, and with Pinkerton detectives. These last, lacking the hirsute adornment of true Texans of the seventies, were under a ludicrous disadvantage. Forced to adopt disguise, the scene abounded with false whiskers and mustachios, and in the nature of things, several were lost. Galloping steeds had to be reined in, while riders clambered down and groped in the dust for mixtures of hair and sticky gum. For years, the theatrical symbol of a detective was a slick city outfit and a set of taped mustachios. The sympathy of the audience, as it watched vaudeville or melo-

---

[12] Captain Hall's telegram to Adjutant General Steele, Galveston, March 5, 1878, *ibid.*

drama, was inevitably with the brigand. The pursuing detective, a villian, was hissed.

The firm of Bass, Jackson, and Barnes divided its time, not unpleasantly, between Cove Hollow and the brakes of Hickory Creek. Bass was better natured than the fox of song and story. On his raids, he shared equally with his men. So liberal was he in paying for provisions and entertainment that soon another robbery was necessary. The ill-fated Number 4 of the H. & T. C. was attacked at Hutchins, a few miles south of Dallas. This time, the robbers were met with a fusillade of shots, for passengers were armed. Bass and his men escaped, but with less than $500 to show for a risky episode.

Their brazen activities were disconcerting to the small detachment of Hall's Rangers, whose movements were hampered by instructions to "keep close under cover." Parrott wrote to his Captain:

"Still we toil in hopes of future reward." They had done lots of riding, and hoped there would not always be failure. Sheriffs and detectives were arresting many innocent people, but Parrott wished to avoid unwarranted arrests. His men were suffering from chills and fever. They were eager for long-due pay. He added,

"It's nearly impossible to get Sam Bass for Tom Gerren, who is the damndest rascal of the two. He brags of seeing and knowing all of Bass's movements and says he can't be taken out of Denton County so long as he is there."[13]

In the next month, Everheart, in Sherman, stated that Gerren told James Lucy, of Hall's Company, of having given Everheart away at San Antonio. The Grayson sheriff appealed to the good people of Denton to remove Gerren from office. Until the end of the chapter, the bandits worked in better harmony than did the officers of the law.

On April 4, Dallas was infuriated by another nearby robbery, that of the T. & P. at Eagle Ford. Before the week was over the same road was robbed thirteen miles from Dallas at the little town of Mesquite. The T. & P. was Jay Gould's railroad. He had inspected it in Texas the year before with Russell Sage.

13 Sergeant A. L. Parrott to Captain Hall, Sherman, March 30, 1878, *ibid.*

[155]

To his august offices in New York City was flashed the name, Sam Bass. Gould, seeming small behind his massive desk, pompous in broadcloth pantaloons and Prince Albert, opened and shut beady, black eyes, and gave a downward stroke to his black whiskers. He'd get that fellow, if he were on the ground!

The day of the latest robbery, officials of Texas railways conferred with Governor Hubbard. Texas needed railroads and wished to keep their friendship. The State doubled its offer of rewards. She would have liked to send her best men against the bandits, but Adjutant General Steele, though he could find money to finance the campaign, was restricted in his use of Rangers. Governor Hubbard had to face a nominating convention that summer, and dared not antagonize his eastern enemies.

Such matters explained why Hall, in attendance in San Antonio at the trial of the Brazell murderers, received no favorable response to his dispatch of April 15:

"I see the train robbers are still active in Northern Texas. If you have made no other arrangements, I can within the next four or five days get together ten or fifteen of my men who will by that time be through with the work I know of in this section, and will go up there, if you think with such information as Parrott and Cavin are possessed we can do anything. I have no doubt if I was able to remain there long enough I could catch or kill some of them.

"It will probably be best, if local peace officers are able, to let them manage it, as it might arouse the ire of politicians of North Texas if we were sent there."

Steele's opinion was the same. Because of eastern dislike of Hall's Company and of the Frontier Battalion, he decided to organize new troops in the northeast. Junius Peak, with some misgivings, accepted a commission, and on April 16 advertised for men. Major Jones assisted him in selecting thirty brawny boys from nearby farms and added fifty more before the scout for Bass was over.[14]

Though none of the western companies was sent to the dis-

[14] June Peak's obituary, *Dallas News*, April 21, 1934, makes the extreme claim that Peak and his men "broke up the gang at Round Rock."

trict, Hall was allowed to contribute spies and detachments, and had the satisfaction of knowing that Major Jones of the Frontier Battalion was on the ground, searching for trails, advising Peak, interviewing those who had information, and using the Ranger device of getting inside news from first one and then another of the band that followed Bass—from Billy Scott, and from Jim Murphy. Yet the Major could not bring order out of chaos. He could not make a unit of divergent elements, but he did coördinate the movements of the Rangers. Bass ridiculed Pinkerton men, sheriffs, and marshals. He had respect for the valor and intelligence of Major John B. Jones.

On April 22, with Peak and twenty Rangers, the Major succeeded in depriving the bandit of any further service from Sam Pipes and Albert Herndon. To avert danger of straw bail, Jones made Federal prisoners of these members of the band on the charge of rifling the United States mails. On April 28 he sent Peak to Denton with warrants for Bass, Barnes, Frank Jackson, Underwood, and Arkansas Johnson. The wanted men were sighted in Cove Hollow by a detachment of Hall's Company working with Sheriff Everheart. Bass opened fire with his gun, "the Tiger." A rapid exchange of bullets showed both groups to be ready for a skirmish. They were separated by a cañon five hundred yards wide. If either had descended and tried to climb the banks for an attack, it would have meant death. To skirt the ravine would have given time for the opponents to escape. As darkness closed down on the men, they ceased firing. No lives were lost and neither side claimed victory.

Near Cove Hollow, Everheart took as prisoners Jim and Bob Murphy and their father for having harbored outlaws. Their trials, with those of Pipes and Herndon, were scheduled at Tyler for May 21. After a significant conversation with Jim Murphy, Major Jones agreed that the latter's prosecution and that of his father would be dismissed if Jim would join the outlaws and bring about their capture. Murphy, then, was allowed to skip his bond, his bondsmen being given protection. So

"Murphy sold poor Sam and Barnes
And left their friends to mourn."

[157]

Indeed, he made six distinct attempts to sell them out. From Tyler, he sent his offer to Major Jones, to Captain Peak, Captain Hall, Sheriff Everheart, and the Marshal of Sherman. Captain Hall described him as "a veritable Judas in every sense of the word."[15]

The pursuers doubled and re-doubled on their tracks. The *Denison News* of June 4 stated that Everheart had an encounter with Bass and his men on the prairies of Grayson County; that before nightfall they were reënforced by the sheriff of Tarrant County, Captain Hall's Rangers, and Sheriff Eagan and his squad—"Dad Eagan," for whom Bass once had worked. Bass and his men were routed, and they retreated toward Hickory Creek. On June 13, Peak's farmer-Rangers encountered Bass's group in Wise County on Salt Creek. Not until two days later did the sheriffs and their posses begin returning to Denison. They reported that Peak's Company, "with a number of Rangers from the west supposed to be Captain Hall's men, were in hot pursuit of the gang."[16] The pursuit began while Peak was watering his horse. When he reached the scene of action, the six bandits already had fled to the underbrush. Only one had time to mount. Arkansas Johnson, of the Bass group, was killed. The hazard of darkness and rain, and the officers' unfamiliarity with hideaways, conspired to save the robbers from night attack. Next morning pursuit was resumed, but without success.

The day after the return of this discouraged posse, Jim Murphy joined Sam Bass. He was welcome, for the outlaw had only two men left, Seab Barnes and Blockey Jackson. The trap was closing, and from this time on Bass was hunted less eagerly. Major Jones and other Ranger officers believed capture would be surer if details as to plans for the next crime could first be learned from Murphy.

It was not to take place in northeast Texas. Murphy discouraged the idea of attempting a bank in Waco, suggesting that instead one should be tapped in Williamson County. After some delay, this was agreed on. Bass was tired of playing fox to the

---

[15] Hall, *Semi-Weekly Express*, September 13, 1895.
[16] *Denison News*, June 15, 1878. The participation of Hall's command is noted also in *The Daily Democratic Statesman*, May 10, 1878.

Rangers' hounds. It was a new and unpleasant experience to have them invade his retreat at Cove Hollow. Even such pranks as capturing four farmers, out after Bass for the reward, hardly made it desirable to continue in the neighborhood. Sam Bass had never killed a man. He might have to, if skirmishes continued. He preferred to "cash his old white pistol" for the coin of Uncle Sam, not use if for bloodletting. In Rockwall, he saw a gallows tree. He didn't like the looks of it.

Sam Bass and his men journeyed south. The outlaw suspected Murphy. Had it not been for Jackson, Murphy would have lost his life. From Belton, he managed to send an agonized wire to Major Jones; from Georgetown, he sent another. The wording was about the same:

"We are on our way to Round Rock to rob the bank. For God's sake, be there to prevent it."

The message reached Major Jones on July 17. The nearest body of Rangers he could summon was Company E, under Lieutenant N. O. Reynolds, seventy-five miles away at Lampasas. Corporal Vernon Wilson set out with the Major's orders to report at Round Rock. Dick Ware, Chris Connor, and George Herold, in the Ranger camp on the Capitol grounds, likewise were ordered to Round Rock by the Major. They were to leave their horses at the livery stable, keep a lookout for Bass and his men, and not allow themselves to be seen.

And then the Major made a mistake. He asked the Deputy Sheriff of Travis County, Morris Moore, to do a few days work at Round Rock. The Deputy agreed to go on the promise that the work would pay. The object of the scout was not revealed, but on the afternoon of July 17, when he left with the Major on a special train, he may have suspected that the prey was young Sam Bass.

In Round Rock, Major Jones made a second mistake. He added a second deputy to his force—A. W. Grimes, banker, Deputy Sheriff of Williamson County, and leader of the faction that opposed the other half of the town organized under Ross. The Major revealed no more to Grimes than he had to Morris. The two deputies had opportunity to talk alone, for the Major had to spend some time at the telegraph office and preferred to do this by himself. He learned there that Reynold's Company could not reach him as soon as expected. Corporal Wilson, after sixty-five miles of stiff riding that killed his horse, had found that the Company had moved fifty-five miles farther and were encamped on the San Saba. This distance Wilson traveled in a tedious stagecoach. When he delivered the orders to the Company, the men saddled and set out with all speed to make up for the delay.[17] Major Jones worried for fear of what might happen before their arrival. He telegraphed the I. & G. N. agents at Hearne and Austin to guard all trains against robbers, but did not name Sam Bass.

Murphy was also in communication with Captain Hall. He had promised to talk with him at Austin, where Hall, disappointed at not finding him, was serving as Sergeant-at-Arms of the State Convention. On July 19, Adjutant Steele sent for the Captain, told him of Major Jones's departure for Round Rock, and directed him to follow and again try to communicate with Jim Murphy. Hall gathered together as his posse Lieutenant Armstrong, one or two Rangers of Special State Troops, and James E. Lucy, who had served as its scout. To these he added his brother, Richard Hall, and Netteville Devine of San Antonio. Together the men rode to within three miles of Round Rock, where Hall directed them to make camp. He entered the town alone, riding straight to the hotel to talk with Major Jones. The two exchanged what information Murphy had given. They hoped to talk with him in person before the crime. Since the Captain was known by sight to Jackson, Bass, and Barnes, it was agreed that he should remain indoors until the next day, when the outlaws were expected to enter the town to rob the bank. The Ranger officers directed the deputies, Grimes and Moore, to go down to the street and, if they should see any suspicious characters, to come back and report. Major Jones returned to the telegraph station, some blocks distant from the thoroughfare.[18]

[17] Stuart Lake, after attending a Ranger reunion at Eastlake, Texas, wrote an account of the Bass affray that was published in *The Saturday Evening Post*, April 11, 1931. See also J. B. Gillett, "The Facts in the Case," *Frontier Times*, October, 1927; J. B. Gillett, "Vernon Wilson Was a Texas Ranger," *Frontier Times*, April, 1929.

[18] Hall, *Semi-Weekly Express*, September 13, 1895.

The afternoon was scorching, and those who could remained indoors. One small boy was in the street holding the reins of a team while his father bought provisions. At Highsmith's livery stable an older boy unloaded fodder.[19] The rhythm of his movements, the regular fall of the hay, gave drowsy pleasure to Chris Connor and George Herold, watching from inside. Dick Ware, his face well covered with lather, was somnolent in a barber's chair.

Fifteen minutes after the deputies left the hotel, a blaze of gunfire, swirling smoke, and smell of powder, turned the sleepy street into a pocket of inferno. Captain Hall grabbed his Winchester and ran towards the men behind the smoke screen. Other Rangers nearer the scene, came "like hot shot off a shovel." The Major, too, ran a double-quick from the telegraph office. But the two deputies had wrecked the Ranger plans.

Moore, who survived to tell the tale, records that, with Grimes, he watched some strange men enter Henry Koppel's store, and remarked, "There are three men wearing guns. Over in Travis, I usually take them away."

"I do the same thing in Williamson County," boasted Grimes.[20]

And there and then, Grimes walked towards Koppel's store. Moore followed. Because of the way the three were dressed, Grimes did not think them the "suspicious characters" he had been told to watch for. He stopped in the doorway, whistling, hands in pockets. Grimes asked the men if they were wearing guns. Before he had time to draw pistol from holster, his own body attested that they were. He fell, pierced by six bullets. Morris Moore discharged five bullets and a last one in the street. None of his shots took effect, but he himself was wounded in the lung.

If Captain Dan Robert's surmise is correct, the two deputies had learned from Ware what prey they stalked, and had attempted to gain the reward alone.[21] If so, they paid dearly for their avarice.

---

[19] This boy was Jefferson D. Dillingham of Austin, who tells the story in *Frontier Times*, November, 1933.

[20] Morris Moore, quoted by "Citizen of Denton," *Authentic History of Sam Bass and His Gang* (Denton, 1878), 170, 171.

[21] Roberts, *Rangers and Sovereignty*, 145-51.

Hall saw Grimes fall on his face in front of the store and Morris Moore stagger to the support of a wall outside. A man running toward Hall shouted that there was a fight between the Ross and Grimes factions.[22] Much of the smoke in front of the store came from shots fired by Dick Ware. He had been the nearest Ranger and was first in the fray. Firing began a fraction later in the yard of the livery stable, for Chris Connor and George Herold joined the fusillade as the bandits ran for the alley and the hitching rack to mount their horses. It was almost impossible to tell what was happening.[23] In the street lay one body—that of Grimes. In the alley was another—that of Barnes.[24]

Hall could not distinguish one man from another, but he heard one man call, "Come on! Come on!" as he made for the hitching rack. The one who followed had one bullet in his body, and two fingers torn and bleeding from a second. His friend kept back the Rangers with a pistol in his right hand, and with

[22] Hall, *Semi-Weekly Express,* September 13, 1895.

[23] W. S. Adair, "Former Texas Ranger [John D. Rains] Tells of Early Days," *Dallas News,* June 10, 1928: "It seemed to me that every man and boy in town was shooting at the outlaws as they rode out of town." J. B. Gillett, Second Sergeant of Company E, says that "every citizen in town that could secure a gun joined in the battle"—"Last Fight of Sam Bass," *El Paso Herald,* August 12, 1902, reprinted in *Frontier Times,* October, 1932.

[24] Gillett, who reached Round Rock with Nevill's squad, believes that it was probably Dick Ware who killed Sam Bass, though Herold swore at the inquest that he did. Captain Roberts also believed it was Ware. Captain Hall and Morris Moore have stated that it was Herold. Wayne Gard in his recent biography accepts the verdict of the coroner's jury and of the "Citizen of Denton," that Herold killed Bass. Stuart Lake, after hearing the Rangers' reminiscences at their reunion at Eastlake, stated in his article in *The Saturday Evening Post* that Ware not only killed Bass, but also killed Seab Barnes. Major Jones, Captain Hall, Captain Roberts, and Wayne Gard, state that Barnes was killed by George Herold (Harrell). Morris Moore says that Barnes was killed by Dick Ware. Another account is that a one-armed man, named Stubbs, came out from the livery stable, leveled his Winchester on a fence, and killed Barnes at first fire.

The verdict of the coroner's jury was that Grimes was killed by Jackson. Hugh Nugent Fitzgerald in "Did Sam Bass Kill Grimes?" *Wichita Falls Record,* May 21, 1927, claims that the slayer of Grimes was Frank Murphy. The indictment against Murphy, it is said, was drawn up by Colonel W. K. MacKemson.

Although Deputy Sheriff Moore fired five shots at close quarters within the store, and one in the street, not one of them has been accounted fatal. These divergences in the various accounts bear out Hall's testimony as to the brevity of the fight and density of the smoke. As to who killed Sam Bass, it is well to imitate the ballad makers, who, in all their hundred stanzas, refrain from judgment: *"They* pierced poor Sam with rifle balls."

his left helped the wounded man mount a gray pony, jumped on his own, and the two were off. To the Captain, he appeared the coolest one in the affray. Hall unhitched Grimes' horse from the hitching rack and with Rangers Connor and Herold started in pursuit. They did not know which men they followed.

Jim Murphy knew. On an excuse, he waited in a doorway in Old Round Rock while the others, Barnes and Bass and Jackson, entered the new town to reconnoiter for next day's robbery. In the shadows he watched for their return. He heard the clatter of hoof beats and saw Jackson, sitting far to the side of his saddle, one arm supporting Bass to keep him steady. He saw Bass, pale and bleeding, slumped and shaking. When they passed, in a flash of blood-spattered horror, the man who had betrayed them knew his plan had gone awry. Yet Bass was wounded, and Barnes was not riding at his side. Before a cloud of dust had settled on the bloody trail, Jim Murphy slunk away.

> *"For Murphy sold poor Sam and Barnes*
> *And left their friends to mourn;*
> *Jim Murphy will a roasting get*
> *When Gabriel toots his horn."*

At one place, the horsemen found a glove with fingers shot through, its mate lying beside it. After six miles, the blood trails led into rocks and cedar brakes. It was dusk, tired horses were stumbling, and the Rangers decided to return to Round Rock and pick up the trail at sunrise with better mounts.[25]

In the night an old Negro came into town and said that a wounded man was lying in front of his cabin. The Negro had been about to chop some wood when a high, weak voice called to him to go to Round Rock and tell the Rangers to come and get Sam Bass, that Bass was dying. When he reached town, the Negro had been too frightened to remember all his message. Only after he told his story was it known that the wounded fugitive was he whom all were seeking.[26] Lieutenant Reynold's Company had arrived, and Major Jones ordered out a detach-

---

[25] "Hall Assists in Capture of Sam Bass at Round Rock," *Galveston News*, July 21, 1878, and issue of July 24, 1878; "Citizen of Denton," *op. cit.*
[26] Hall, *op. cit.*

ment under Sergeant Nevill.[27] They found the outlaw stretched beneath a live oak.

"Don't shoot!" he called, "I am unarmed and helpless. I am Sam Bass."

Sergeant Nevill's message to Major Jones, reporting the capture, was relayed at once to Austin and read to the Democratic Convention. Delegates suspected a political hoax for the glorification of Hubbard, the Rangers' friend, who was seeking renomination. To end all doubt, Adjutant General Steele telegraphed:

"It is claimed that your dispatch is an election trick. Bring Bass here if possible. Answer."

The answer could not be sent by the Major, for he, with Captain Hall, Dr. Cochran and others, had gone to bring Bass in to Round Rock. It was Morrow, the telegraph operator, who wired that Bass was really captive.[28]

The Doctor found that the body wound was made by a bullet from a Colt six-shooter—not a deep wound, but it had cut its way through the intestines and would serve. A bullet had torn away two fingers from one hand. Bass told Lee Hall that he received his wounds before running for his horse.

The outlaw was carried into town in the wagon of a vegetable gardener[29]—a poor equipage for the man that legend was to make a Robin Hood.

And yet he made his end in a fashion that did not incommode the ballad makers. From the time that he received his wounds, he lived three days. Major Jones questioned him about his family and the members of his band. He told him that he was born in Indiana, but of his family he would say nothing. He told how he had tried to get water during the long night. He expressed his admiration for Jackson, who wanted to remain, bound his wounds, tethered his horse, and left his saddle where he could reach it, if strength remained.

As to the men who shared his guilt, Bass gave no information

---

[27] Ranger James B. Gillett was a member of this detachment.

[28] W. A. Morrow was the agent and general utility man at Round Rock, E. M. Ainsworth, "Old Austin and Round Rock and Fort Concho," reprinted in *Frontier Times*, July, 1929.

[29] J. D. Dillingham's story quoted in *Frontier Times*, November, 1933.

—"wasn't built that way." He'd die with what he knew inside him. He was going to hell, anyway, and wouldn't take any one with him.[30] He had not killed any man, unless it was Grimes.[31] Through long, hot, July hours, he lingered on. They had laid him on a cot between clean sheets, but for such things Sam did not care. The monotony of the questions worried him. Finally, the Doctor told him he was dying and had only one more chance to aid the cause of justice.

"Let me go," said Sam.

There was not long to wait. "The world is bobbing around," said Sam, and took his leave of it.

The day was the Sabbath, his birthday, the beginning and the end of the twenty-eighth year of his life.

[30] Hall, *op. cit.*
[31] "Citizen of Denton," *op. cit.*, 175-78.

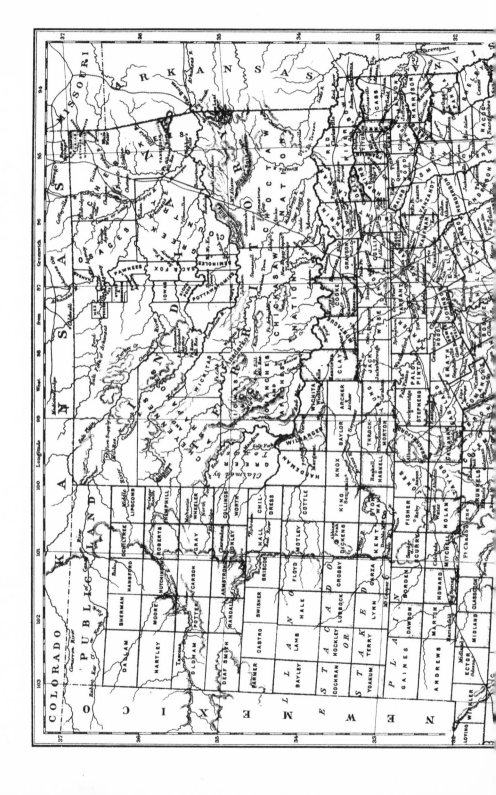

TEXAS
and
Indian Territory
in the Eighties

Scale of Miles

Railroads

County Towns

WESTERN PART OF
T E X A S.
(Continuation of Map.)
Same Scale as the larger Map.

From the Encyclopædia Britannica, Ninth Edition

XIII

The Decision of "the Old Alcalde"

(July, 1878-March, 1880)

"*The district judges, state's attorneys, grand jurors, sheriff and county officials of every district west of the San Antonio River and northward to the Red River have urged upon the Executive the retention of these commands, and in their official capacities have said that had they been withdrawn in a large majority of cases, their courts could not have been held, and the settlements would have been driven eastward one hundred miles.*"—Excerpt from Governor Hubbard's Message, January, 1879.

"*There was in the administrations of Governor Coke and Governor Hubbard, running through five years, a remarkable improvement in all the departments and functions of government. Under their influence a splendid prosperity dawned upon the country, and the people of the state were inspired with general gratitude at the restoration of good local government.*"—DUDLEY G. WOOTEN, *Comprehensive History of Texas.*

XIII

The Decision of "the Old Alcalde"

WHEN Chief Justice Roberts of the Supreme Court was nominated governor,[1] there was rejoicing in East Texas that "Spread Eagle Dick" would be succeeded by "the Old Alcalde," who would inaugurate a régime less bellicose and more economical. Sergeant-at-Arms Hall of the convention was not impartial. He had the viewpoint of a Ranger Captain and was disappointed at the defeat of the governor who constantly had supported Special State Troops. It was gratifying, however, that the convention unanimously endorsed Hubbard's retention of Hall's command and declared that those whose money had kept it in the field should be reimbursed. Officers foresaw lean months to come. There would be no more recruiting, companies would be cut, and, when the legislature convened, might be abolished. It was more than ever necessary that the conduct of the troops should not encourage criticism.

George Talley of Hall's Company inopportunely "got into trouble." What had started as a practical joke ended in his killing an irate farmer, one Joshua Peters of Banquette.[2] The man, unarmed and "hog wild" at being laughed at, had forced Talley's pistol down to shoot the Ranger in the leg after he, himself, had received a death wound. George Durham of Hall's

[1] The circumstances that occasioned this nomination were unusual. See Dudley G. Wooten, *Comprehensive History of Texas*, II, 226.

[2] County Court, Nueces County. In chambers at Court House, August 9, 1878. *The State of Texas vs. G. W. Talley, Charged upon the Verdict of Coroner's Inquest with the killing of Joshua E. Peters at Banquette on August 1, 1878. Adjutant General Papers*, Archives, Texas State Library.

The scene at the bunk house is picturesquely described by George Durham, in Clyde Wantland's article, "On the Trail," *West Magazine*, 1935.

Company arrested Talley and jailed him in the railroad station until the two could leave for Corpus. Before the train came, the Sheriff talked to the prisoner and found him full of remorse. Talley said he had supposed that Peters and all of his friends were after him, believing they could run him off, but that he was a member of Red Hall's command and none of the Company knew how to run. Newspapers exaggerated the affair and Hall protested to the Adjutant General.[3] As Captain, he had to discharge George Talley. The penitent Ranger was indicted for murder in the second degree and bound over on a $10,000 bond. Fearing a life sentence, Talley "skipped," and for forty years was "on the dodge" in Mexico.

Captain Hall, with a dozen men, pitched camp at Collins, forty-five miles from Corpus. It was the terminus of the narrow gauge railway, a dumping place for cutthroats, thieves, and gamblers. Lieutenant Armstrong, with six members of the Company, remained in Cuero, DeWitt. A correspondent to the *Galveston News* reported that, since the indictment of the Brazell murderers, lawlessness was no longer a boast and DeWitt was as quiet and orderly as any county in New England. This he ascribed to "the untiring efforts and unflinching courage of Lee Hall."[4]

Some of the Company guarded jail at Corpus Christi. It was not as full as the amount of crime warranted. The County Judge was the father of some of the criminals and the friend of others. By the end of September, 1878, nearly a thousand cattle had been captured by the Rangers, but few arrests were made. In that section, it seemed that criminals even enjoyed the aid of nature. For when the Captain planned to surprise a band on St. Joseph's Island, a storm prevented passage of the reef between the island and the coast. In Live Oak, Corporal Rudd and his detachment recovered hundreds of stolen cattle and gathered evidence to clinch indictments.[5]

Not only from the Captain's monthly reports could the need

[3] Captain Hall's telegram to Adjutant General Steele, Corpus Christi, August 8, 1878, *Hall Ms.*
[4] *Galveston Daily News*, October 4, 1878.
[5] Report of Captain Hall to Adjutant General Steele, Collins Station, Nueces County, August 28, 1878, *Hall Ms.*

for the Company be gauged. The United States surveyors at Fort Ewell stated that the county was terrorized by outlaws who did their work in daylight. Civil authorities were powerless; army officers at the Fort equally so, because Congress had forbidden them to serve as a *posse comitatus*. The report recorded that citizens were appealing to United States officials for Hall's Rangers or any other body that would be able and willing to make arrests.[6]

Across the frontier on the national holiday, September 15, the Mexicans shouted for war against the United States. Minister Foster was present at the time of the *grito,* and entered formal protest with the government.[7] President Diaz's message, read next day at the opening of the Mexican Congress, in seventeen paragraphs discussed border conditions and again voiced resentment at the Order of June 1.[8] Hall's men, with little success, were still trying to induce observance of the extradition treaty of 1861. In November Corporal Rudd and two others, following the Captain's instructions, arrested Martino Rodriguez, murderer of the Deputy Sheriff of Nueces. The arrest was made in Matamoros. Although Rodriguez was an American citizen, Mexican authorities refused extradition.[9]

Much as the Company was needed, neither the State, railroad officials, nor stockmen were providing adequate support. Had the Rangers been "military retainers of baronial stockmen," as a certain "Agricola" claimed in a July issue of the *Austin Democratic Statesman,* this might have been forthcoming. Certain cattlemen were aggrieved that Hall extended protection to sheep raisers, whom they preferred to see run from the land. Also, the Company was strangely assisting Mexicans to retrieve cattle stolen from their small ranches! Railway officials

[6] *Galveston Daily News,* September 24, 1878.

[7] J. Fred Rippy, *United States and Mexico,* Chapter ix.

[8] Message of President Porfirio Diaz on opening of the Sessions, September 16, 1878, *Un siglo de relaciones internacionales.*
The Minister's difficulties can best be understood by studying his memoirs in the volume in the New York Public Library, *Archivo Diplomatico, Numero 29, Las memorias diplomaticas de Mr. Foster sobre Mexico, Publicaciones de relaciones exteriores* (Mexico, 1929).

[9] Captain Hall's telegram to Adjutant General Steele, Laredo, November 27, 1878; Captain Hall's report to Adjutant General Steele, Corpus Christi, December 1, 1878, *Hall Ms.*

thought that the command should devote its attention more exclusively to matters connected with the welfare of the railroads. The reason for financial weakness was the very reason for Ranger strength: the fact that the men regarded themselves as unselfish guardians of the safety and interest of the State. It was this, also, that weakened their foes: "The worst thief and the most desperate criminal," wrote a correspondent to the *Galveston News*, "has some respect for the majesty of the law."

By October, 1878, funds were so low that Hall received orders to cut his company to fifteen privates and two sergeants.[10] Each Ranger was furnished with a copy of the order on which the Captain acted. In determining which men to retain, he followed the principle of seniority in service,[11] discharging some whose work was very valuable and whose loyalty was unquestioned, and retaining Rudd and Durham, who had always felt that McNelly's successor should have been Lieutenant Armstrong. The paper at Corpus published news of the reduction without explanation. A protest meeting was held but with no encouragement from Captain Hall.

Cavin and Holden were two of the newer members whom, most reluctantly, he had to lose. Cavin was attending court at Lampasas, as witness in a jail-breaking case. Holden was busy with detective work. Both were to appear in November in Uvalde, as witnesses against King Fisher and other criminals whom they had helped indict.[12] Hall advised the State to keep them employed in order to afford protection. Anxiously Hall visited Laredo himself in a last effort to strengthen their evidence.

Since the Company was to be disbanded, the men redoubled their efforts, making arrests of thieves in Live Oak, McMullen, Nueces, and San Patricio, and capturing more than seven hundred cattle with blotched brands.

The Captain's annual report described conditions in each

---

[10] The order was dated September 21, 1878, *Daily Democratic Statesman*, October 19, 1878.

[11] Captain Hall to Adjutant General Steele, Corpus Christi, October 22, 1878, *Hall Ms.*

[12] Captain Hall to Adjutant General Steele, Corpus Christi, November 7, 1878, *ibid.*

county where detachments had been stationed. Its laconic statements offered the best of arguments for the existence of the Company. As the date approached for its disbanding and that of the Frontier Battalion, editorials, letters, and petitions attested their value. Citizens claimed that as soon as the companies ceased to exist, an increase in crime would cost the State more than the Rangers' maintenance.[13]

Judge Henry Clay Pleasants, when alleged to oppose retention, published a vigorous denial:

"There is scarcely a man to be found in those counties in which Hall's command has operated who will deny that these troops have contributed loyally to the suppression of crime in this section of the State. Indeed, their presence has been indispensable, in this and other counties, to the peace and tranquility of society ... I should deprecate the disbandment of any portion of the state troops at the present time or within the next one or two years. ... I would advise, if permitted to make a suggestion, that Hall's command be increased to the number of one hundred with headquarters in the city of Austin, and be detached thence in detachments of sufficient strength to such districts and localities as emergencies might require."[14]

Nevertheless, on January 2, 1879, Hall's Company of Special State Troops was mustered out.[15] In various hidden places there was obscure rejoicing that the "hoodoos" no longer could cause trouble.[16] Their ultimate fate depended on the Sixteenth State Legislature. When this convened on January 14, Hall's star seemed declining. He was defeated for the position of sergeant-at-arms,[17] and listened in the visitors' gallery with men of no authority to debates as to payment and reorganization of his Company. He scouted for support outside. The counties of the northeast and of the southwest were joined in battle, and the fight was hot.

His arguments were strengthened by the Governor's final

---

[13] *Galveston Daily News*, October 23, 1878.
[14] Judge Henry Clay Pleasants' letter published in *Galveston Daily News*, October 16, 1878.
[15] *Galveston Daily News*, January 1, 1879.
[16] Letter signed "A. M. O." *Galveston Daily News*, January 23, 1879.
[17] *Daily Democratic Statesman*, January 15, 1879.

message and the report of the Adjutant General. Hubbard made the Rangers' cause his own:

"It was believed that the extension of our settlements as rapidly as possible to the westward, the consequent reclamation of large districts of country from the savages to civilization, the consequent additions to our taxable property and the last, but not least, consideration of the protection of the lives of women and children and men of our border—these were considerations involving life and liberty which could not be measured by the 'red tape' of the national war department or by the dollars and cents of our state government.

"The treaty of annexation required that the Federal government should protect all our frontiers, and yet since 1845 to 1879—a period of more than thirty years—Texas has been compelled to spend over $2,000,000 of money in her defense."

As to Hall's command, the Governor reminded the legislature that it had been created under the Act for Suppression of Crime and Lawlessness. In his opinion, the reasons for its creation still existed. They had existed when, appropriations being nearly exhausted, he had reduced the Company to half its original size; and they had existed when, late in 1877, he was forced to order its disbandment. Citizens of the west, the Governor reminded the legislature had volunteered, at this time, to support the force if, by executive authority, it could be retained. He had agreed to keep it in the field with the proviso that the State should not by his act be held responsible either to the men or those who had advanced supplies, but that the Company's backers should await legislative action. The Governor recommended that the equity of their claims be recognized.[18]

The accompanying report of the Adjutant General described the lawless condition of the seventies and stressed the economic effect of the Rangers. He showed they had increased the value of taxable property in every county where they worked.[19]

These valedictories were succeeded by Governor Roberts's inauguration. Press articles embodied in their congratulations the recommendation that the new Governor should consider

[18] The Governor's message, quoted in *Galveston News,* January 17, 1879.
[19] Report of Adjutant General in issue cited above.

carefully old border needs. A correspondent for the *Galveston News* claimed that to deprive Maverick County, for one, of the protection of Hall's Company would throw it back into such a state as had filled the earlier files of the *News* with accounts of criminality:

"Surely Governor Roberts cannot see anything in the present state of society anywhere leading to the belief that the want of an asylum for outlaws has ceased to exist. Surely he must know that the demoralization growing out of cattle transactions has not yet sufficiently subsided to permit the wheels of local government to work smoothly as elsewhere. If the Governor can stop a real leak anywhere, it will be true economy to give the saving to Captain Hall for future service."[20]

Governor Roberts's message, delivered in February, showed understanding of the need for protection.

Responsibility, however, for advances made to the Company was not coveted. The legislature was disposed to defer the question of the legality and equity of the claim to members of the executive department for quasi-judicial inquiry. The executive, in his turn, was not disposed to clean up this unfinished bit of business.[21] In addition to passive negativism, there was an active wish on the part of members from east Texas to return to their constituents with such political capital as defeat of the payment of Hall's command, prevention of its reorganization and that of the Frontier Battalion.[22] Through March and April, the wrangling continued. Claims advanced by merchants of the southwest for provisioning and support of Captain Hall's Company for the last seven months of 1878 amounted to $46,000.

George P. Finlay, in a long speech to the legislature, urged payment. He asserted that Hall's men brought peace and security to as many counties as there were men in the Company. He reminded his hearers of the time when Suttons and Taylors came into a certain courtroom "with a written treaty of peace, hundreds on each side, and forced the District Judge to come

20 "A. M. O." *Galveston News,* January 23, 1879.
21 Editorial: "Afraid of Responsibility," *Galveston Daily News,* April 2, 1879.
22 Gillett, *Six Years with the Texas Rangers,* 131-34; *Galveston Daily News,* April 10, 1879, quoting *San Antonio Express,* April 8, 1879.

down from his bench and sign the treaty as a witness"—a treaty that was broken an hour after it was made. Hall's men, he claimed, had changed all that.[23]

Early in May, the legislature included, in its appropriations, the item of $46,000 for the seven months' expenses and supplies of Captain Hall's Company. This, along with many other appropriations, the new Governor promptly vetoed.[24]

Meantime, the organization of a *Santa Hermandad* on the Mexican side of the border caused an exodus to the Texas side of a flock of itinerant jailbirds in search of no man's land. With the disbanding of the Ranger companies, the border outlaws resumed activities.[25] King Fisher regained his freedom, re-entered his kingdom, and again was "on the prod." Warren Goodin escaped jail in Lee and reforged the broken chain of the relay system.[26]

In June, 1879, the legislature convened in special session and made reasonable appropriations for Ranger services. To these, the Governor gave approval. Very rapidly the Rangers were reorganized under Major John B. Jones, who long had been their commander. Captain in the Confederate Army, he had migrated, after the Civil War, to Brazil. Priests there seeming to him far worse than carpetbaggers; he returned and was given command of the Frontier Battalion. In addition to the dash and valor of a cavalry officer, he had tact, courtesy, and exceptional administrative ability. Measured by scale and yardstick, the new Adjutant General was small—five feet seven in height, and weighing less than 125 pounds. No one could think of him dimensionally. He rode magnificent stallions, and he rode them magnificently; and he guided and controlled his dangerous men with even greater skill.[27]

Captain Hall telegraphed in July to ask what decision had been made as to the captaincy of the company for southwest Texas.[28] He learned that Governor Roberts had authorized the

[23] Speech of George P. Finlay quoted in *Galveston Daily News,* April 1, 1879.
[24] *Ibid.,* May 8, 1879.
[25] Letter from "A. M. O." dated Eagle Pass, May 8, 1879, quoted in *Galveston Daily News,* May 9, 1879.
[26] *Daily Democratic Statesman,* July 4, 1879.
[27] Roberts, *Rangers and Sovereignty,* 16; Gillett, *op. cit.,* 60-62.
[28] Captain Hall to Adjutant General Steele, Corpus Christi, July 16, 1879.

mustering in of a Special Force for the Suppression of Crime and Lawlessness. Lee Hall was to command. Names of members of his old company reappeared in the new: W. L. Rudd, ("Colorado Chico"); C. M. Dibrell; S. N. Hardy; John McNelly, nephew of the late Captain of the Company; S. A. McMurray, later to have a company of his own; H. Maben; C. B. McKinney.

A half year's separation and the "hoodoos" came together, a quicksilver specific against corruption!

Of the twenty-seven, less than half were native born.[29] The rest were Southern, with the exception of one recruit from New Jersey, one from Missouri, and Rudd, the Englishman. A composite picture of the Company would show a man of twenty-five, blue-eyed, about six feet in height. Nine of the new Special Force had been in the squad of Sergeant T. L. Oglesby at Carrizo Springs, the surviving remnant of a company hard hit by reduction. Hall welcomed Oglesby as First Lieutenant. Some half dozen of the men were raw recruits. Each furnished his mount, saddle, and bridle. Wagon team and pack mule waited at Carrizo Springs while the force was mustered in. Captain Hall read the oath,[30] the men signed it, and he pronounced them Rangers. They received rations of flour, bacon, coffee, sugar, rice and beans, soda, salt, and pepper. The Company was sure to find all the wild game it "could say grace over." Sharps .50 carbines, and Colt .45's were dealt out, and the latter charged against the men's accounts. Equipment was of the simplest. There was less chance for fuss and feathers than ever now that the "Old Alcalde" was ensconced as Governor. The *Galveston News* observed that the Captain did not want his men "to sport ivory-handled pistols nor wear spurs that looked as though they were built for a horse twenty-seven feet high."[31]

Speed was the need. Red Hall, as well as every man of the Company, was unpleasantly conscious that King Fisher was throning it in the saddle; that King Fisher had reorganized; that his men had long ropes and longer records. As for Red

[29] Muster-in Roll, *Adjutant General Papers*, Archives, Texas State Library.
[30] Captain Hall subscribed to the oath, August 1, 1879, before Z. T. Fulmore, notary public, Travis County.
[31] *Galveston News*, August 17, 1879.

Hall, he had the authority of the state behind him and danger ahead.

The summer of '79 was lush with vegetation and with criminals. Grass was abundant, mosquitoes "more hellish than common," and flies were everywhere. Cook had his troubles in making fires and drying out provisions in a sodden camp. Swollen streams impeded the work of detachments. Two teams were used to prevent the Company's wagon from bogging in the roads. When the rains delayed arrival of camp supplies, the men borrowed from the good people of Carrizo Springs.

The new Lieutenant, Oglesby, had been in the region some time and had won the confidence of the citizens. He had enough evidence to send King Fisher to the penitentiary, if King Fisher could be captured.

If, in addition, the outlaw could be brought before Judge Paschal, the prospects would be better, for the Judge intimated he would change venue to San Antonio. Hall hoped that a San Antonio jury might impose capital punishment, since there its members would be safely outside the royal domain.[32]

Taking with him one Ranger, the Captain set out for Eagle Pass, King Fisher's capital. The outlaws whom he had rounded up two years before were again comfortably plying their trade of thieving. They stampeded at the news of his arrival. Judge Paschal recorded the obliterating effect of the announcement:

"Lee Hall came in last night!"[33]

Streets became quiet; so safe and so deserted that children played marbles near saloons and crawled beneath the swinging doors. Every one who dared went to "Sunday meetin'." Others wished to. They wanted Red Hall to see that the town was made up of such God-fearing, law-abiding gentry as made his presence superfluous. They prayed silently and fervently that Red Hall would return to Austin and ask to be sent far off to some district worthy of his steel.

[32] Captain Hall to Adjutant General Jones, August 17, 1879, and report of August 20, 1879, *Hall Ms.*

[33] Judge Tom Paschal's account of Captain Hall's achievements appeared in the *San Antonio Express* after the Captain's death and was enclosed in a letter to members of the State Cattlemen's Association in a request for contributions for a monument to be erected over the grave.

There was no real change. All indictments against King Fisher were dismissed. They would not be renewed, since the next grand jury had been chosen from the outlaw's obliging friends. As for the Sheriff, criminals could put their trust in him.[34] The others could only keep their powder dry. With a mental promise to return when conditions were propitious, Hall rode back to his camp. From there, he led a detachment to San Diego in Duval County, a part of the Nueces Strip. Smallpox was raging, so the Captain pitched camp a mile away and imposed a quarantine.[35]

He visited Corpus and towns in DeWitt and Goliad to learn what had developed during the Company's disbandment. District court was in session in DeWitt when he arrived, but the State lacked witnesses and was not ready to come to trial. The county was reverting to its condition at the time of the Brazell murders. Good citizens lived in fear of short lives, and the life of crime was long. The men scoured the adjoining counties and brought in frightened witnesses.

In the southeast portion of DeWitt, the chief malefactor was Bill Taylor—that same Bill Taylor who had occasioned Hall's first scout with a detachment of McNelly's Company—Sergeant Warren ran down one of Taylor's bands after a mile-and-a-half chase through timber and thorny underbrush. The leader himself made off towards Karnes County. On September 20, Warren captured him and lodged him in the County jail of De-Witt.[36]

Bill Taylor was still a dandy in dress, light, wiry, with a temper so hot that it always got him into difficulties, and a brain cool enough to get him out. Captain Hall swore out a warrant on the old charge of the Goliad bank robbery of 1876. So many other indictments had accumulated for horse and cattle thefts that Taylor's bail was high. He had willing bondsmen, but he knew that if ever he was brought to trial conviction would be certain.

[34] Captain Hall to Adjutant General Jones, August 24, 1879, *Hall Ms.*
[35] Captain Hall to Adjutant General Jones, San Diego, September 2, 1879, *ibid.*
[36] Captain Hall to Adjutant General Jones, Cuero, September 20, 1879, *ibid.*

He was far from hopeless. Daring friends, he knew, had a simple plan for freeing him. The night after his arrest, they set fire to the town. They had not much liked Cuero since Lee Hall had begun coming there. In the confusion of a general conflagration, they hoped Bill could break jail. He had escaped before when a hurricane destroyed Indianola where he was jailed for murdering Gabe Slaughter. Fire proved not so helpful as wind had been. The attempt failed and Bill's plight was worse. In solitude, he reflected that the last grand jury had indicted him for theft, forgery, and assault to murder.

To gain immunity, Bill turned State's evidence, naming the incendiaries and those who had helped him in earlier crimes; giving away future plans and present hiding places. With the cool, pitiless eyes of a killer, he offered to decoy his friends by whatever plan Hall might propose. The band consisted of the three Day boys and six others, all under indictments in DeWitt, Karnes and Goliad.

The Captain arranged to let Taylor regain freedom and agreed on a plan for the robbery of a bank either at Victoria or Cuero. Bill Thompkins, formerly of Major Jones's escort, was to join the gang, and with Taylor's help make his report. Hall expected then to catch the men red-handed.[37] He returned to camp at San Diego, leaving behind Sergeant Warren, Sam Graham, and two others. They "did considerable scouting after the old Sutton-Taylor outfit."[38]

The success in September of gaining Taylor's confession, and bagging fifteen criminals, was offset by the escape of King Fisher.[39] The Captain had captured and held him prisoner, even though he knew the grand jury would set him free. Though guarded by a corporal and detachment, his detention was not long. King Fisher was harder to hold than the Company's four mules. Bill Cavin, who had gathered the most evidence against him, rejoined Hall in November. Cavin was known now as a

[37] Captain Hall to Adjutant General Jones, San Diego, October 4, 1879; Cuero, October 17, 1879, *ibid*.

[38] *Manuscript of Reminiscences of Mr. Sam Graham*, Archives, Texas State Library.

[39] Captain Hall to Adjutant General Jones, Cuero, September 20, 1879, *Hall Ms*.

spy and had to be provided with a strong guard when he attended court.[40]

With the springs of man-traps set against old foes, the Company scouted for new offenders. Fresh recruits to Warren Goodin's relay system were stealing cattle in DeWitt, Victoria, Lavaca, and Gonzales. The herds were pastured on the Colorado below Columbus and shipped to Houston. Thirty miles above Fort Ewell, the Moon gang was operating on a larger scale. Jim Moon, its head, had under him about sixteen Mexicans and Americans. Their pens for livestock were in the river bottom. As soon as these were filled, the outfit drove the cattle east and returned to gather more.

In Nueces County, ten or twelve known as "the Dunn party" committed sixty murders in two years. Citizens were so terrorized that the Sheriff—a good one—could not get together more than three men as a posse. Hall succeeded in getting one Ranger in the band so that he could expose it. Mexicans were asked by Hall's men to go with them through pastures of the Nueces to identify and recover their steers. For weeks the Mexicans were fearful and refused.[41] By November, when court sessions were held, owners had gained confidence and took the witness stand. Nearly all of the Dunn party were indicted and jailed. Mexicans, and even Negroes, dared go with the Rangers to identify stolen stock and accept delivery. When the pasture men made difficulties about giving up the cattle, owners held out "for the last hoof."[42]

Lieutenant Oglesby and his men at Carrizo were so successful that work there in the future would be light. Joe McCampbell, under eight indictments, and four of his followers, who long had stolen cattle from Mexicans, all were arrested. Only Sergeant Rudd, at Santa Maria on the border, found little to report. He complained that all the wanted men took flight on the arrival of his detachment. They had "gone off somewhere and no one appeared to know where." Scouting expeditions on

[40] Captain Hall to Adjutant General Jones, Cuero, October 13, 1879, *ibid.*
[41] Captain Hall to Adjutant General Jones, San Diego, October 4, 1879; November, 1879, *ibid.*
[42] Captain Hall's report to Adjutant General Jones, November, 1879, and January 1, 1880, *ibid.*

the Rio Grande between Edinburgh and Brownsville revealed that everything in his district was "very dull."[43]

In contrast, there was some spectacular gun play early in November at Campbell's store in Atascosa County. Located twenty miles north of Pleasanton at a little settlement called Wolfe City, the store had a monopoly of trade for miles around. Besides supplying the needs of stagecoach passengers traveling to San Antonio, it did some business in selling cattle for ranch customers, depositing the money against their accounts and keeping the surplus until they could come in to claim it. When they did come in, they made large purchases. One division of the store was stocked with liquor and salt goods, one with canned goods and staples. The till was often full. A scout of Hall's learned details of a plan for robbery. Before the scheduled time, Hall, with his Oakville detachment, rode to the store. He stationed two men inside, and three others outside between the walls of the store and a mesquite timber fence.[44] Let Ranger Sam Graham tell what happened:

"When we arrived, the proprietor had been notified by the Captain. The Captain came about fifteen minutes after we arrived. It was all timed to arrive after night and by different routes. One outfit was lost and did not arrive until after the whole thing was over. We were secreted in the store. Martin and I inside a room with a door opening in about the center of the store. The robbers came about eight o'clock, took the drop on the clerk, took him outside and started to loot the store. We stepped to the side door and ordered them to surrender (thinking they would—they generally did), but the answer was a shot. They dropped behind the counter. Our shots brought them out of there. Then it was a running fight, they running for the door. One, a Mexican, fell dead in the door with his pistol full cocked in his hand; he had fired all the loads out of it. One of the others fell about fifty yards in front of the store. He died

---

[43] Captain Hall's report to Adjutant General Jones, January, 1880 (for Lieutenant Oglesby's work); Sergeant W. L. Rudd to Captain Hall, Santa Maria, November 12, 1879, *ibid.*

[44] The description of the store and some particulars of the plan I learned from Mr. Sam Crowder, an Englishman and former Ranger scout, who talked with me in San Angelo, Texas, in August, 1938. Mr. Crowder heard of the affair from Mr. Campbell, owner of the store.

about three days later. Another was wounded so badly he could only get about seventy-five yards away. He lived to go to the penitentiary. The man that took the clerk out got away on his horse. None of us were injured."[45]

That they escaped was amazing, for thirty-five or forty shots were fired, and so rapidly that the store was illuminated by the gunfire. The clerk, a nephew of Dr. Hugh Young, also was fortunate. One citizen, in a misguided effort to come to Campbell's assistance, was badly wounded. The account Hall telegraphed to Adjutant General Jones did not mention that the plot was exposed by two of the Rangers.[46] Newspapers were less discreet, and by stating their suspicions hampered the Captain's plans. The Rangers who had exposed the robbers were also working within King Fisher's band. After reading the newspapers, they realized such association no longer would be healthy.

Years afterwards Hall told the story of the fight to Frederic Remington as they sat in the San Antonio Club. Remington included it in an article published in the *Harper's New Monthly Magazine* of Christmas, 1896.

So many scouts were made that for a part of the time the camp at Cuero was deserted by all but the Negro cook. He slept there unafraid, for the "hoodoos" were on his side and no one dared molest their property. When the boys did come back, they bragged of "square meals" they had eaten at Buck Pettus's ranch, a "regular Ranger home." Pettus was "white." He branded no animals that were not his own, and he lent the rangers his cowboys to help in locating criminals.[47]

Hall needed men and he needed arms. Half a dozen of his Company were using borrowed carbines and pistols.

The winter was cold. Sam Graham records that for a time his mustache was stiff with icicles. Grass and water were scarce. The Company was forced to buy hay. On one cold scout in February, it was necessary for Corporal McKinney to kill a Mexican cow-thief, Manuel Martinez.[48] The relatives of Martinez

---

[45] *Ms. of Reminiscences of Mr. Sam Graham.*
[46] Captain Hall's telegram to Adjutant General Jones, November 5, 1878. The Captain's November report adds further information, *Hall Ms.*
[47] J. W. Warren to Captain Hall, Cuero, November 11, 1879, *ibid.*
[48] Captain Hall's telegram to Adjutant General Jones, February 28, 1880, *ibid.*

in San Antonio charged that this was unjustifiable homicide.[49] McKinney felt his cause was so clear that he did not trouble to send in a detailed statement until a month later when he laboriously penned the following:

"While in camp on the 28th, Pierce Johnson wrote me a note to come up and arrest a Mexican that had shot a Mexican and stoled a horse. I went up not taking anyone with me, as I had two other prisoners in camp to guard. In making the arrest, the Mexican's friends come out and made fight. Peter Johnson went with me to show me the Mexican and do the interpreting. Peter Johnson was seriously shot. I killed the Mexican that shot him."[50]

Hall's report for the year gave credit to his men for their scouts and the good results of the court sessions they had attended. In San Patricio, for the first time since the Civil War, a white man was convicted and sent to the penitentiary, the scout, Holden, supplying the necessary testimony.[51]

No one in the Company was more active than its Captain. The same night that he took part in the Atascosa affair, he made another arrest and lodged the criminal in jail in Yorktown in DeWitt, then rode to Goliad. During November and December, 1879, he was never in camp for two consecutive days. This was not enough. King Fisher was at large; Bill Taylor, also; and the promises Bill made, he was slow in fulfilling.

[49] Captain Hall gave his version of the affair to a reporter in Austin. This was reprinted in *The Dallas Herald,* March 8, 1880.

[50] C. B. McKinney's letter to Captain Hall, Souce [Sauz?] Ranch, March 30, 1880, *Hall Ms.*

[51] Captain Hall's report to Adjutant General Jones, November, 1879, *ibid.*

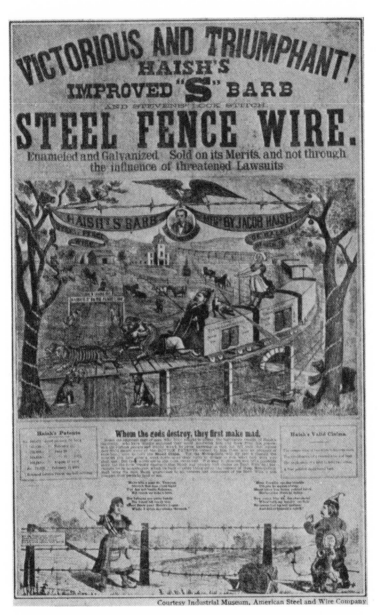

ONE OF THE TRINITY OF STEELS

With steel of rails and steel of Rangers
it served to tame Texas.

CAPTAIN L. H. McNELLY
Who called the tune—a rousing one—for
Special State Troops.

SPECIAL STATE TROOPS

"Men with the bark on." Lee Hall third from left, top row.

AN APPEAL

BY

THE PEOPLE OF THE STATE OF TEXAS,

OF THE TERRITORY BETWEEN

The Nueces River and the Rio Grande,

PREPARED BY CERTAIN

CIVIL AUTHORITIES OF THAT DISTRICT,

AND ADDRESSED THROUGH

THE HON. SECRETARY OF STATE OF THE UNITED STATES,

TO THE

PRESIDENT, TO CONGRESS, AND TO THE COUNTRY,

FOR PROTECTION

AGAINST INCURSIONS OF THE

Savages of the State of Cohahuila, Mexico,

AND, ALSO, THE HISTORY OF A LATE

MURDEROUS AND DEVASTATING RAID,

WITH

Affidavits of Eye-Witnesses

TO THE

ATROCIOUS CRIMES COMMITTED.

Those wrongs, those bitter injuries
I doubt not with honor to redress."
SHAK.

CORPUS CHRISTI, TEXAS:
FREE PRESS PRINT.
1878.

AN "APPEAL"

Calculated to rouse Indian war whoops and
rebel yells.

KING FISHER

Who could twiddle his handle-bar mustache with
one hand and send a man to glory with the other.

GENERAL CANALES

The Rangers never saw him with a book.

IN THE DAYS BEFORE CANDID CAMERA

Lee Hall, gentleman, who could spin a yarn to net securely the interest of companions.

REACTION EQUALS ACTION

As understood by Frederic Remington, who might have
taken it from Ranger memories.

Photo by Brady from U. S. Signal Corps.

GENERAL E. O. C. ORD

He could ride the frontier with any corporal.

BESSIE WEIDMAN HALL

The lovely lady, appointed superior officer by a
former Captain of Special State Troops.

SIDNEY PORTER

Who as Lee Hall's guest stored away
material to use for O. Henry.

THE BEEF ISSUE AT ANADARKO

By Frederic Remington

QUANAH PARKER

More esteemed in Washington than on
the Reservation.

LEE HALL

Ranger, Manager of the D.H.&D. Ranch,
Indian Agent.

OFFICERS OF THE 33RD INFANTRY, IN CAMP AT PRESIDIO, SAN FRANCISCO, SEPT. 23, 1899.

LIEUTENANT HALL'S BROTHER OFFICERS IN THE FAMOUS THIRTY-THIRD

IN THE PHILIPPINES—A BAYONET RUSH

By Frederic Remington

THE RURALES

As seen by Frederic Remington

XIV
Blooms on the Cactus
(May, 1880-1882)

"Life, God wot, like the cactus blows,
Silkeny saffron and satiny rose."

—H. R. R. Hertzberg.

XIV

Blooms on the Cactus

In 1880, spring scouts were made on the Upper Nueces, in Frio
Cañon, and other sections of the southwest. Lieutenant Oglesby
and the men did well. Their Captain was captured. For the
usual good reasons that the troubled port constantly provided,
he went in May to Corpus Christi. There at the home of Captain Halter of the Coast Survey, he met a visitor from Pennsylvania, Mrs. Halter's sister, pretty Bessie Weidman. Carbine
and pistol shots, Red Hall could hear without flinching, but the
tap of her heels and the swish of her skirts on the stairs seemed
fearsome sounds. When her fingers fluttered over piano keys,
he almost forgot his Scottish songs. But he did sing them, and
there were brief glances and lingering ones, and touch of hands
upon the music rack.

Lee Hall knew now why wild flowers bloomed in spring on
the Nueces, why spiney thorns of gray-green cacti sheltered
poppy-flowers of rose and gold, why yellow balls dotted the
huisache with fragrance, why bluebonnets drew down to earth
the blue of cloudless skies. It was difficult to write reports, to
plan for scouts and vigils, to plot to capture thieves and murderers. He became fastidious in his dress. The Company opined
that Red was "goin' gallin'." They wished him all the joys that
men in lonely places visualize.

One night in a friendly home in Corpus Christi he danced
with this new disturber of the peace. And then he had to take
her away from the others, had to lead her into darkness where
the sky would be his roof and the whiteness of her dress would
gleam for him alone. When walls did not shut around her, when

[187]

she was in his world, he could ask, with no further waiting, what his fate might be. They were standing by an old well, and the lady was deep and cool, as coveted as water dipped from earth's hidden bosom for the solace of a thirsty man. The well was sheltered. It could reflect the stars, but it could never know the plunge and fall of tidal waves. A pebble, splashed into its surface, would have been rebuked by a grave echo, primordial, impatient of man's crude intrusion. The lady seemed aloof and far removed from such a life as Hall had known. The lashes fringing her gray eyes drooped low to hide her answer. And yet she was not unconscious of the spring, nor of night's magic, nor of the spell she wove around the Captain of State Troops. She knew that she had met no man so handsome, and none so humbly worshipful. There was prayer in his eyes when she raised her own to look at him, and the tone in his voice was the tone of a pilgrim whose journey ends before a shrine.

She was twenty-one and thought, not as a girl, but as a woman. Her answer was "Yes," but an Eve-woman's "Yes" with a sweetly cadenced condition. There would be no marriage unless he abandoned his work as a Ranger.[1] King Fisher was at large. The trials continued of the murderers of Dr. Brazell and young George; Judge Pleasonts and Judge Paschal had need of the Captain for the guarding of jurors, witnesses and prisoners. Bill Taylor's scheme had not developed. Border depredations still vexed the people of the Rio Grande. And there was Hall's Company—more truly his than ever, reorganized after an interval so anxious. All these seemed trivial. Dumbly they let themselves go down beneath desires long dormant, now awake and clamorous. A pebble splashed into the sea was more momentous than all the arduous, uncompleted efforts of his Ranger years.

His answer was "Yes;" the "Yes" of a man who had starved himself of an ecstasy that now he realized existed; the "Yes" of a pioneer who thought no price too high that a woman named.

And, so, he "took her into camp."

[1] Mrs. Isham Keith, Captain Hall's daughter, was told by her mother of this request.

[188]

BLOOMS ON THE CACTUS

"Peaches in the summer time,
Apples in the fall,
If I can't get the girl I want,
I won't have none at all."

Inside, the dancers were singing a play-party tune. There was laughing, stamping, and gay exchange of partners. When the Captain and his lady stepped over the sill into the lighted room, they faced smiling and curious glances. The doorway framed them, a picture of radiant romance. Lee Hall felt touched with glory, yet on confessing his joy to a young matron he spoke in halting fashion, as have other moon-mad mortals.

"I went out trembling, unengaged, and came in beaming with joy, engaged to Miss Bessie."[2]

Late in May, he sent the Adjutant General his resignation:

"Owing to private and business engagements of my own, it is impossible for me to remain longer in the service. ... To yourself and to his Excellency the Governor, Commander in Chief, I beg to convey my grateful and lively appreciation of the favors and kindnesses uniformly received at the hands of the administration, and to assure you of my lasting friendship and regard."[3]

Influential friends, not understanding the nature of his private engagements, wished to solicit a commission in the army. They were dissuaded. Bessie Weidman did not wish it.

At twenty-nine, the would-be benedict set out on a new pilgrimage. It was money that he now desired. Search for black sheep yielded to search for land on which to pasture white ones. He planned to establish himself in Crockett County,[4] to sink artesian wells, to build canals, and make a home for Bessie. Heavy rains preceded his expedition. While his men watered their horses in a creek bed, a flood descended so precipitately that they could barely clamber up the bank in time to save their lives.[5]

---

[2] The story of the proposal is from a letter to Mrs. Keith from Mrs. Sam Rankin, dated October 26, 1928. Miss Weidman's charm and beauty are attested in the *Frances Wier Hall Ms., supra,* Note 2, Chap. VII. See also, Hyder E. Rollins, "O. Henry's Texas Days," *The Bookman,* October, 1914, 154-65.

[3] Captain Hall to Adjutant General Jones, May 24, 1880, *Hall Ms.*

[4] *Daily Democratic Statesman,* August 10, 1880.

[5] *Ibid.,* August 24, 1880.

In October he was back in San Diego, and prospering so well as a sheep raiser that he could set an early date for his marriage.[6] Before his wedding day, he undertook the management of a sheep and cattle ranch. The owners, A. J. and J. J. Dull, wished to extend their holdings in LaSalle and McMullen.

With his mind appropriately filled with connubial longings and schemes for money making, Lee Hall entrained in November for Pennsylvania. And if any errant wind whistled a tune of fresh adventures, he kept his windows tightly closed. He banished it to the oblivion of the prairies. Yet to Miss Bessie's friends and family, he appeared far different from the orthodox. He was still a pilgrim, still a stranger.

The man and maid were married, Ranger and pretty conqueror, in the Lutheran Church in Lebanon.[7]

Texas friends gossiped that it had been a fashionable wedding. The bride's friends gossiped too. Some said Lee Hall had killed men, and they shook their heads. The women liked the curl and color of his hair. His manners they found perfect. The men liked the humor of his western stories. They wondered if, away from Pennsylvania, they could have matched his exploits.

"And forsaking all others ... Till death do us part."

These were words. Facts were that Texas had lost a valued officer, a man signally equipped to struggle for justice and security; that the lady had gained an ardent lover. The Captain's worth as a husband had yet to be proved.

The first house to which he took his bride was a frame structure of a single room, twelve feet by eight. From that they soon moved to another of logs and 'dobe, two rooms fronted by a wide gallery where stood a guncase stacked with rifles and re-

---

[6] Captain Hall to Adjutant General Jones, San Diego, October 19, 1880, *Hall Ms.*

[7] Eli Merriman, in a letter to Mrs. Robert Kleberg, Sr., February 28, 1935, says that the marriage was solemnized in the Presbyterian Church of Corpus Christi. Two small photographs made in Corpus Christi at this time by Louis de Planque seem to be of the Captain and his groomsmen, since all of the men are in unaccustomed fashion decked out with canes and boutonnières. Each holds a long cigar. The Captain so habitually smoked cigarettes that only the exigencies of the festivities occasioned by a wedding can reasonably account for his cigar. However, Mrs. Isham Keith is certain that the marriage took place in Pennsylvania.

volvers, loaded, ready for instant use.[8] Saddles and other cowboy paraphernalia were piled there and the place was redolent of leather. To Lee Hall the house seemed adequate, for he compared it with a camp. Only gradually he learned that it should be compared with other dwellings—with homes in Pennsylvania. If the house was too small, even for a family of two, the ranch itself was lordly in extent. Most of it was situated on the rolling prairies of LaSalle County, watered by the Nueces. Northward, its chaparral pastures stretched into Frio, and were enriched by the river of that name. To the east, they reached into McMullen. By 1881, the Ranch comprised about 250,000 acres.[9] In April, 1883, a correspondent of the *Corpus Christi Caller* estimated its area at 400,000 acres.[10] One hundred and twenty miles was reckoned as its circuit. Lee Hall's knowledge of country and people enabled him to buy and lease at a price lower than the owners would have paid by direct dealing. Since he worked for a percentage of the increase, he labored to stock it rapidly and well.

Identification of stolen cattle had initiated him early into the mysteries of brands and earmarks, and his herds were of authentic ownership. Steers, in 1881, sold at $12 a head, range cows for more, and prices were steadily mounting.[11] The ranch pastured about 12,000 head of cattle and 6,000 sheep. Mustangs were native and not counted. The cattle were of the old breed of Texas longhorns, pioneers, tough, better able than any others to weather Texas northers and Texas drouths, bad-tempered, arousing in old time cowboys such emotional reactions of hatred and affection as the shorthorn Herefords or Brahmas never can produce. The old breed provided danger, hard work, and excitement until the end of the trail, and those were the elements on which a cowboy lived.

Cowboys know range cattle as individuals. They describe a steer or an old cow not only as to the "critter's" appearance but

---

[8] *Frances Wier Hall Ms.;* C. Alphonso Smith, *O. Henry Biography* (Garden City, Doubleday, Page & Co., 1916), 98, 99. Mr. Smith quotes from a sketch by the Captain's wife.
[9] So stated in a newspaper clipping in the collection of Captain Hall's mother.
[10] *Corpus Christi Caller*, April 1, 1883.
[11] Raine and Barnes, *Cattle.*

as to idiosyncrasies of behavior and character as well. Being mounted, the cowboy felt the superiority always experienced by one who can look down on the pedestrian, but some part of his sense of well-being came also from the fact that he dealt with "ornery, horned jack rabbits and pitiful, potbellied, motherless dogies," and no matter how picturesquely scornful his language might be, he esteemed his charges as supremely interesting and important.

Since no work was more desirable than his own, he was indifferent towards outsiders. The cowboy was leisurely and soft spoken, but he made no effort to conceal his sense of superiority. He knew that the worth of the ranch itself was determined by the worth of its cow-punchers. An old ranch has time to develop traditions of service. Mexican cowhands train their sons painstakingly, and have no fear of outside competition.

To increase 12,000 cattle to an adequate number for stocking 400,000 acres was not to expect from Lee Hall the impossible, but to provide a seasoned bunch of cowhands was a "tall order." He could fill it only because he was able to recruit from his former Rangers, and because his reputation made it possible to supplement their number with others of like breed. Cavin, one of the best scouts of Hall's former Company, became ranch pilot, and for two years, using stars as his guides, took short cuts as he pleased. North Star, Morning and Evening Stars, Big Dipper, Little Dipper, and several others that "he didn't know the names of," he made do service for the ranchmen, as earlier he had put them to work for Rangers.[12] Jake, Tom, and Sam Platt, three brothers, who with one other, were later valiant Rangers under Captain McMurray, worked now with Hall.[13] Sam Platt had been one of the best of his former Company. Another recruit was Netteville Devine, who had been in Hall's posse in the scout after Sam Bass; Charlie McKinney, active in Hall's Company in '79, performed services as hazardous on the Dull Ranch.[14]

In 1883, young Tom Adams joined the outfit. Just seventeen,

[12] W. T. Cavin's letter, May 8, 1935, to Mrs. Isham Keith.
[13] Letter to the author from the late John W. Bracken, dated Austin, Texas, May 25, 1935.
[14] W. T. Cavin's letter cited *supra*.

was Tom. He had come to Texas soon after his father, the Chief of Police of New Orleans, was killed by the Mafia, and had worked for Frank M. Edwards on a ranch west of San Antonio.[15] Among the new men was Ed Brockman, a North Carolinian, who felt an almost proprietary affection for the Captain. Ed, like other boys in Greensboro, had been reared on a judicious diet of pone bread, lye hominy, chicken, hoecakes, simlins, and Lee Hall stories. Ed knew nothing about cowpunching, and was therefore put in charge of the commissary tent.[16] For a while, Will Hall, the Captain's younger brother, was of the group.

Two other brothers, Richard and Frank, looked after a sheep ranch, which was included in the acreage of the pastures owned by the Dull Brothers.[17] Dick Hall was six feet one, and had much the same coloring as Lee. He had been trained as a civil engineer. With Devine, he had been one of the posse sent to Round Rock against Sam Bass. He was a good man to have near in time of trouble.

And trouble there was—a state-wide struggle between those who built fences and those who cut them down. In 1880, forty thousand tons of steel barbed wire of the Haish and Joseph Glidden star varieties were sold to Texas ranchmen.[18] Asher Richardson on his ranch in Dimmit County, east of LaSalle, early had seen the advantage of barbed wire and been among the first to use it.[19] Adjoining the Dull pastures, was the ranch belonging to the father of Colonel E. M. House.[20] This, too, was enclosed by fencing. But the ranchman whose name was most often mentioned in connection with the struggle against fence-cutting was Lee Hall. Great reels of the wire were unloaded at Cotulla and hauled by mules over the sandy roads.

[15] Letter to author from Mr. Frank M. Edwards, dated San Antonio, Texas, May 25, 1935.
[16] C. Alphonso Smith, op. cit., 110.
[17] Frances Wier Hall Ms.
[18] Dobie, Vaquero of the Brush Country, 117, 118; A. G. Warren, "Barbed Wire," reprinted from The Iron Age, June 24, 1926.
[19] Paul S. Taylor in "Historical Notes on Dimmit County, Texas," Southwestern Historical Quarterly, October, 1930.
[20] "We owned an adjoining ranch but both were of such proportions that the two ranch houses were many miles apart."—Letter of Colonel E. M. House to Mrs. Isham Keith, February 23, 1929.

Miles and miles of it were strung to make the circuit of the ranch.[21]

Cattle and sheep, in 1881, brought especially high prices. Outfits were being bought, "sight unseen," by the English, Scotch and Australians. For now refrigeration was making possible long distance shipping. The year was very dry, so that the higher cattle were rated abroad, the more valuable to the owners were water holes and grass. Grangers, too, had been quick to string up the new fences. One old-timer, especially disgruntled at the fence building of farmers, complained that:

"These fellows from Ohio, Indiana and other northern and western states ... have made farms, enclosed pastures and fenced in water holes until you can't rest. ... They are the ruin of Texas and have everlastingly, eternally now and forever destroyed the best grazing land in the world."[22]

When the old-timer thought of onions and Irish potatoes growing where mustang ponies should be exercising, and where two-year-old steers should be getting ripe for market, he denounced fences as the supreme curse of western Texas. Some had no gates, except at unreasonably long intervals. They cut off water supply from water holes for those whose own property had none. The cry of "Free Range and Free Grass" was raised.[23] It did not stop the work of the fence builders.

A man who had strung up a four-strand fence to enclose property to which he had a legal right, experienced the same austere indignation, when his fence was cut, that has been felt through time eternal whenever landmarks have been altered or destroyed. The fence symbolized ownership. It afforded opportunity for improving crops and stock breeding. "Horse high, pig tight, and bull strong," barbed wire had come to stay.[24]

It meant the end of four-county round-ups, the end of winter drifts. The fences interfered with cattle trails and made the use

21 J. A. Wright, "Looking Backward through the Years," *Frontier Times*, September, 1936.

22 Sweet and Knox, *On a Mexican Mustang through Texas*, 172.

23 Captain Hall's conversation with Frederic Remington, "How the Law Got into the Chaparral," *Harper's New Monthly Magazine*, December, 1896.

24 R. D. Holt, "Saga of Barbed Wire in the Tom Green Country," (*West Texas Historical Association Year Book*, Abilene, Texas, June, 1928.)

of freight cars a necessity. And freight cars spelled the doom of the longhorn. No more would herds of the old-time cattle be started up the Trail, increased on the way, and when the market was reached, gain double profit. In LaSalle, conditions were especially bad. The county was not organized, and Captain Hall could not expect such assistance as Judge Paschal and Judge Pleasants had given elsewhere. The Dull, Hall and Dull outfit enclosed pastures that only a little while before had been free range for the enrichment of the men who were now dispossessed. Cattle thieves had found their trade in LaSalle richly profitable. They did not mean to lose it through a Ranger captain who had caused trouble enough already for themselves and friends.

Some depredators were cowmen, who had from a dozen to one or two hundred head of stock, and needed free grass. On occasion this meant free right to brand mavericks and increase their herds by a method used formerly by some of the men who had come strongly to support closed pastures. Nesters also— farmers who had made a home for themselves in some remote section of a great ranch—did not want to be discommoded by a fence that signified "Private property! Keep out!"

Like others with whom Hall contended, the fence cutters knew the benefit of organization, took orders from Jim McCoy, and made their plans in concert.[25] There was "big war talk" as to what they would do to the former Ranger and his cowboys. To this, the men on the ranch did not object, but the destruction that the fence cutters carried out at night—wires clipped between their posts for miles and left curling on the ground, while hundreds of cattle strayed or were driven off—this was serious. Sometimes a roughly scrawled message fluttered an insult from a denuded fence post:

"If your bull you hunt for, call at the first ranch this side of Hell, and brand him when you get him."[26]

The Captain sent his cowboys to "lie on the fence" and await the coming of fence cutters. "Riding the fence" of a ranch with

[25] C. Alphonso Smith, *op. cit.*, 98; Kleber Miller's interview with Judge Brooks, Falfurrias, Texas, April, 1935.
[26] Paul S. Taylor, "Historical Notes on Dimmit County, Texas," *Southwestern Historical Quarterly*, October, 1930.

such a circuit as that of the D. H. and D. could not be done in less than three days, so preliminary work was carried on to discover which section was in danger of attack. Of all the men, Cavin was best at getting to the appointed place in the nick of time.

Captain Hall's pretty bride found that her husband's life was no less in peril than when he had been a Ranger. She showed, moreover, that she had courage and wit. Perhaps she believed, as did one of her young visitors, Frances Wier Hall, that her husband traveled at night to avoid vengeance of veterans of the Taylor-Sutton feud. More probably, she knew that he traveled at night for the reason that he preferred to meet danger, rather than avoid it. For night was the working time of the fence cutters. Mrs. Hall said afterwards that "his life was threatened in many ways, and the mail was heavy with warnings, generally in the shape of crude sketches, portraying effigies with ropes around their necks, and bearing the unfailing inscription 'Your Necktie'."[27]

Because of danger, the Captain could not let her ride with him as he had hoped to. She grew lonely. As soon as he could he had bricks hauled to the Ranch and a comfortable home built, twenty-five miles from their first small dwelling place. After that she shared her adventures with visitors.

One moonlit night when the Hall carriage reached the fork of two roads, it was stopped by mounted men who demanded the names of those inside and where they were going. It happened that the occupants were two young ladies who had been guests at the ranch, and were being driven to Cotulla by Dan Dull, a college boy, son of one of the owners.

"Drive on," they were told, when the men were close enough to see their faces. They entrained for San Antonio with fearsome shudders at the dangers besetting Bessie's husband.[28]

Nor was the glimpse of Cotulla reassuring. It was a gawky town where the I. and G. N. stopped to take on or let off an occasional passenger, or to allow its freight cars to be loaded with cattle or with wool from the nearby warehouse. Passengers,

[27] From Mrs. Hall's sketch in C. Alphonso Smith, *op. cit.*, 99.
[28] *Frances Wier Hall Ms.*

looking out, saw a yellow pine hotel, wind-bent, discouraged looking mesquites, dogs, Mexicans, and a sprawling commodious saloon in which there was a floating population. The saloon was the town's bright spot. Big lamps flooded light over and under swinging doors and on the tables where men played poker, monte, *con quien*. They talked good horse-talk, and drank whiskey which the soldiers from Fort Ewell greatly preferred to the "white mule" of scabtown.

One night in 1881, Captain Brooks of the Rangers was "liquoring up" when word came that Lee Hall and Netteville Devine were in from the Ranch. Around one table were six of the town's bad men. They opined that the visitor would stay in the hotel at the other end of town. This was *their end*. A few minutes later, the doors swung open, and Hall and Devine entered, hands on guns, eyes on the bad men. The two walked to the bar, gave their orders, drank, and backed out, never letting their eyes stray from the table where six desperadoes gaped and made no move.[29]

There were not many opportunities for going farther than Cotulla during the first year. Ranch stores and commissary tents had to be stocked for cowboys, for the outfits that were stringing fences, and for the Mexicans who had been set to grubbing wooded land to increase the acreage. To add to the troubles caused by fence cutters, no rain fell until the fall. So little grass survived that thorns were burned from the cactus and its roots and succulent leaves hacked with spades and machetes and fed to the cattle. The strange food could not fatten steers for market, but it did keep life in them.

Innumerable trails led to the low, muddy waters of the Nueces and the Frio. On the brush, the leaves curled wanly in the heat, turned from green to brown, then ashen gray with dust, dried and drooped, as though fire had been laid at the roots to run its searing way through every tender vein. For the young wife, it was hard to believe that Pennsylvania still existed, that there were cities where one could see new people every day, hear

[29] From Kleber Miller's interview with Judge Brooks in Falfurrias, Texas, April, 1935.

[197]

women's voices, where ice and fruits and vegetables were not great luxuries.

When the time approached for the birth of her first child, she made the journey to San Antonio and stayed at the old Post House. The baby was a girl, and was honored by being given her father's name. When she could toddle, the cowboys gave her instruction in natural history.

> *"Old Joe Clark has got a cow*
> *She was muley born;*
> *It takes a jay-bird forty-eight hours,*
> *To fly from horn to horn."*

Lee Hall sang her songs that always she would remember: "Skip to my Lou," "All the Pretty, Little Horses," "The Old Gray Goose" and "What Folks are Made Of." He did not sing any longer of being a pilgrim and a stranger, but his wife noticed that at evening when he stood on the gallery near his gun rack, his blue eyes looked beyond the ranch—beyond barbed wire that closed in muleys, dogies, steers, and Ranger-cowboys; sheep and their Mexican shepherds; camp outfits; a wife and baby; and, with all of these, closed in Lee Hall.

XV

Hero for O. Henry

(1882-1884)

" 'I've heard of fellows what was wedded to danger, but if Bob Buckley ain't committed bigamy with trouble, I'm a son of a gun.'

" 'Peculiarness of Bob is,' insisted the Nueces Kid, 'he ain't had proper trainin'. He never learned how to git skeered. Now, a man ought to be skeered enough when he tackles a fuss to hanker after readin' his name on the list of survivors anyway'."

—O. HENRY, "An Afternoon Miracle."

"Bunch the herd at the old meet,
Then beat 'em on the tail;
Whip 'em up and down the sides
And hit the shortest trail."

—Old Range Song.

XV

Hero for O. Henry

A CHARACTERISTIC of a Texas ranch in the eighties was the large number of the manager's family living on it. Lee Hall had with him on the D. H. and D. his brother Dick and wife, his brother Frank, and, in the spring of 1882, his father and mother. The parents came for a visit, bringing for a longer stay Willie Porter, a youth of eighteen. Porter had clerked in his uncle's drug store and had exercised his story-telling powers by retailing to the youth of Greensboro Dr. Hall's occasional accounts of the activities of his Ranger son. The split-second escapes of the North Carolina Captain lost nothing in the telling.

With uncles and fathers of the small boys, Will was unpopular. He seemed unsocial—a fault they did not share. They did not come to Clark Porter's drug store to purchase, but to play chess, enjoy the warmth of the big store, smoke free cigars, and pass judgment on the policies of the President of the United States. Will Porter caricatured these loungers and wrote a satire to accompany his drawing. After that, it was just as well that he left Greensboro for Texas. Dr. Hall invited him to go to the Ranch because he knew the boy's heritage was tubercular and he was grieved by his anæmic condition and hacking cough.[1]

Richard Hall and his wife were occupying the second house that Lee had built, and it was at the sheep ranch of this younger brother that Will Porter lived.[2] In the two years he spent

[1] C. Alphonso Smith, *O. Henry Biography,* 93, 94, and Mrs. Hall's sketch in same, 98.
[2] Hyder Rollins, "O. Henry's Texas Days," *The Bookman,* October, 1914, 154-65.

there, he became well. The price was boredom. He described
the ranch as bounded by the horizon and situated in the lone-
somest part of the sheep country. Existence there made clerk-
ing in a drug store seem a glamorous career. After a man had
lived on a ranch for a while, he would split his ribs laughing at
"Curfew Shall Not Ring Tonight,"[3] and would really enjoy
playing cards with ladies. His own sheep, he wrote home, were
"doing finely . . . never were in better condition. They give me
very little trouble, for I have never been able to see one of them
yet."[4]

He spent much time on a canvas cot, shaded by hackberries.
There he read and drew, strummed a guitar, and learned the
songs of Mexican sheep herders. It was fortunate that his illness called for outdoor treatment. For one of the two rooms in
the house was Mrs. Richard Hall's, the other was kitchen or
dining room, depending on the dividing line of a heavy curtain.

When he had read through the little stock of books the ranch
afforded, he eagerly awaited installments of reading matter supplied by Bessie Hall. He perused almanacs and mail order cata-
logs and assiduously studied the dictionary. He had no thought
of writing, but he caricatured men and animals and described
his work with a gusto that gave it double value. One pony
seemed to have a "Dante Alighieri face." The rider had tucked
chaparral twigs beneath the bridle to keep away deer flies.
"Thus crowned, the long-faced quadruped looked more Dan-
tesque than before and judging by his countenance seemed to
think of Beatrice."[5]

On an afternoon when Porter lay drawing, a bull snake fell on
the cook's ironing board. The Negro left, with voluble expres-
sions of relief at getting away. Porter regarded her as a coun-
tess or duchess in disguise from the way the pots and pans made
way at her approach.[6] With humility, he volunteered for service
at the stove,[7] and wrote the Vesper Club in Greensboro of lim-

[3] O. Henry, "The Hiding of Black Bill.
[4] O. Henry, *Rolling Stones,* (New York, Doubleday, Page and Co., 1914),
253.
[5] Hyder Rollins, "O. Henry's Texas Days," *Southwest Review,* July, 1919.
[6] C. Alphonso Smith, *O. Henry Biography,* 110.
[7] Rollins, *op. cit.*

ited success in cooking mutton steak and gravy. "Please send by express to the ranch," he added, "seventy-five cooks and two hundred washwomen, blind or wooden-legged ones preferred. The climate has a tendency to make them walk off every two or three days which must be overcome."[8]

Sometimes he rode in to Cotulla, and reported progress there: The town had grown wonderfully—thirty or forty new houses had gone up and thirty or forty barrels of whiskey gone down. The barkeeper was planning to tour Europe next summer and thinking of buying Mexico as a plaything for his little boy.[9]

Whatever he did and wherever he went, Porter stored away impressions. He teased stories from Mexicans and cowboys and beguiled Lee Hall to talk of service on the border—to tell such tales as that of vengeful Blas, his faithless *novia* and her Ranger lover.[10]

Much later when, as "O. Henry," Porter wrote of the four million and for the four million, the two ranch years proved fecund in material. His practice of exaggeration was not needed to bedizen stories of the patrol of the Nueces and the Rio Grande, but he let his sense of the dramatic enliven the events of No Man's Land, inspired with his imagination figures of Rangers, Mexicans, and outlaws, so that they came to life, and spoke and acted. With the lordly swing of a toreador, he swept around their shapes a shimmering cape of high romance.[11] Of them all, none is more romantic than the Ranger modeled from Lee Hall:[12] "blond as a Viking, quiet as a deacon, dangerous as a machine gun" . . . "agile, broad-chested,"—a man who could "heft his sixes in their holsters as a belle gives the finishing touches to her toilette,"—a man who had "committed bigamy with trouble."[13]

As soon as he was able, Porter deserted his cot and guitar to bestride a saddle, but he did not ride enough to curve his chaps into the horse collar that marks the leather of the old cowhand

---

[8] O. Henry, *Rolling Stones*, 253.
[9] Smith, *op. cit.*, 110.
[10] Ranger George Durham told Clyde Wantland that this was the origin of "Caballero's Way." Wantland, "On the Trail," *West Magazine*, October, 1935.
[11] Rollins, "O. Henry's Texas Days."
[12] C. Alphonso Smith, *op. cit.*, 99.
[13] O. Henry, "Caballero's Way," "An Afternoon Miracle."

—not enough to appear bow-legged. When horses were to be broken, Porter climbed the fence of the corral to sit as "rail bird." He watched the antics of bronchs with "bellies full of bedsprings," and noted the brimstone language of their riders. Porter knew when to yell encouragement and when to be quiet. He heard one cowboy will away his boots, saddle, bridle, chaps, and sombrero, thinking he would be "thrown so far he couldn't get back to his own funeral." It was the horse that died. He ruptured a blood vessel.[14]

Porter learned that ankle-deep mud in the corral was not the only reason why a tenderfoot should keep outside. He learned how to dip his drink from a hole that was nearly dry and not muddy the water for the next fellow. And he made the cowboys like him. They even let him talk about the weather. He could describe a norther with such diversity of incident and epithet as left his listeners gaping.[15]

When his rhetoric became too rambunctious and his criticism too caustic, the cowboys punished him with the excessive courtesy that they reserved for the lowest of the low. And after duly testing him, considering his oddities and weighing them against his grit and stamina, his gift for friendship, his admiration for courage and talent for kindness, the cowboys gave him their initiation. They fired six-shooters, let out wild yells, and one of them, dragging a saddle, galloped across his bed. When he protested, they stretched him over a roll of blankets and thrashed him with leather leggings. After an hour of it, they let him go.

Later, in a lively story, he described it all—"The punchers' accolade. From then on he had won his spurs and would be 'pardner' and stirrup brother, boot to boot."[16]

He added to his costume spurs and a sombrero, and when his hair had grown to pioneer length, he boasted that only a benevolently amiable expression saved him from arrest on general suspicion of murder and horse stealing.[17] The cowboys of Lee Hall's former Company were too occupied with fence cutters to

[14] *Frances Wier Hall Ms.*

[15] O. Henry, "The Higher Abdication;" Letter to Vesper Reading Club, quoted by Smith, *O. Henry Biography*, 108.

[16] O. Henry, "The Higher Abdication."

[17] O. Henry to Dr. W. P. Beall, February 27, 1884, *Rolling Stones*, 259.

consider endangering young Porter's liberty. A force of sixty was making new enclosures and restringing wires previously cut near their staples. Ed Brockman ran their commissary. For a time, Will Porter substituted.

He counted at the tent "nine niggers, sixteen Mexicans, seven hounds, two six-shooters, four desperadoes, three shot guns and a barrel of molasses. Inside there were a good many sacks of corn, flour, meal, sugar, beans, coffee and potatoes, a big box of bacon, some boots, clothes, saddles, rifles, tobacco and some more hounds. The work was to issue the stores to the contractors as they sent for them, and was light and easy to do. Out at the rear of the tent they had started a graveyard for men who had either kicked one of the hounds or prophesied a norther. When night came the gentleman whose good fortune it was to be dispensing the stores gathered up his saddle blankets, four old corn sacks, an old coat and a sheepskin, made all the room he could by shifting and arranging the bacon, meal, etc., gave a sad look at the dogs that immediately filled the vacuum, and went and slept outdoors."

For diversion, Will Porter "had an offer to gamble from the nigger cook and was allowed as a special favor to drive up the nice, pretty horses and give them some corn. And the kind of accommodating old tramps and cowboys who constituted the outfit came in to board, sleep, smoke, cuss and gamble, lie and brag, in short, did all they could to make time pass pleasantly and profitably to themselves."[18]

When Ed Brockman quit the store, he donned a red sash and swore so fluently that he was mistaken for a member of the legislature. This signified, Will Porter added, that he had gone "to work for Lee among the cows."[19]

The two boys from North Carolina were no more than amused, and amusing, outsiders. They were too young to be ripe in their judgment; they were still untested by danger; too ignorant to appreciate the problems facing the Ranger cowboys and their Captain. The men Will Porter ridiculed were not unlike the later heroes of O. Henry. Years mellowed his tart judg-

[18] C. Alphonso Smith, *op. cit.*, 110, 111.
[19] O. Henry to Mrs. Hall, November 31, 1883; *Rolling Stones*, 252.

ment. Disgrace brought charity and understanding. Meanwhile, the real work of the Ranch continued, unaffected by his presence. This was the building of fences to diminish cattle theft.

From an article in the *Corpus Christi Caller* of April, 1883, it appears that Hall's efforts were strengthened by support won from the farmers:

"Dull and Hall have run their fences around us, taking in besides small tracts, 400,000 acres, and we find the gentlemen exceptional to the general rule. ... They have gone to each one who owned land outside their pastures and offered him more than a liberal price for his land, with the privilege of free rent for five years. We are all satisfied."[20]

The men who coveted the herds grazing on enclosed pastures were increasingly dissatisfied. Lee Hall had learned a good deal about state law, and he carried his struggle to the courts. His legal battles were persistent. In a single year, 1882, he added to the dockets of courts in Bexar County four cases against destroyers of property and against horse and cattle thieves. He was striving to work within the framework of the law, but he demanded of this framework considerable elbow room.

Billie Tompkins, Sheriff of LaSalle, was a friend of the outlaws. Hall decided to supplant him with a man from his group of cowboy-Rangers—Charlie McKinney. Tompkins got his band together and announced that he would keep the Captain and his men from the polls. The night before election, Hall rode into town with a troop of dusty, determined looking cowboys. He had them sworn in as peace officers. At an early hour next morning, they were at the voting places. They made the other citizens vote one at a time. When the opposition tried to rush the polls, the peace officers fired. Cavin, describing Tompkins' attacking cohorts, says laconically, "They stopped."[21]

Far away from the Dull Ranch, along the Colorado and its sources, the weather was exceedingly dry, good cattle brought high prices, and fence cutters became more active. In 1884, Governor John Ireland called a special session of the legislature to solve the problem. In O. Henry's burlesque account, the rep-

[20] *Corpus Christi Caller*, April 1, 1883.
[21] W. T. Cavin's letter to Mrs. Isham Keith, May 8, 1935.

resentative from the Rio Grande Country gathered up his palm leaf fan and his linen duster to set out for the capital, while the Panhandle solon wrapped his muffler about a well-buttoned overcoat, kicked the snow off his well-greased boots, and set out also.[22] Once in session, the legislature enacted a statute that made fence cutting a felony, punishable by a five-year term in the penitentiary.[23] The law provided that fences should be of a certain height, and reliably built, right of ways preserved, and gateways made at intervals of every linear three miles. Those failing to conform with the law were heavily fined.[24]

The Captain's activities, a good sheriff, and good laws brought peace to LaSalle County. Lee Hall took a holiday. He went to Austin to attend a cattlemen's convention. He had many friends there, but he was not a friend of the most notorious of Austin's citizens, Ben Thompson. The story of why Ben Thompson's enmity was momentous would make a saga in itself. He was of English stock and born in Nova Scotia. He had seen much of Texas since he entered the state, a boy of ten, with his brother and sailor-father. "Drunken Thompson" gave his sons no education. They shifted for themselves. In Austin, Ben became a printer's devil, drove a water cart, fought with Cortina, served in the Civil War, and in the smoking seventies perfected his skill at gambling and shooting.[25] His hall of chance in the capital was long immune from molestation. When he staged his escapades outside, he still enjoyed protection.

In January, 1883, he was acquitted in San Antonio of the murder of Jack Harris, proprietor of a notorious vaudeville house. At the time of the crime, Ben Thompson was City Marshal of Austin—the office being the award of citizens for a career that had won notoriety at the cost of many men. After his

[22] One of his characters describes the legislature as a body that "sets up there at Austin and don't do nothing but make laws against kerosene oil and school books being brought into the state."—Hyder Rollins, "O. Henry's Texas," *Southwest Review*, July, 1919.

[23] W. P. Webb, *The Texas Rangers*, 426; "Muzzle-Loadings," *Frontier Times*, November, 1936.

[24] "Introduction of Barbed Wire into Texas," reprinted from *Texas Industrial Review*, *Frontier Times*, November 1, 1931.

[25] Ben Thompson's obituary, *San Antonio Express*, March 13, 1884, quoted in *Frontier Times*, September, 1934; Eugene Cunningham, "Rangers Tell of Old Days," *Houston Post Dispatch*, October 23, 1927.

acquittal in San Antonio, he returned with his wife and little daughter and was met at the Austin station by a large delegation. When the family were seated in their carriage, admiring friends, envious of the honor of drawing it, unhitched the horses, and with great acclaim pulled the vehicle up the Avenue and to Ben Thompson's home.

In view of the desperado's activities, Captain Hall suggested that it might be well to name the capital Thompsonville. The remark was recorded in an Austin paper with the observation that "Mr. Ben Thompson didn't offer to take this up with Captain Hall as was usually his custom when such disparaging remarks were made."[26]

Hall's path had never crossed that of the desperado, and after the Captain resigned his commission, it seemed unlikely that it ever would.

"In Texas," O. Henry has written, "you may travel a thousand miles in a straight line. If your course is a crooked one, it is likely that both the distance and your rate of speed may be vastly increased."

Ben Thompson's course was jagged and, in dramatic fashion, it crossed the Captain's. But Ben was no fugitive. Early in 1884, the cattlemen held their convention in Austin. It was attended with gusto by men of broad acres of all the southwest portion of the state. At its sessions they discussed problems connected with branding, fence cutting, refrigeration, pasturage, and celebrated the conclusion of their business with a banquet at Simon's Café on Congress Avenue. They came attired in what O. Henry describes as Texas full dress—"black frock coat, soft white hat, and lay down collar three quarters of an inch high, with black wrought iron necktie." Stockmen did not want to be mistaken for members of the legislature, so color lightened their apparel in shirt or vest. They seated themselves at a banquet board opulently supplied with food and drink. On the other side of the café at small tables were the patrons not belonging to the Cattlemen's Association. Captain J. E. Lucy, formerly of Hall's Company, was one of these. He was dining

[26] "Front Page Fifty Years Ago," newspaper clipping in the collection of Mrs. Isham Keith.

with three friends, one of whom was a noted newspaperman, Colonel William Greene Sterrett.

The evening was convivial, and it must have been outlandishly noisy, for Shanghai Pierce could not make himself heard when he called for some turkey at the other end of the table. Now Shang had a voice! According to the legend, when he bellowed his orders from the gallery of his ranch house, they reached to the men at cattle pens a mile away.[27] When he greeted friends at the Menger in San Antonio, tramps, slumbering on distant benches in Military Plaza, stirred in their sleep.

The unaccustomed lack of attention at the banquet induced him to shed his shoes—he was six feet four without them—and proceed down the top of the table to his wanted supplies. Impromptu speeches were attempted and howled down. Knowing of Lee Hall's gift for impersonations and the telling of good stories, some one wishing to quiet the din, suggested that he entertain the company. He was willing to oblige. What followed is best described by Lucy:

Hall "was a rare entertainer and those present on the side of the café reserved for functions were uproariously applauding his remarks ... Captain Lee Hall had been my pal. We had served together in the Rangers. We had bunked together in North West Texas. He was almost as close to me as a brother ... While the merriment was at its height around the banqueting board and Hall was using a chair as a rostrum for speaking purposes, one of the screen doors was pushed inward, and revolver in hand, Ben Thompson walked toward Hall. Hall was one of the bravest men I ever knew. He had been given the acid test as a Ranger many times. Thompson was in an ugly mood. He had not been invited to the banquet. He looked upon Hall as a personal enemy. He used his gun as a club, smashing the glass and other tableware and was to all intents and purposes bent upon deadly work. Then happened the most remarkable stampede I have ever witnessed. Thompson was known from border to border as one of the most dangerous men of the period. Ban-

27 Joseph McCoy, *Historical Sketches of the Cattle Trade of the West and Southwest* (Reprinted by The Rare Book Shop, Washington, 1932), 142-44; Dobie, *Vaquero of the Brush Country*, 27.

queters deserted their long table. They deserted the place. Hall never drew his gun. I felt that he was in a most precarious place, that his life was in danger and I drew and cocked my pistol and covered Thompson.

"He said to me, 'Captain, this is not your fight. You have no business in it. It does not concern you!'

"Now, I had no ambition to kill Thompson. I do not think that he desired to kill me. Lee Hall was the man I was thinking of. He was my loyal pal and friend. As I have said, those interested the most had stampeded the place. Like the Arabians, they had folded their tents or cloaks about them and the place that they had occupied at the beginning of the affair was a banquet hall deserted.

"I held a cocked gun in my hand. In the rear of the tables was a vacant space and against the wall was a large safe. Thompson placed his back against the safe. My gun was cocked and covered him. Indeed, I was taking no chances but I was not there to slay if I could avoid it. He continued to tell me that it was not my fight, that I was not concerned, that it was his and his alone. There was a rear entrance, and then something happened ... I did not dare turn to peer into the rear section of the place. All at once there was a rustle or rush and a sound of footsteps. Then a voice rang out,

" 'Ben, give me your gun.'

"Then I did look. The man who had stepped in between us was Congressman William Henry Crane. Without a word Thompson handed Crane his gun. This done, Crane turned to me and said,

" 'Will you give me your gun, Captain?'

"Thompson had complied with his request. There was nothing left for me to do. Into Crane's hand I placed my pistol. Then the gentleman from Cuero, one of the Democratic leaders and orators of his day, departed with the guns. Thompson called out at the top of his voice,

" 'Mack, where are you?'

"A large Negro, who was employed by Thompson at his gambling house, joined our party of two. He was the personal valet and attendant of Thompson and he handed Thompson a gun. . .

"Thompson had me at his mercy. He had a gun and I was unarmed. Of course, I did not lose my presence of mind. I merely remarked to him,

" 'You have a gun. Where do I come in?'

"He looked me squarely in the eye. He did not show a trace of anger. He merely stated,

" 'There are bad men on the outside. Here is my gun. Are you ready to go? If you are, there is a horse and cart on the Avenue in the same block.'

"He was as good as his word. He placed the gun that the Negro Mack had given him in my hand. We walked to the main exit. On the outside were four or five as desperate men as I knew in Texas. They had no use for Ben Thompson. Regardless of this, they exhibited no signs of hostility. We walked to the place Thompson had indicated. We entered the cart and I drove Thompson to a place where he had asked to be taken for the night."[28]

Unfortunately, O. Henry was not present to immortalize the episode. The entertainment Hall provided induced a silence deeper than had been expected. He did not finish his story. Ben Thompson did not finish Hall's life.

[28] Captain J. E. Lucy's account, the most reliable of many, appeared in *The Austin American,* March 14, 1927. Captain Lucy served in Captain Hall's Company from December 1, 1877, to January 1, 1878, and after that seems to have served the Company as a detective.

Other versions of the eventful banquet appear in W. M. Walton's *Life and Adventures of Ben Thompson* (Austin, privately printed, 1884), 88; and in *Frontier Times,* October, 1934. The latter is by Captain J. B. Gillett, who was not present and whose account differs markedly from Captain Lucy's.

XVI
At Las Islas Crossing
(1884-1885)

"Where the coffee grows on the white-oak tree,
And the rivers flow with brandy—
Then it's fare-you-well, my own true love,
Foh I'm bound foh the Rio Grande."

—E. L. SABIN, *Range and Trail*, Crowell Co.

"I knew your Father, Captain Lee Hall, and admired him much. In my opinion, he and Captain Bill McDonald were the greatest of all Texas Rangers and that is high praise."— COLONEL E. M. HOUSE to MRS. ISHAM KEITH, February 23, 1929.

XVI

At Las Islas Crossing

A FEW WEEKS after the unusual entertainment afforded cattlemen at Simon's Café by that strange team, Ben Thompson and Lee Hall, the Deputy Sheriff of Uvalde County reached the capital. Although he came on business connected with the struggle against fence cutters, he had been a malefactor who himself had long engaged the attention of Lee Hall. This was King Fisher. A superfluity of indictments, and extended visits to county jails and the old Bat Cave in San Antonio, had sobered the gentleman of the tiger-skin chaps. At twenty-seven he had aligned himself with the forces of law and order, but old ways were not easily set aside. During the day, King Fisher consorted with Ben Thompson, for whom earlier he had often expressed contempt. Thompson was flush, boasted of his friends, denounced his enemies, presented King Fisher with his photograph. They quarreled, for Austin's former marshal was drinking. His mind was full of thoughts of his latest victim, Jack Harris. The killing had been due to bad blood caused by the claim that an associate of Harris, Joe Foster, had cheated when winning Thompson's money in a faro game. Foster was King Fisher's friend, and had sent him free meals during the time the outlaw had been a reluctant guest in old Bat Cave. He did not like to hear him slandered.

In the afternoon the Deputy Sheriff and the former marshal started off together on a train, but not for the same destination. Again they quarreled, for Thompson was going to San Antonio with the intention of visiting the Vaudeville Theatre, once owned by Harris, and trying to humiliate Foster publicly. King Fisher decided that he had better go along to prevent trouble, since in Thompson's holster was an ivory-handled, silver mounted revolver. As a precaution, the Deputy Sheriff of Uvalde remained sober. In San Antonio the two dined and witnessed the performance of Ada Gray in *East Lynne*. It was a pathetic play on which to end the evening. Ben Thompson commended the sprightlier entertainment at the Vaudeville Theatre. King Fisher reluctantly agreed to go.

The quarrel on the train had been overheard and Harris's associates, Billy Sims and Foster, had been warned by a San Antonio citizen of Thompson's threats. Sims, on their arrival, pretended to receive the two visitors with tolerant good humor, but Foster, when summoned by Ben Thompson, would neither drink with him nor shake his hand. Some say that Fisher was attempting to bring them to good terms when Thompson, either with his hand or a pistol, struck Foster and the fracas began. Jacob Coy, the theater's policeman, grabbed Thompson's gun. Just before this or immediately after (no accounts agree), two shots were fired from this gun. Coy held on grimly. The matter might have ended there had not another man, probably Sims, drawn also. King Fisher ordered him to put up his pistol. And these, perhaps, were his last words. For he fell, as did Ben Thompson, wounded mortally. Foster, Coy, and Sims have variously been accused of the killings. *The Austin Statesman* preferred to charge that the "assassins" were men who had been posted earlier in boxes and on the stage. The coroner's jury held the shots were fired in self-defense. A few days later Foster died from a wound inflicted, probably, by Thompson's pistol as it was forced downward by Jacob Coy.

Men who looked at the dead bodies, riddled by many bullets, described Thompson's expression as stern, the upper lip drawn taut across the teeth, waxed mustache curling upward, gray eyes set in a ghastly stare. The feet were small and carefully shod with shoes such as the cobbler, Lucchese, made in San Antonio. The hands were the white hands of a gambler. When Thompson's body was taken to the old Bat Cave, city prisoners on their way to be tried by the recorder, hardened as they were, shuddered and edged away. But Fisher, even in the tawdry vaudeville house and in the jail, managed to cheat dread death of horror. A picture of Ben was found in his pocket. Thompson's admirers claimed that he lay with an arm across Ben's body, as though unwilling, even in death, to desist from defending his "friend." Those who thought Joe Foster the better man to die for, preferred to think King Fisher's efforts were for him. Whatever the case may have been, "The most noted desperado on the Rio Grande frontier from New Mexico to the Gulf" wore, at last, "a pallid and peaceful expression." He had been shot several times. His own pistol was in its holster.[1]

Outlaw, deputy sheriff, enigma, compact of knavery and bravery, this was King Fisher!

Captain Hall read at his ranch of the garish night that ended the lives of the desperadoes. He felt far removed from the days when the capture of King Fisher seemed more momentous than any event in all the state. The ex-Ranger, now twice a father, found life strangely tranquil. He marveled that citizens and the press still spoke of him in terms of his former career. The new Adjutant General, W. H. King, in praising the Rangers for resolute and prompt enforcement of the law and for such fairness and honesty as were an inspiration to the state, listed twenty-one officers and men as worthy of especial praise. Among those named was Hall.[2] Reporters noted that he had not transmitted his ability to lead a company of Texas Rangers. His children would never give commands. For the second baby was another girl, Elizabeth.[3]

Hall and his wife carried the little daughters to visit with his parents. His presence in Greensboro notably increased attendance at Sunday services. In North Carolina, the new devotees were small boys instead of such desperadoes as he had influenced in Eagle Pass. The fact that their Ranger hero was now a *pater familias* did not decrease his worship by young tar heels. They tried to duplicate his smart carriage, his quick glance from left to right. They speculated as to whether he carried pistols. They somehow sensed that his days of adventure were not over. And the boys were right.

[1] W. M. Walton, *Life and Adventures of Ben Thompson*, 89-104.

[2] Adjutant General W. H. King, "The Texas Ranger Service and History," in Dudley G. Wooten's *A Comprehensive History of Texas*, (Dallas, W. G. Scarff, 1898), II, 366 ff.

[3] *Corpus Christi Caller*, November 23, 1884, quoting *Houston Age*.

Events were shaping towards the end of his career as a ranchman. The year 1885 was the last of the era of high prices. Fortunately, during the previous spring, the Captain had sold over two thousand head of cattle to a buyer from Colorado.[4] Hall's brother, Richard, bought land in Williamson County and shipped there his flocks of sheep.[5] Thither Will Porter did not follow. His affection for sheep had been negligible. He was well now and eager to cast his lot among men of the cities. His beginning was modest. He went to Austin. The Capital took no note of his arrival. It still was arraigning San Antonio for what it termed "the assassination of Major Ben Thompson." For the rest, it was much concerned over the fence cutters.

From executive offices to executive mansion and back again, Governor Ireland carried with him anxieties caused by these men and by conditions on the frontier. Diaz, in his second term as president, faced heavy criticism.[6] Citizens complained that the government had granted too many concessions to gringoes. The Mexicans did not welcome the signing of the new convention on reciprocity. Its strictures, when communicated to their agents revived old issues:

"To speak of permanent or desirable commercial relations with a government thus estranged from us in sentiment is without hope of success. . . .

"The duty and responsibility of protecting our own people from the effects of constantly recurring revolutions in Mexico and on the borders thereof must transcend and precede all others in treating with our neighbors. . . .

"Every citizen knows by heart that our citizens on the Mexican border have been long exposed to depredations and lawless bands invading our country in arms, and after committing spoliation and murder, returning to find a safe asylum in Mexico. . . .

"The establishment of the Zona Libre was itself a revolutionary act in violation to the Constitution of Mexico."[7]

[4] *Daily Democratic Statesman,* May 15, 1884.
[5] Rollins, "O. Henry's Texas Days," *Southwest Review.*
[6] J. Fred Rippy, *The United States and Mexico* (New York, Knopf, 1926, Chapter xix. Partly due to an indirect sale by the Mexican Government to Americans of concessions in Lower California.
[7] "Adverse Report on Mexican Treaty of January 20, 1883, submitted by Mr. Maybury from the Committee on Ways and Means," *U. S. Foreign Affairs, Forty-ninth Congress, 1885-1887,* Part 2, Vol. XCII.

In 1884, the Diaz government still further reduced its popularity. Many Mexicans believed that the Nueces was their legal frontier. To these the Morteretos treaty, concluded with the United States in 1884, was anathema. It accepted as rightful boundary the middle of the channel of the Rio Grande of 1848. Mexican customs officers on the Island of Morteretos had seized Texas cattle there, and the national spirit was aroused by the necessity the Treaty created of acknowledging that the seizures were illegal. These officials knew that border rustlers were well organized, that the head of their bands was not a Mexican, but a hard-drinking, murderous ex-cavalryman, John Kinney of Mexico.[8] Conditions being what they were, it took daring to renew with the United States the convention for reciprocal passage of troops across the international boundary for pursuit of hostile bands. But daring was a characteristic that Diaz did not lack, and he renewed the convention.

Believing that the government unduly favored the northern nation, Mexicans on the border, in 1884, took matters into their own hands. They raided above Eagle Pass, killing many American citizens.[9] They planned to invade as far as Carrizo Springs in Dimmit County to effect the rescue of five Mexicans who were jailed there. From bandit camps across from the county, continuous and lucrative raids were made. The Mexicans felt relatively safe, for the extradition treaty had been suspended.[10]

Texans were about ready to begin reprisals. There was grave need for caution and for men of determination and good will. Citizens wished that Lee Hall would resume his border services.

A reminiscent account of his activities that appeared, in 1914, in the *New York Times* claims that he took command of all border Ranger companies and cleaned up the Rio Grande from Brownsville to El Paso,[11] killing Mexicans without num-

8 "Santa Fé, New Mexico," quoted in *Frontier Times*, October, 1936.
9 James A. Wright, "Looking Backward through the Years," *Frontier Times*, September, 1936.
10 On July 29, 1882, an agreement was made which was thereafter frequently renewed. It provided that regular Federal troops of the two republics might reciprocally cross the boundary lines when in close pursuit of savage Indians. The crossings were to take place only in "unpopulous or desert areas." It will be noted that no such privileges were accorded State troops.
11 "The Red Ride," *New York Times*, March 15, 1914.

[219]

ber. Just so much of this account is true as states that Governor Ireland sent for the ex-Ranger and asked for his assistance. Hall conducted no "Red Raid." He preferred to gain his ends through peace. This was the wish of responsible citizens on the other side. The Mexicans solicited negotiations.[12]

Across from the borderland of Dimmit County, one hundred and fifty of them had established camp. Each day brought fresh recruits. Facing them, on the American side, were detachments from a regiment of United States cavalry and from Company D, Frontier Battalion, commanded by Captain Seiker. These, the ex-Ranger decided to supplement by thirty well mounted men from the D. H. and D. Ranch. It was February 9, 1885, when he set out with his men. The weather was very cold. It was good to be again at the head of a troop with a purpose that, if accomplished, would benefit the State. It was a mixed troop, members of his former company, cowboys, and such nesters as he had won by consideration in the building of his fences. His men, with Seiker's detachment, entered Carrizo Springs at midnight. When the sun rose, they were near enough to the river to see, in silhouette, the bands of Mexicans on its banks. An old nester, with whiskers reaching down to his saddle, cried out, "No defalcation, boys, by God, they're thar!"

Cold and excitement set the old fellow's teeth to chattering. In wooden stirrups, his feet beat a regular tattoo. Impatiently the old man looked down at them, and spat,

"Darn your hide," he scolded, "if you were on the ground, you'd run away with me."[13]

Next day, near Las Islas Crossing on an island midstream in the Rio Grande, representatives of Mexico met with representatives of the Texas citizens of the border. Both groups were unarmed and unattended, but the crowds that lined the river's banks covered the island with Winchesters and revolvers and the Americans were ready to fight on signal—the drop of a handkerchief. Captain Hall and Charlie McKinney, whom he had elected Sheriff of LaSalle County, spoke for the Texans;

[12] "An Arbitration on the Rio Grande," dispatch dated Eagle Pass, February 11, 1885, *Dallas Daily Herald,* February 12, 1885. This dispatch is the best source for the events recorded.

[13] Related to Mrs. Isham Keith by former Ranger Ben F. Riely.

Dr. Pope and two Mexican officials represented the other side. The former Ranger rolled and smoked many brown paper cigarettes before the consultation ended. At one time it seemed that tension was unendurable and fighting would break out. The result of the negotiations, though not recorded in any compilation of treaties, was accepted by both sides: four of the five Mexican prisoners jailed in Carrizo Springs were to be liberated and restored to Mexico; there was to be no more shooting of Mexicans in Dimmit or in Maverick Counties without due investigation of charges; the Americans were to deliver all American raiders who were running off Mexican stock or committing crimes across the river. On their part, the Mexicans promised to do everything possible to prevent robbery and pillage of Americans; agreed to break up the bandit camps opposite Dimmit County near the boundary; and to restore to Texas owners the stock then pastured at the camps.

According to Ben F. Riely, a member of Captain Seiker's detachment, one incident marred the idyllic nature of the settlement. It accounts for the spread of a rumor that Lee Hall had been killed, a rumor that came near precipitating heavy fighting. As Ranger Riely tells it, after the "treaty" was signed, the Texas representatives and some of their men were invited, with malice prepense, to dine with the Mexican *Commandante* at Presidio de San Juan Bautiste just beyond the *Zona Libre*. They accepted, thinking they were to participate in something of a love-feast. Food and drink were abundant, toasts were exchanged, and then, well satisfied with their entertainment, the Americans rode off to cross the *Zona Libre* and ford the Rio Grande. When they had gone about a mile, they were halted by a squad of Rurales with weapons drawn. The Mexicans announced that the Alcalde had ordered arrest because the Americans had passed beyond the *Zona Libre*. They knew then why the *Commandante* had entertained them. They would be released and, doubtless, apologies would be made, but their horses —and they were good horses—would remain with the Mexicans. On the border, a man without a horse was a man without legs. Such thoughts flashed through their minds while their eyes looked into the ominous barrels of the Mexicans' Winchesters.

"Boys, I move we don't go! Quick, make a run for it!"

The words were Hall's, and all with one accord dug heels into their horses' flanks and raced across the chaparral to reach the river.

Furiously, the Rurales pursued, firing as they came, but the stampede had been sudden, the Mexicans were not able to take aim, and their shots went wide. When the Americans came in sight of the Rio Grande, they found it far below them. There was no time to reach the ford. The horses jumped the bluff and swam, the riders guiding them, cowboy fashion, by splashing water at their sides. After half a mile, they reached the Texas side. The cold ride did nothing to cool their rage at the treacherous hospitality of their Mexican host. They wanted to pay a return visit of a different character. Captain Hall dissuaded them by pointing out that whatever joke there was, was on the Alcalde.[14] Reports of the episode did not diminish ill will. Petitions asked retention of the Ranger force and the dispatch of a detachment to form a permanent garrison in Dimmit County.[15] Such petitions no longer concerned Jesse Lee Hall, ranchman.

Home again!

"My love is a rider, wild bronchos he breaks
Though he's promised to quit it, just for my sake."

Lee Hall did not find zest in the songs his cowboys sang. Spring was around the corner, a brief spring. O. Henry has left a picture of how the ranch gave welcome to it: ambient prairie, murky patches of brush and pear, lay like a darkened bowl in which the sky, with turquoise cover, closely penned dregs that were men. The air was sweet with leagues of flowerets, and breath had tang and savor. "In the sky was a great round, mellow searchlight ... no moon, but the dark lantern of summer come to hunt northward cowering spring." Yapping of coyotes,

[14] Ben F. Riely's account cited *supra*.

[15] *Dallas Daily Herald*, February 12, 1885. Mexico diminished the reasons for such action by negotiating a new extradition treaty with the United States which reciprocally prevented criminals from gaining immunity from punishment. Diaz referred to this in his message of April, 1885, (*Un siglo de Relaciones Internacionales*).

twittering of whippoorwills were dissonances that could not long prevail against the rippling harmony of mocking birds' notes falling from shrubs and trees. Nights were for miracles when stars hung brightly imminent and challenged men to grasp them.[16]

Lee Hall was not the age of Will Porter, and he had never cared for dwelling in Paradise and plucking at stars. He read the papers when, tardily, they reached the ranch. His thoughts were on the world outside his fences, not on phenomena of nature. In April he read the message Diaz delivered to the' Mexican legislature. He saw that the President commended the new extradition treaty which placed his country and our own under reciprocal obligations against allowing criminals immunity. The ranchman liked to think that his recent arbitration had helped make possible the formal treaty. Border "incidents" diminished. Next year, on his ranch in the Dakotas, Theodore Roosevelt scented the possibility of "trouble with Mexico" and offered "to raise some companies of horse riflemen from among the harum scarum rough riders of the West." There was no need for them.[17]

And yet, in '85 and '86, these men that Roosevelt wrote of might well have welcomed war. Jobs were scarce, cattle prices on the toboggan. Choice beef sold in Chicago at two dollars and forty cents a hundredweight. Grass was scant in Texas, and cattle, where not stopped by fences, drifted downward to the Rio Grande. The drouth of '86 was for West Texas a calamity as costly as the Civil War. One of the stories of the day was that the farmers carried salt in their jeans, booted potatoes from the soil, and found them baked and ready for seasoning.

Before the drouth reached its height, the Messrs. Dull in Pennsylvania had become discouraged over their ranching properties. Instead of allowing Hall, as general manager, a percentage of increase of stock, as first agreed, they proposed that he receive a quit fee of five thousand a year for the work that he had done. There was an accounting and a settlement.[18]

[16] O. Henry, "The Missing Chord."
[17] Walter Millis, *The Martial Spirit* (New York, Houghton Mifflin, 1931), 217.
[18] Letter of W. T. Cavin to Mrs. Isham Keith, May 8, 1935.

Since he could no longer serve the State as Ranger, his desire was to serve the Federal government. He would walk in the ways of peace, as his wife requested, but he would choose a path not altogether free from danger—not so far removed from combat but that by a stride or two he might come within hailing distance of his old acquaintance, death.

In May, at Seguin, he mailed a letter to Washington. It stated that Jesse Lee Hall, native of North Carolina, had been resident in Texas more than seventeen years; that he was a Democrat, living in LaSalle County; that for five years, he had commanded a Ranger force on the frontier, and "had much experience among Indians." The letter formally applied for the post of Indian Agent and was accompanied by noteworthy endorsements: letters from Senators Coke and Maxey, Governor Ireland and Lieutenant Governor Barnett Gibbs; O. T. Holt of Houston, member of the National Democratic committee; William Bate, Senator-elect from Tennessee; Chief Justice Willie of the Supreme Court of Texas, and Associate Justice J. W. Stayton; Congressman Charles Stewart of Houston; J.C.Brown, General Solicitor of the Gould system of railways; Governor Scales and Senator Vance of North Carolina. Several repeated the phrase used often to describe Lee Hall: "terror to evildoers." His sponsors declared that his knowledge of frontier conditions, his hardihood, his bravery and sense of justice qualified him in an unusual degree for dealing with the Indians. President Cleveland made the appointment promptly. The Senate, when it next convened, confirmed it with practically no opposition.

Hall received his commission, bearing the date of July 28, 1885.[19] In August he took leave of his friends in southwest Texas. There were vigorous hand-shakes with ex-Ranger cowboys, men "that had man in them," men "fit to ride the River with." Then, once again alone, the Captain rode away. Brick home, the barn-like store of the Ranch, thatch-topped *jacals* faded into the distance. His strenuous life as a cattleman was ended. He began a state-long journey; up through the country

[19] "Jesse Lee Hall," dispatch dated St. Louis, October 21, 1887, *Dallas Morning News*, October 22, 1887.

where knights of the road had waylaid Concord coaches bound for San Antonio; north to districts where men had no use for Rangers, and state representatives bragged of crippling the companies by scant appropriations; north to the swamps where will-o'-the-wisps led frightened boys to swear Sam Bass still ran from his pursuers, and doubled and laughed to deceive them; north towards the state line, where, as guardians of the gate, stood Denison and Sherman, cautiously respectable, but still remembering a young North Carolinian to whom they had afforded early experience with Indians and bad men; north and west through the grand prairie, fast becoming cattle country, new to Lee Hall. At Henrietta, the rails of the Fort Worth and Denver ended. Horseback, he followed the Chisholm Trail to Anadarko. There the Agency awaited him.

And so, good-bye to Texas!

XVII
Eck-Hob-It Paph—"Red Head"
(August, 1885-1887)

"*The old West, the old time,*
The old wind singing through
The red, red grass a thousand miles . . ."

—WILLA CATHER, "Spanish Johnny."

"*I believed him to be the best of all the Indian agents* . . .
'*Eck-hob-it Paph*' *was as a father to his child-like Indian wards*
and they—with a few exceptions—loved and obeyed him. A
thoroughbred western man in his manner, true to his friends
and yet firm and square in his dealings as Indian Agent."—
J. EMMOR HARSTON, to the author, May 29, 1937.

XVII

Eck-hob-it Paph—"Red Head"

LEE HALL, in a report sent to Washington, numbered his wards at the Indian Agency at Anadarko at 4,256. The government reserved for their communal use some 2,903,040 acres of prairie country, covered with long, blue-stem grass, most excellent for grazing. The Agency was on the road that ran between Fort Sill and Fort Reno and was watered by the Washita River. Its nearest station was Henrietta, terminus of the Fort Worth and Denver railroad. From there and from Fort Reno, mail came to Anadarko by a circuitous route several hundred miles in distance and several days in time.

Most numerous and powerful of the reservation tribes were the Comanches, on the Little Washita, southeast of the Agency. In the western part on Elk and Rainy Mountain creeks were the tepees of a thousand Kiowas. The Wichitas, who had brought with them the Caddoes, were so reduced by warfare and disease that they occupied small space. Three hundred and forty-eight Apaches, and one hundred and sixty-five Wichitas, lived in the central section on Cache Creek.[1]

From the time when the whites first traded with the Indians, they had shown an economic interest only in the tribes that once possessed the continent. General Sheridan was not exceptional in rejoicing in the extermination of the Indian's "commissary department," the buffalo. The opinion was almost universal that the red man retarded the march of civilization.[2] Though outsiders failed to distinguish signs of progress in the

[1] Captain Hall's "Report on the Agency," August 26, 1886, manuscript in the possession of Mrs. Isham Keith.
[2] "When MacKenzie Swept the Plains," *San Angelo Standard Times,* quoted in *Frontier Times,* October, 1937.

tribes, the signs were there. They could be seen if one conceived that civilization did not always march. It was in attendance at the smoke talks; not far distant from law-makers. Of the company who furthered its development were those who shaped and stained rude pottery; squaws who wove colored grasses garnished with beads and fringed the supple doeskins; and carried, on tribal wanderings, seeds to enrich new lands.

The new Agent at Anadarko had lived much of his life in solitude. He was discerning. He had his own sense of values. He studied the problems of the Indians, evaluated capacity for development.

The dealings of typical Texans with the red man had not been so leisurely as to conduce to a study of their virtues. The typical Texan thought of the Indian as a dirty savage, given to scalp lifting and cattle stealing. The typical Texan sang of him:

> *"One fine day they found a dead man*
> *Who in life had been a Red Man*
> *So it's doubtless he was nothing else than bad."*

Lee Hall was not typical. In applying for his position, he stated that his experience with Indians was "considerable." It was not his experience with them as an officer of the law that made him unusual as their agent. Rather, he was unusual because of salient personal characteristics: he had independence of judgment, he was daring, and he was capable of sympathetic understanding. He conceived of his wards as neither the good Indians who lived, and nobly died, in the pages of J. Fenimore Cooper, nor the tomahawk-wielding devils who snaked their way through "Blear-eyed Dicks."

Soon after he began his residence in August, 1885, he formulated his aims. They were not those of an official who regarded his job as merely the necessity attaching to a salary of $2,300 a year.[3] Hall's ambitions were to bring about a better balance in vital statistics, to improve living conditions, to make the Reservation self-supporting, as nearly as possible, and to assist in the physical and mental development of his wards. As to the

---

[3] *Corpus Christi Caller*, August 2, 1885, quoting a dispatch from Washington to *The Fort Worth Gazette*.

future, he was optimistic. Before the year was over, the press quoted him as saying that more could be made of the Indians than was supposed. He liked them for their fidelity to those who won their trust. He liked their childish ways and their simplicity. He sympathized because of the impositions they long had borne. If they could be protected, if bad men could be kept away, and if practical education could be given by the honest and industrious, he believed their future would be bright.

Texans were amazed to read his statement in the *Dallas News*[4] that the chief hope lay in the Comanches. Though these had forsaken the warpath more recently than the others and still painted themselves and sometimes donned scalp locks and war bonnets, they had learned much. No Indians in America had ranged so widely. They were brave; they were trustful and teachable. They did not beg like the Kiowas. Hall claimed that they were clean in their personal habits and that their women were true to their husbands.

The Agent rode much on the reservation. It was his habit to stop at the trading store and call out the Comanche name for his interpreter, "*Nod-e-ma Tao-yo!*" Then young Emmor Harston would come running and return the salute by greeting him with his own Comanche name, the word for "Red Head"— "*Eck-hob-it Paph.*" If the two drove in a buggy, a shotgun sometimes stood against the seat, because there might be a chance for bringing down a wild turkey. If they rode, Hall slung a Winchester under the stirrup leathers and buckled on a "six-gun." Emmor Harston says that Lee Hall liked to carry arms because they reminded him of Ranger days when he rode out "high, wide, and handsome."

Hall greeted the braves with a hearty "*Hi Hites!*" ("Howdy! How's my friend?"). He lifted grave little G-string toddlers to his saddle; he shook hands with the chieftains, the braves, and the squaws; and he had a comradely word for the white man who had accepted Indian ways and become a member of a tribe. Not by kindness only did he win the confidence of his wards.

4 "Captain Hall on his Wards," *Dallas Morning News,* December 31, 1885. This is a long article consisting of a dialogue between Captain Hall and a reporter.

They trusted his prowess and determination when he broke the power of the reservation bully, Lone Wolf, who had alike defied the previous agents and the Indian police. To use the phrase of a Comanche, Hall "took him in his shirt sleeves"—made the arrest unarmed. Lone Wolf equalled the Captain in physique, and at the time had two guns stuck into his belt. Between falls, Hall got a grip on them and threw them out of reach. After that, he knocked the great Lone Wolf under a nearby wagon, dragged him out, hoisted him by the seat of his pants into a buggy, rolled a cigarette and drove off on a trot for the Agency.

Kiowas, Wichitas, and Comanches came in from their tepees to see the great Eck-hob-it Paph who had conquered Lone Wolf. They shook his hand, patted his back; a few attempted to embrace him.[5]

Shortly after this he strung up miles of barbed wire fencing with no fear that Indians would cut it down. It was needed, for Agency records revealed the theft in three years of seven hundred ponies. And the records did not tell all of the story.[6] Before Hall's coming, Indians had found that little good resulted from reporting the crimes of white men. In retaliation, the braves had stolen. Fences, the Agent believed, would protect reservation property and deter the Indians from slaughtering the beeves of others. Lee Hall worked for the security of their possessions and the increase of their wealth by stock raising and agriculture.

Near the tepees that irregularly dotted the reservation, the Agent watched squaws with crude implements, or none at all, carry on whatever farming was done by Wichitas and Comanches. He taught that most of this should be man's work. He urged the government to allow the schools twenty or thirty plowboys to help in instruction. Many of the men did not know the use of a trace chain and were uncertain whether to hitch the head of the horse or its tail toward the plow.

[5] The author is indebted for the material in this and the two preceding paragraphs, as well as for scattered facts in this and the next chapter, to the author of *The History of Comanche Land*, Mr. Emmor Harston, now a grand old man of San Antonio with a clear memory, a clear head, and clear handwriting. Mr. Harston is the author of *Biography of Dr. J. J. Sturm, the Old Comanche Doctor, History of Clay County*, and *Manual of Metallurgy*.
[6] Mr. Harston's note on first draft of this book.

Somewhat amusing were the former Ranger's efforts to win assistance from the squaws. He had added to his understanding of womankind, and had respect for the stabilizing influence of matrimony. A woman made a man settle down. She bore him children and these made transportation difficult. She cared for "things," for finery. She was not willingly a wanderer. A wife whose trunk was lost or delayed was a creature desolate. So among the Comanches, the greatest wanderers of all, when a squaw obtained a fine doeskin, or a silk or calico dress, she did not wish to trudge, years long, over mountains and into valleys, as her tribe sometimes had done. To reach a land where there was always summer, and "little men lived in trees," seemed less desirable than to live in a tepee. Her papoose had a better chance for life where there was no more travel than the moving of a wigwam to a place of more abundant grass. The roving Indians had several wives to dress their buffalo hides, to build their fires and dry their meat. Lee Hall urged the women to discourage the taking of number two and number three wives.[7] The braves resisted. Number two and three wives were younger than the first. They could work harder. They were more comely and better able to afford enjoyment. The powerful chieftain, Quanah Parker, had five wives and made himself happy by taking a new one whose voice was like the tinkling of small bells.[8]

Though the Agent approved the work of Methodist and Catholic missionaries and attended the services of visiting ministers, his chief interest was in schools. In them, he found vitality. He wanted more good Christian teachers.[9] His early experience in Sherman assisted him when on Mondays he made assignments for the week. In addition to study of the three R's, he furthered the teaching of sewing and cooking for girls and of farming and gardening for boys.

When he acted as judge of a court of appeals for Indians and as judge of first instance for cases involving whites and Indians,

[7] "Captain Hall on his Wards," *Dallas Daily News,* December 31, 1885.
[8] This and other details concerning Quanah Parker were given me by his former friend, Mr. Fred C. Dolcater of Washington, D. C., a gentleman of the "ripe young age of seventy."
[9] Captain Hall's report, *Reports of Agents in Indian Territories, 1887,* collection of manuscripts owned by Mrs. Isham Keith.

he vividly recalled attendance on court sessions. At intervals, detachments of Regulars were summoned to uphold decisions, and this was reminiscent, also, of occasions when his Rangers straightened the course of justice in the Nueces Strip.

He erected saw and grist mills, sheds for agricultural implements, a smithy and a carpenter shop. He planned stables and barns to shield stock and store hay; he planned a dormitory for the fourteen white employees, a council hall for the chiefs. He began erecting a residence, to be in readiness on the arrival of his family. Bricks, lumber, windows and furniture were hauled from Henrietta, terminus of the railway. His was the first brick building in that area.[10]

Just before their arrival, the state press recorded a "slight encounter" that boded ill for Mrs. Hall and her young daughters. In September, two deputy marshals came to the Agency with warrants from the district of Graham. Two were for service on Ka-ma-ta and Po-tan-te, Kiowas accused of horse stealing. Captain Hall sent for the men and tried to detain them until troops arrived from Fort Sill. The Indians were restive. They attempted to leave. Hall shoved them into chairs, using the butt of his revolver. When again they tried to go, they drew six-shooters. The Agent and his clerk covered and disarmed them. The Indians broke for the door. The white men held fire. At that moment, the two deputies came up the path to the Agency. The Indians shot past. Men of their tribe met them and gave them Winchesters. Ka-ma-ta and Po-tan-te turned to fire, but seeing the Captain and the deputies regarding them with leveled pistols, the braves ran on toward their tepees.

Quietly as prairie dogs appear above their holes, the Indians assembled. In less than five short minutes, hundreds surrounded the Agency. Their burnished figures were as impassive and impersonal as plinths of rock upon a desert. Captain Hall had ten men at his command. He ordered them inside. There they took up their positions and for half an hour expected fight. Then a chief strode to the door and entered. For long, Hall talked to him, explaining the arrests and why the Kiowas had forfeited

---

10 Mrs. Isham Keith's manuscript, "Jessie Lee and 'Lizabeth." This is the only source used for material on the daughters.

the protection of their tribe. The chief listened, said nothing, went away. And soon the hundreds that had gathered vanished as quietly as they had come. But with them went Ka-ma-ta and Po-tan-te. Hall threatened to withhold rations, and arrests were finally made.[11] He advised the establishment of a telegraph station. Military wires in front of his office passed directly to Fort Reno and Fort Sill. The service of an operator could be had for fifty dollars a month,[12] but the Agent's recommendation was not favorably received.

Early in October, the Captain met his family in Sherman and brought them to Anadarko. The little daughters liked the brick house, its galleries and shade trees. They ran to the stable to see the carriage horses, Dan and Ginger. And they peered between the pickets of a high white fence. Outside was story-book land.

Their father took them into it, took them through tall, blue, swaying grass to visit the tepees. Naked children played outside, squaws were always working. Old men sat by the fire, but with no genial warmth of firelight in their faces. Sometimes they smoked long pipes, their faces sombre above bright woven blankets. Sometimes they did nothing, and thoughts of days gone by so glazed their eyes that they looked at the Captain's children without seeing, looked through them and on, as impersonally as they looked beyond the lines of jerked beef that squaws hung in the dry air. Not from such men as these could the Captain expect success for a program of work for man as well as squaws.

The little girls watched curiously when the Indians swarmed to the dispensary to receive the beef issue. Dressed in buckskin, their faces painted, the men rode in from every section of the reservation. If the day was sunny, they held above their heads bright paper parasols, not for protection, but because they liked the display of gayly colored flowers. Squaws came afoot, dressed in calico, with dusty, sleepy papooses strapped upon their backs and small boys and girls walking on either side.

[11] *Corpus Christi Caller,* October 4, 1885, quoting a Dallas special dispatch of September 22 to *San Antonio Express.*

[12] Captain Hall's report on the Agency, manuscript collection of Mrs. Isham Keith.

Children were everywhere, dodging ponies, being trampled on, standing apart to eye each other until a sudden sound or a flying pinto broke their gaze.

Yet with so many children, the tribes did not increase. Hall thought that if the food supply were more abundant, deaths would diminish. He planned, at the same time, to save the government the expense of dispensing beef. His project was to have the cowmen who leased grass lands pay their rental in heifer cattle.[13] The "grass money" (about twenty dollars) which each Indian received was foolishly and quickly spent. White men who preyed upon the Indians continually caused trouble.

While the Agent's family was new to the reservation, a cowboy galloped in one afternoon to warn them that the Indians were on the warpath. Outside the picket fence of the residence there formed in the moonlight an ominous circle of a hundred braves. They danced in solemn unison, bodies stiff, legs raised and lowered in measure with the monotone of a weird chant. Bronze skins were daubed and striped with war paint—ochre and red clay. The sight was like an apparition, its beginning and end so quiet and so sudden.

In the gray of dawn, the Captain had government mules hitched to an ambulance, and the family started towards Fort Reno. It was spring and the prairies were carpeted with wild flowers, harebells, Indian blanket, winecups. The air was sweet. This, only children noticed. Their elders were preoccupied with the dangers of the forty-five mile journey. Heavy rains had swollen the Washita into a torrent. The river had a quicksand bottom, so the ambulance was lightened of its load before the mules could swim and drag its heavy weight. The limb of an oak, broken by the storm, with one end lodged in a tree fork on the other side, spanned the river. Elizabeth was carried, but Jessie was the name-child of her father and kept her eyes on him and followed without glancing at the swirling water. When the family reached the officers' quarters of hospitable Fort Reno, Hall left them and returned to Anadarko. He held pow-wows, smoked long, clay tribal pipes, and restored peace.

[13] "Captain Hall on his Wards," *Dallas Morning News*, December 31, 1885.

It was at a quiet time that a third daughter, Dorothy, was born to Mrs. Hall. Indians who came to see the baby marvelled at her white skin and golden hair, and this admiration further endeared them to the Captain. They were of another world, these wards of his, devoted, blundering, yet developing, sometimes, an ominous cleverness in contrast with their child-like ignorance.

The chief of the Comanches was a more complex personality. His mother had been Cynthia Ann Parker. She had been captured as a child and taken on the journeys of the tribe. Peta Nacona, "the Wanderer," made her his wife, and Quanah, their son, combined the traits of two peoples. He was the "Washington Chief" of his tribe, who acknowledged as their lineal chief, Champion Rider, or Horse Back, as his name more generally was translated.[14] Quanah had come to Anadarko from Fort Sill after General Mackenzie's departure. The Comanche did not like Mackenzie's successor:

"Old squaw no good!" the Indian said of him and departed.[15]

Very tall, very dark, well-built, commanding in appearance, was Quanah Parker. Over magnificent shoulders, he draped whatever garments suited his fancy. Sometimes he wore an army coat with a major's epaulets; on the reservation he wore blankets, and wore them regally. With Captain Hall, in Dallas or Fort Worth, he wore "store clothes" and a derby hat, beneath which hung his braids and earrings. He was proud of a thick gold watch and the chain that dangled from his pocket. Thus appareled, he claimed that he was on the "white man's road."[16]

It was beset with dangers. He and Yellow Bear, in December, 1885, had their first experience with gas. They blew out the lights in their hotel room in Fort Worth and lay down to slumber. Yellow Bear never wakened. The Captain came from the Agency and took the body back for tribal burial. That

[14] This and the preceding paragraph are from manuscript notes by Mr. Harston.
[15] Charles Goodnight, "True Sketch of Quanah Parker's Life," quoted in *Frontier Times.*
[16] *Frances Wier Hall Ms.* Miss Hall visited the Agency; conversation with Mr. Dolcater, Washington, July, 1935.

Quanah could journey home was due to his phenomenal constitution.[17] He stayed over night at the Agency and treated his lamp with great respect, allowing it to burn all through the night. In the morning, when he emerged, the stench of a burnt wick followed him down the hall. As befitted a chief returning to his people, he was in full regalia—war bonnet, turkey fan, buckskin robe and moccasins. He ordered his squaw to hitch the team to his buggy and drove away through clean grass in clean air, his Indian blood well in the ascendant.[18]

On another occasion when he appeared more like the son of Cynthia Ann Parker, Mrs. Hall told him gently of the religion of his white grandfather, an elder. Quanah listened eagerly. He seemed docile until she told him that, as a Christian, he must give up all his wives but one. And then Quanah turned presbyter! He would keep his wives. He preached that the Captain should take a number two and number three wife. Mrs. Hall could be "boss wife" and live in idleness. As it was, he sympathized.

Other Indians felt pity for their Agent. The greater grew his reputation for bravery, the greater was her own. And this was due to stories from the tongue of Ta-ba-naw-a-ka. Mrs. Hall had accused him of the theft of a silver knife. He came to her husband glowering under war paint, denied his guilt and threatened to kill the Captain's woman: "To-ba-naw-a-ka kill many men and women too."

On Lee Hall's neck was a shallow wound made when a stretch of wire had broken in a fence he was building and a barb had cut into his flesh. Said the Captain,

"Ta-ba-naw-a-ka, I have killed men and women,—more than you have fingers and toes. I never saw any man I feared, but I am afraid of that woman. Look at my neck. She came near cutting my throat this morning. I am going to tell her what you say. You keep away from that house, if you know what's good for you!"[19]

[17] *Corpus Christi Caller,* December 27, 1885, quoting *Dallas Herald.*
[18] *Frances Wier Hall Ms.*
[19] Senator Robert L. Owen to Mrs. Isham Keith, letter dated March 10, 1935.

Ta-ba-naw-a-ka departed, wondering. And great were the tales of Ta-ba-naw-a-ka.

Another fillip to her reputation came from the war chief of the Kiowas, Sun Boy. One summer afternoon, servants had filled a tub and she was bathing. Dim light filtered through the closed shades of her room, which grew brighter as the door slowly opened, and when she turned and looked, she met the scrutiny of Sun Boy. He stood, very tall and straight, within the entrance. At first, she screamed, and then with as much dignity as nudity and anger would permit, she ordered him to leave. The Indian gazed for hour-long minutes.

"Ugh, just squaw," he grunted as he departed.

Next day, he saw the husband. It appeared that the Captain's face was scratched from riding in the brush. The Indian regarded the marks with real concern.

"Heap brave squaw!" sympathized Sun Boy.[20]

Laughter was needed for danger stalked among the Agency's tepees with tread as soft as any Indian's. Chiefly it came from white men, such men as Hall had struggled with in Texas. He had aroused the fear of cattle thieves and of grass-hungry, greedy cattlemen who preyed upon the Indians. As a Ranger, he had been successful. For two years on the reservation his luck still held.

A Texas stockman, Colonel Malone of Bee County, long accustomed to driving cattle through, praised Hall as the best Agent who had ever been at Anadarko:

"He has the Indians under good control and does his best to prevent depredations upon trail herds. ... The Indians regard him as a bigger man than old Cleveland, and whatever he says goes."[21]

A way existed to undermine such loyalty and confidence, and someone found it. A way existed to make the Indians feel that the time had come when they must turn from teachings of the white man and force from him a restoration of freedom and ancient rights. And someone found the way. It was an occult way, shrouded with fears, shadowed by superstition. It was

[20] Mrs. Isham Keith, *op. cit.*, and manuscript notes.
[21] *Corpus Christi Caller*, July 11, 1886.

planned that the Indians should be led astray and Hall confounded through the powerful medicine man, Pa-ying-yah.[22] He came among the Kiowas, and back and forth among the tribe's tepees, he wove his magic. He awed them by prophetic vision, he frightened them with minor miracles. And then he told them that such powers as he had shown were nothing. On a day that soon would come, he promised, lightning would flash from his eyes, and burn to ashes the Agency, the schools, the puny Christian missions. The white people would perish with their works. Again the plains would be covered with buffalo grass, again the buffalo would roam the prairies.

There were war dances around blazing logs, and when ryhthm, fire-magic, and the constant beat of tom-toms had worked his people to a frenzy, Pa-ying-yah on hands and knees bellowed like a calf, and told the warriors that what they heard was a buffalo crying from under the earth for the Indians to kill the white men. There were war-whoops and shrieks from the braves, and long-drawn cries, *"Hi-e-ya, Hi-e-ya, Hoon-ya Hi-a-ka!"* Each tribesman felt himself a prophet: the Kiowas would come into their own. Their horses would be swift and sure, the envy of all tribesmen; they would have more corn than the Wichitas, more cattle than the Comanches, and they would not have to gain their wealth by working: Pa-ying-yah would bring about this thing, Pa-ying-yah, medicine man of the Kiowas, he whom the Kiowas must obey. The people looked to their chiefs for guidance; when Sun Boy accepted as a verity the prophecies, they too believed them. And great was the power of Pa-ying-yah in the land of the Kiowas!

The older chieftain of the Kiowas saw his tribe fail in their loyalty. For he was alone in rejecting the strange new teachings. A snare and a delusion, he accounted them, and the blackness of Pa-ying-yah's magic, he feared, would engulf the tribe in war. This man was Stumbling Bear. He was practical, but at this season he was without honor among his people. They elected with one accord to follow Sun Boy.

---

[22] Mr. Harston, disguised as a Comanche brave and accompanied by some Kiowa boys, watched Pa-ying-yah at his mystic rites. It is from Mr. Harston's information that I have written my description.

Captain Hall, as he came and went among the Kiowas, was conscious of a strange tension. Its source, he could not fathom. Young Emmor Harston gave him news of the medicine man and his actions at the war dances, but it seemed incredible that such rantings and absurdities were the basis of the trouble.

He disliked to summon soldiers from Fort Sill until he could succinctly state some reason for anxiety. And Pa-ying-yah's brew of poison simmered and its fumes grew sinister, and its stench pervaded the tents of the Kiowas.

The hill in front of the Agency was a vantage point from which the Captain often surveyed the pointed tops of the tepees and thought of how to help the child-like people entrusted to his care. On a sultry afternoon, he climbed to its summit to strengthen himself as men had done since the time when there were hills and human need of them. He found no peace. A party of Kiowa braves was waiting. They circled round him and their looks were ominous. Light touched the metal of their knives, and the line of bows and arrows was added to their silhouette.

The Captain was unarmed. Below him, a mile and a half away, he could see the Agency. In the doorway stood his wife. The sun that glinted on the Indians' knives picked out in cheerful contrast the friendly whiteness of her apron.

"That is the last I'll see of Bessie," thought her husband.

What the apron stood for made life very dear, and thoughts raced forward to elude the death that waited on a hillside in the sunny morning.

His hands were in his pockets as he climbed the hill. He kept them there for he needed to convince the braves he felt no fear. What could he do to show contempt for the men and their knives and murderous bows and arrows? He stood his height, threw back his head, and with his gray-blue eyes challenged the sullen dark ones. The red men crowded close, their gestures menacing. Then full into the face of the nearest Indian, Lee Hall spat. Nor did one brave alone receive this symbol. His marksmanship was unerring, and he accompanied it with ridicule of fools who thought they could harm the Agent of the Great White Father. He motioned them to open their circle, to make way. They obeyed, and without haste the Captain strode between two braves, and rolling a cigarette walked toward the Agency.[23]

Never, perhaps, had he been so close to his old neighbor, Death.

Before their prophet could sting the Indians by the venom of his ridicule, the Captain acted. He had the horses harnessed and his wife and children driven to Fort Sill. It was good, at last, to see the stars and stripes flying above the trim parade-ground. Major Upham was in command. The Captain left the family in his care and returned to Anadarko with a detachment of the Twenty-fifth.

He knew now why a council of Kiowas had been summoned, why children of the tribe were absent from the mission school. The Agent had not been invited to Elk Creek, but he attended with chieftains and medicine men, the creatures of Pa-ying-yah. In full panoply, the prophet dominated all. Again, he told of the great day that was to come when his secret powers would be revealed. Captain Hall listened with every appearance of respect. He inquired, and he found that the great day was not to be the morrow nor the day after. And then he spoke. It was obvious that the entire tribe could not remain on Elk Creek to await the portents. Already the feast of dried meats had been consumed. Tepees deserted were tepees open for plunder. He advised that the Kiowas return to their tents till the appointed time. Their day of destiny was predetermined, anticipation could not speed its coming. The Kiowas agreed, and they departed.

The great day came and went with sunrise and with sunset, as any lesser day. There was beauty of billowing blue grass, but buffalo grass did not spring up to clothe the prairie. Nor did the herds of buffalo appear. The Agency, the missions, and the schools remained. Night came, a spring night with bird-songs and the fragrance of wild flowers. But the "might, majesty, power and dominion" of Pa-ying-yah were as withered leaves that fluttered down, with none to mark their passing.[24]

[23] Mrs. Isham Keith, *op. cit.*, and manuscript notes.
[24] Mr. Harston states that the "Sun Boy rebellion" was "the last of the reservation troubles."

XVIII
Indian Agent *vs.* "the Sons of Boone"
(1887-1892)

"*These dissatisfied cattlemen probably intend by some concerted action to thwart us in keeping them out of this territory. I will keep a watch on them and request you hold any herds that may have crossed into it. The intention seems to be to just drive through to Kansas, but some only wish to graze their herds.*"—Letter, dated May 29, 1880, from Colonel P. B. Hunt, Indian Agent at Anadarko, to Commanding Officer Colonel Mizner, Fort Sill, I.T., quoted in *History of Comanche Land*, by J. Emmor Harston.

"*I have been an Indian agent and not a white man's agent, and if I had been vice versa I do not believe there would have been any charges filed against me in Secretary Lamar's department.*"— LEE HALL in a statement to the press, October 22, 1887.

XVIII

Indian Agent *vs.* "the Sons of Boone"

CAPTAIN HALL's main problem at the Kiowa, Comanche and Wichita Reservation was not how to deal with the Indians, but how to deal with certain white men. It was a problem inherited from Colonel P. B. Hunt, the active and intelligent Agent who preceded him.[1] The Colonel had begun the struggle against predatory whites in 1878. It was continued and extended. Men who leased the grasslands, contractors, marshals, squawmen, a small number of employees, a few teachers and missionaries— these alone had the right to live upon the reservation. Hall expelled the rest, but steadily they drifted back. Some were outlaws, others were squatters who, to keep their land, claimed to be working for the Indians.[2] To arrest those who resisted expulsion or persisted in returning, he used the Indian police. Its

[1] Mr. Emmor Harston's note on first draft of the manuscript of this book. Additional material on this is in his unpublished *History of Comanche Land*, extracts of which were sent the author.

[2] The problem was complicated by the fact that cowboys, "going up the trail," drove their herds through the reservation. By the autumn of 1878, the buffalo had vanished. The cattle came along the Canadian River and the herds spread over all the Panhandle and into the Indian country, where with Indian ponies they fattened on the long buffalo grass.

Mr. Harston claims that hundreds of horses were lost to white men, and "including those taken, divided up, and shot, by the Army" should be more than 7000. "The Comanches knew it did no good to report the theft for, in fact, the government not only wanted to destroy their buffalo, but the Indians themselves. It had a surplus hang-over of idle army officers who wanted to hold their jobs and it was cheaper to bury an Indian than it was to feed him, so the horse stealing business was winked at until the arrival of Captain Hall as agent." Mr. Harston's note on first draft of the manuscript of this book.

On December 30, 1885, Captain Hall was in Dallas for the prosecution of thieves who had stolen ponies from the Indians and run them into Texas. It was at this time that he gave the revealing interview in which he outlined his policy as agent. *Dallas Morning News*, December 31, 1885.

chief, Azook R. Rushe, not only was of service on the reservation, but went with the Agent to testify and assist in prosecution in the Texas law courts.[3] So active were the two that in October of Hall's first year, the *Dallas News* reported that, because of this new policy, there was a "prospect of serious trouble, if not bloodshed."[4]

Among the outlaws were cattle thieves of the kind that Hall had fought in Texas. One night he drove with his wife across the prairies toward Fort Sill. The scattered lights of the tepees were like weird jack-o'-lanterns. The Captain liked the far-off beat of the tom-toms, and he liked the monotone of distant Indian chanting. Mrs. Hall could distinguish sounds but vaguely, for her hearing had already become dulled. Suddenly her body stiffened. She detected the vibration of a horse coming towards them at full gallop. Then a voice called, though no one could be seen,

"Is that you, Captain Hall?"

"Yes, who are you?"

"A friend." And the friend warned that in the next arroyo men waited to rope the Agent from the buggy and make an end of him.

"Who are the men?" Hall asked.

One name was shouted—that of a man believed to be a cattle thief. Then the friend, invisible still, wheeled his horse, and galloping hoof-beats grew faint in the distance. At his wife's persuasion, Hall turned the horses and drove back to the Agency. He could not desert her to go forward, and he could not take her into danger. Later he found that the men who were lying in wait that night were members of a gang whose leader Mrs. Hall had befriended during an illness.

"Don't hurt Mrs. Hall, boys," he warned the others, "she was good to me; but kill the Captain."

It was a stupid attempt and it resulted in a stupid failure[5] —one distasteful to the lords of the ranges of northwest Texas. They regarded the Agent's work as distinctly a menace to their

[3] *Dallas Morning News,* July 13, 1886.
[4] *Ibid.,* October 12, 1885, quoting Little Rock dispatch of October 11.
[5] Mrs. Isham Keith, "Jessie and 'Lizabeth," and manuscript notes.

own activities. They wished to be rid of him, but they did not wish a telltale body on the prairie, or an abduction with Hall's own wife as witness. It had not been necessary to resort to such crimes in their struggle with Colonel Hunt. In that, they had used subtly the old device of divided rule—favoring Quanah Parker over Champion Rider.

Champion Rider, one of the chiefs of the Comanches since 1862, had apprised Agent Hunt of his anger at the practices of the white cattlemen. They were pasturing their cattle on reservation grass, paying a few of the Indians and ignoring the rights of the tribes to benefit from the use of land held in common. As Champion Rider put it, he was "heaps o' Goddam mat" that a few of the chiefs were pasturing thousands of cattle and appropriating the money for themselves. When he himself was approached by would-be bribers, he was even more "heaps o' Goddam mat." He called a council of the headmen at old Fort Cobb in the spring of 1878. Whiteman, chief of the Apaches, and Stumbling Bear, chief of the Kiowas, declared to the assemblage that Champion Rider spoke their thoughts when he denounced the greed of this secret partnership of Indians and Texas cattlemen.

Quanah Parker was present, but at first said nothing. The others knew well that he was pasturing stock for one of the richest of the cattlemen. This man continually made him presents, paid him money monthly, and was building him a residence with separate bedrooms for each of his half dozen wives. The council asked Quanah whether he stood with the Texans or with the Indians. He assured the chieftains that he felt as they did. He stalked from the council with the others, but he did not act with the others. He did not change his practice.

To rid the southern district of white men holding cattle there, and of white men's cattle held by Indians, Colonel Hunt had found it necessary to use the Indian police and a detachment from the regiment of Colonel Hatch. Champion Rider worked with them. Quanah did not. And so powerful was Quanah, and so influential his benefactors, that, though Colonel Hunt reported his misdeeds, the government made no mention of him in any of its orders.

In appreciation of his value and further to enhance it, the cattlemen succeeded, two years later, in having him appointed a chief of the Comanches, the title being conferred by General Mackenzie on advice from Washington. The tribe could not accept him, since by their law their chieftains must be chosen by themselves from men of undiluted Indian blood. Quanah Parker absented himself from smoke-talks held to deprive him of his title, but never before the death of Champion Rider, did he presume to act as chief upon the reservation. Until 1885, wherever he rode, Quanah, fearing tribal hatred, was accompanied by a bodyguard.[6]

When Hall inherited the struggle, he "found one cattleman trying to build Quanah a summer residence on the north bank of the Red River with its blood-red waters for a swimming pool." Another was hauling in lumber to build him a winter residence south of the Wichita Mountains." Undoubtedly, he was "a heap big Injun," but with too much white blood in his veins to be an "honest Injun" in dealing with his tribe.[7]

This chief was profitably conformable. Captain Hall was not. In the southwest, the same class had regarded him as a friend and a protector, but even there he met with disapproval because of his concern for the property of small ranch-holders of Mexican blood and for the lives of isolated shepherds. On the reservation, he seconded the constant protests made at smoke-talks and induced the Washington authorities to send him orders to burn illicit camps, and gather all cattle not legally belonging on the reservation. The latter were to be redeemable by their owners only by payment of a dollar a head to defray expense of the round-up. For this work, Hall was to have the assistance of the Indian police and detachments from Fort Reno and Fort Sill. He acted on his orders with vigor and dispatch.[8]

---

[6] Harston, *History of Comanche Land,* and manuscript notes.

[7] Quanah "seemed to take on the nature of a white man ... entered business and became a successful stock farmer. He built a palatial residence."—Max Coleman, "Transformation of the Llano Estacado," *Frontier Times,* July, 1936.

The late John Bracken, who worked with Captain Hall on the reservation, told me that Quanah had twelve wives housed in a large building. Mr. Dolcater credited him with no more than seven.

[8] Captain Hall, in reporting to the Commissioner of Indian Affairs, named four commanders at Fort Sill as having given efficient assistance in arresting

Stockmen who had been accustomed to controlling affairs in northern Texas, at first believed that nothing more was intended than an occasional shakeup that would result in the reservation's receiving, at intervals, a good round sum of money. They drove their herds out on one side, and in again on another. They meant for them to stay, although claiming they were "jist goin' up the trail" to Dodge City. They hired enterprising whites to become temporary squawmen and set forth a claim to property rights of pasturage. "Sons of Boone," such men were called, and the number of their cattle and the brands these bore made obvious the source of their pay checks.[9]

Lee Hall had known too many honorable cattlemen to think it impossible to make some arrangement that would be fair to them and at the same time benefit the Indians. The very small sum paid for annual grazing privileges, if distributed among the tribes, would result in each Indian's receiving about twenty dollars a year as *"sawmie pohewaits,"* or grass money.[10] In 1885, the year when a Texas drouth made pasturage especially desirable,[11] the effort to maintain the policy begun by Agent Hunt was more than ever difficult.

Yet Captain Hall was succeeding. In 1886, he was quoted as saying that he and his men had expelled 5,000 head of cattle, and that at the next round-up, they expected to rid the reservation of as many more. These were "trespass cattle,"—that is cattle for which the owners had not paid for grazing privilege.[12]

The payment was small and sharks were always at hand to assist the Indians to waste their money. The Agent's preference was that, increasingly, the payment should be made in heifers and the Indians trained to the cattle industry.

"In two years," he said, "the beef or meat supply would be settled. I believe if this course were adopted and Indians taught

---

trespassers and expelling trespass cattle from the reservation, *Reports of Agents in Indian Territory in 1887,* Mrs. Keith's collection of manuscripts.

[9] Harston, *History of Comanche Land,* and manuscript notes.

[10] Captain Hall's interview in *Dallas Morning News,* December 31, 1885.

[11] W. C. Holden, "West Texas Drouths," *Southwestern Historical Review,* October, 1928.

[12] *Corpus Christi Caller,* June 6, 1886, quoting *Dallas Morning News.*

practical farming by practical farmers they would support themselves in less than three years."[13]

For stock raising and farming, the Indians needed their ponies. Of these, hundreds were lost each year, due to the activity of horse thieves who drove them into Texas or the nation of the Chickasaws. Hall prosecuted the thievery. He longed for his Ranger detectives, and requested that authorities in Washington let him have two men to assist in ferreting out thieves. He was not refused but neither was the request granted. The stealing of ponies before he came had been a somewhat routine procedure.

The change the Agent tried to inaugurate was regarded with increasing concern by the cattlemen. If Hall's plans succeeded, they would lose their nearest market. Beef contractors and the government dispensary no longer would be needed. If Indians became prosperous stock raisers, the Texans would have to compete with rivals who were nearer than themselves to the Kansas market. Grasslands would cease to be available for leasing; the transit of Texas herds through the reservation would mean *transit,* not pasturage. Nor could the size of the herds any longer be increased by the addition of reservation cattle.

The problems that the Agent faced were many. The problem of the stockmen was the single one of how to discredit and remove Lee Hall. He was favorably and widely known in Texas. He had been recommended for his office by an exceptionally large number of prominent citizens. He was honest,[14] energetic and intelligent. His appearance in the courts at Fort Worth, Waco, Graham, and Dallas, made known throughout the northern Federal district the vigor and persistence of his efforts. Every legal success he gained against the little men increased the dangers of the men higher up. It was not only what he did but his method of doing it that attracted attention. He possessed news value. Any reporter interviewing him had a good time and came away with material for a good story. He was

[13] *Dallas Morning News,* December 31, 1885.
[14] "His [Captain Hall's] word is like his bond and these ostracized men knew that what he said he did."—Letter to the Editor, *Austin Herald,* January 21, 1882.

excellent as an entertainer. His mimicry, his telling gestures, and the rapid play of expression on his mobile face might have been coveted by an actor. A certain essence of the dramatic seems to have been infused into his very personality. It was this, more than his height and his red hair, that made him the focus of attention. Men described him as magnetic. He had conceived the part of a Ranger and lived it so consistently that O. Henry, when he came to write of the men guarding the border, unfailingly thought of Lee Hall.[15] Lawyers, newspaper men, stockmen, men of the town and men of the country enjoyed the Indian Agent's stories. And what he said was quoted. Men liked him. They wished him success. The *Dallas News* of December, 1885, carried a 1,600-word interview in which he explained the problems that confronted him and how he meant to solve them. Readers were glad to know of his progress. His adventures with his charges, his efforts in the courts on their behalf were noted constantly in the Texas press.

He had the confidence of the officers at nearby forts. When Lieutenant Anthony, with a detachment of troops from Fort Sill, stopped a herd of 2,000 cattle that were going up the Western Trail through the Cheyenne Reservation, he said he acted on instructions from Captain Hall. The Captain had told him to take the cattle back to the line of the Kiowa and Comanche Reservation. There the chief of police was to drive them to the crossing of the "North Fork" in Greer County, Texas. Six men and the trail boss, who refused to take the back track, were arrested. Hall's claim was that the herd and its drivers had trespassed against the Indians. Newspapers reported in headlines that the owner threatened to sue. Since he did not do so, it is probable that the Agent's instructions, though unusual, were well founded. The affair was due to the need of a Texas stockman who had contracted to deliver 5,500 cattle by a specified date and given a bond of $24,000 for performance. The herd numbered 1,960 head when it started through the Agency to-

---

[15] "One does not have to read O. Henry's Texas stories very closely to detect the presence of Red Hall. ... There stands before us a calm and determined man who uses his pistol with instant precision but only as a last resort. This is the real type of the Texas Ranger, dime novels to the contrary notwithstanding."—C. Alphonso Smith, *O. Henry Biography*, 99.

wards Dodge City.[16] Men driving their herds through did not wish to have at Anadarko an agent so solicitous for the property of his wards that he would order arrests outside the territory under reservation jurisdiction.

With Quanah Parker, they determined to discredit Hall so thoroughly that their motives would be well concealed, and then to oust him. They hoped he might be followed by some one who would turn, in their direction, a blind eye and an itching palm. On the main issue, the stockmen were wrong. Lee Hall was right and all knew it.[17] It was another issue that was set before the public.

An inspector of the Indian Department, T. D. Marcum, and a special agent, Eugene White, came to the reservation and began work on the records. The evidence uncovered showed to their satisfaction that for over a year false vouchers had been presented. Their report resulted in a request from Secretary of Interior Lamar that the Attorney General institute criminal proceedings against Jesse Lee Hall.[18] This was done on October 15, 1887, the year in which he had shown his strength over the Kiowas to be superior to that of Pa-ying-yah. While the Captain was attending court in Texas as a witness for the government, he was suspended from office.[19] For four years, the man who had arrested hundreds, assisted in gaining evidence, pro-

[16] "U. S. Troops Stop Herd," undated newspaper clipping in the collection of Mrs. Isham Keith. The owner of the cattle, the paper said, intended to bring suit for damages. He did not sue.

[17] "In his old Ranger days his rôle was as a friend and protector, while in this fight, a child not his own, he was against them and they were wrong, and he was right and all of them knew it. They must get a man they could handle by getting rid of Hall."—Mr. Harston's note on first draft of the manuscript of this book.

[18] *Dallas Morning News,* October 18, 1887, quoting Washington dispatch of October 16. Eugene E. White of Prescott, Arkansas, was Special Indian Agent from 1885 to 1889.

[19] Eugene E. White to Secretary of the Interior, dispatch dated Kiowa, Comanche and Wichita Agency, October 18, 1887, manuscript collection of Mrs. Isham Keith.

"Since the transfer took place while I was absent, attending the U. S. court as a witness for the Government ... and as I have exercised no control over the affairs of the Agency since that date ... I cannot be held responsible for the amount, condition or disposition of the public property of the Agency."—Signed, "J. Lee Hall, Ex-Indian Agent." The letter, an answer to an inquiry of the Acting Commissioner of Indian Affairs, is dated Dallas, Texas, August 21, 1888.

tected witnesses and judges, and guarded prisoners, was himself to face indictments, suits, and their continuances.

Stripped of abundant verbiage, the stark claim was that he had presented fraudulent vouchers in his accounts for a year or more; had, with the collusion of beef contractors, put public money to his own use; and had appropriated large sums placed in his hands by cattlemen for rent of Indian pasture lands.[20] A Washington dispatch, in stating the charges, recalled that few men receiving a position at the hands of this administration had presented finer endorsements. Bonds had been sent to Washington on his nomination, when the Senate approved his appointment and on two later occasions. Two only of these had been held, since to the Treasury, they seemed sufficient to provide security. Under the cumulative plan, they amounted to about $60,000. The alleged shortage was less than half of this. The Washington dispatch added that no alarm was felt since the bondsmen all were solvent.[21]

This was countered by the assertion in the *Dallas News* that the bondsmen felt equally secure because of confidence in Hall's integrity. They had questioned him and his answers were reassuring. In the press, the Agent categorically denied the incriminating charges. As to the chief one, that of defrauding the Indians of "grass money," he claimed that the greatest amount of this had not been paid to him, but directly to the Indians by the men who had pastured cattle on reservation lands. To Indians known to be living there, but not appearing to claim their share, $8,000 had been due. This was paid, on Hall's request, to him as Agent but with the knowledge of the Indians. Less than half of this, he invested in cattle, the value of which had increased. The rest of the $8,000, he said, was deposited in the City Bank of Sherman, where lived the bondsmen, and was subject to order. In concluding his defense, Hall said:

"I have been an Indian agent and not a white man's agent, and if I had been vice versa I do not believe there would have

[20] *Dallas Morning News*, October 18, 1888, quoting Washington dispatch of October 16; *Corpus Christi Caller*, October 22, 1887, quoting Associated Press dispatch from Washington.
[21] The Washington dispatch was quoted in *The Dallas Morning News*, October 22, 1887, from *The St. Louis Republican*.

been any charges filed against me in Secretary Lamar's department."[22]

In Austin, Richard Hall was serving as State Land Commissioner. News of the charges brought him north. In his office, he had learned much of the power of avaricious stockmen and of the vagaries of the law. Sidney Porter, his clerk, remained behind in the pink, castle-like structure on the Capitol grounds where he studied men and manners in the Land Office. Perched high on his draftsman's stool, he watched a little world revolve beneath—a world where powerful land sharks triumphed with the aid of shyster lawyers. He pondered, probably, that a great state permitted these to glut themselves upon its wealth, and a great nation found unfit for service a man whose qualities had made him the Ranger hero of clear-eyed boys in his native state, in Texas, and at the Agency. Porter could picture Richard Hall, alighting from the train and talking to reporters. The Land Commissioner would be dressed in fine black, a suggestion of Roman drapery in ample coat-skirts. Those who talked with him would find his antique courtesy a little chilling. They would not know, as Porter did, that behind the mask of an official sternness, were tender and gentle thoughts, and, for his brother, anxiety and sorrow.[23] The draftsman found it hard to concentrate. He sketched sardonic scenes upon the margin of his ledger pages,[24] and he pondered on the whirligig of fate.

Jointly with Judge R. R. Hazelwood, of Henrietta, who had been retained as Hall's attorney, the Land Commissioner branded the charges as untrue. The *Fort Worth Gazette*, published their statements with editorial approval.[25] In a later issue, Judge Hazelwood, while still denying any shortage, admitted that there might be irregularity as to Hall's vouchers:

"His clerks did make out and present several in exact accordance with statements sent in by them to the department at

---

[22] Interviews with Captain J. H. Britton, one of the bondsmen, and with Captain Hall at the Wakefield Hotel, Sherman, Texas, *Dallas Morning News*, October 23, 1887.

[23] O. Henry has described the Land Commissioner in "Georgia's Ruling," *Outlook*, June 30, 1900.

[24] The records of the old Land Office are still searched for O. Henry's drawings.

[25] Quoted in *Corpus Christi Caller*, October 22, 1887.

Washington, and by following the statements instead of the amount actually expended there was drawn from the treasury between $500 and $600 more than was actually paid out on the vouchers. This money was in Captain Hall's hands, however, when the special agent came there and was counted in his presence, the books showing that the surplus had been accumulating from the date of the vouchers. The reason the money was not converted back into the Treasury was, according to the statements of Captain Hall's clerks, because the latter thought there were some outstanding orders given during the summer when they were out of funds and which had not been presented for payment. The money referred to above was being carried in the safe, as shown by the books for the purpose of meeting the supposed outstanding orders, and the true source from which the surplus arose was not known to Hall or his clerks (as they say) until the facts were brought out in the investigation." The explanation revealed an irregularity but one that was not unreasonable in those days.

Judge Hazelwood referred to Hall's necessity, while serving as a witness against criminals and trespassers on the reservation, of entrusting affairs to his clerks, appointees of the government.[26] Indeed, the chief of these, W. C. Morrill, had exercised considerable authority. Unfortunately—and this the Judge did not mention—the accounts were left unchecked on the Agent's return. The ex-Ranger had been accustomed all his life to dealing in the open with human beings. Men of every kind, he had faced unflinchingly. He could not face the tedium of studying the figures on a page. Drouth, the rigors of a norther, blinding heat, he could contend with, but not the orderly entries in his office ledger. His supervision of Morrill steadily decreased. The clerk came to expect this. Having fallen heir to a considerable power in the making of vouchers and the allocation of funds, he used it.[27] Judge Hazelwood held that, contrary to the charges, Hall had made the best agent the reservation

---

[26] "No Crookedness," undated newspaper clipping in collection of Mrs. Isham Keith.

[27] Mr. Emmor Harston testifies to the hatred the Captain had for all clerical work; Mrs. Keith, to her father's negligence in failing to supervise sufficiently the work of his chief clerk.

had ever had: every cowman on the reservation would testify that he had been rigid and made them more closely conform to agreements than had his predecessors. The Indians' testimony showed the tribes to have been exceptionally prosperous. Not only did they have more property, but they knew better how to use it. Hall had encouraged them to cast aside their blankets, to till the soil, raise cattle, and support themselves. They boasted with touching pride that, unlike any other agent, he had visited at their tepees.

The long-faced Special Agent, Eugene E. White, was a man who understood ledgers. On his information, a deputy United States marshal swore out a warrant, charging that, in November, 1887, Captain Hall had presented false vouchers, and with others had connived to defraud the government.[28] In February, with his wife and three little daughters, he came to Waco. Soon after, he gave himself up to the Federal district attorney, Major Charles B. Pearre. Business men offered to furnish bail, but the accused preferred to give bond in Dallas. In the custody of a deputy marshal, Hall went there in the afternoon.[29]

Lee Hall, once Captain of Special State Troops, formerly head of the Kiowa, Comanche and Wichita Reservation, was a captive, an ex-official cast aside by his government, discredited as a swindler. There was laughter in filthy hideouts and at the meeting places in northwest Texas of the powerful lords of the range.

A month later, at Graham, Hall was indicted on the charge of having embezzled $14,800. Immediately, he gave bond.[30] In April, at Waco, the Grand Jury added to this charge five more bills of indictment. These accused him of embezzling sums amounting to $680 and presenting false claims against the government amounting to $1,000. In connection with the last named charge, his chief clerk, W. C. Morrill, was indicted as accomplice.[31] These second accusations were an anti-climax. It may be surmised that they were made because the charge of

---

[28] *Dallas Morning News,* February 24, 1888, quoting a Waco dispatch of February 23.
[29] *Ibid.,* February 24, 1888.
[30] *Ibid.,* March 23, 1888.
[31] *Ibid.,* April 22, 1888, quoting Waco dispatch of April 21.

embezzling the larger sum, "the grass money," had been found untenable.

When the cases came on for trial, the government was at a disadvantage. Major Pearre had been succeeded by Eugene Marshall. This new Federal attorney for the northern district of Texas studied the papers in some bewilderment. He found listed a hundred witnesses, most of whom resided far from the place of trial. The names of others, whose testimony Mr. Marshall believed would be material were the cases tried upon their merits, strangely were absent from the lengthy list. Furthermore, no names of witnesses appeared endorsed upon the indictment, and this omission was contrary to the practice of the northern district.

The record seemed to indicate that the indictments were obtained solely upon the testimony of Special Agent White. Those for presenting false claims curiously omitted two material charges: that the claims were presented to an officer of the United States, and that they were presented with intention to defraud. The cases for embezzlement of monies of the United States described practically the same transaction. Captain Hall's attorney moved that the indictments be quashed. The Federal judge sustained his motion. The cases were dismissed.

When the trial took place for the alleged embezzlement of "grass money," the government was not prepared. It had no witnesses. Three of those it had counted on were dead. One was insane. The Federal attorney was constrained to admit in a report to the Attorney General that the bills could not have been sustained had every living witness been brought to court. The government lacked as evidence a transcript of the books of the Treasury, such as would show a balance against Hall. Federal Attorney Marshall had asked for this. It was not forthcoming. On the other side, those who had leased the land for pasturage appeared as witnesses and were ready to testify that Captain Hall had turned over the "grass money" to the Indians in their presence, or else had used it for Indians' benefit. Captain Hall was acquitted.[32]

[32] The history of the case is contained in the report of Eugene Marshall, United States Attorney, Northern District of Texas, which was sent, January 5, 1892,

From term to term until the end of 1891, the cases in regard to fraudulent claims were continued.[33] By then most of the indictments had been quashed. The court refused to continue the others. Marshall, himself, admitted that the cases had not been "maturely considered" by his predecessor; that the indictments were based on the sole testimony of Agent White, whose written report showed that they could not be sustained; that White had based his claims on hearsay—"inadmissible as evidence" in any criminal prosecution.

However faulty the investigation, it was considered sufficiently strong by the Department of the Interior to justify the judgment of its agents. They believed, as White claimed, that Hall had been negligent in his duties, frequently under the influence of intoxicants, and with his subordinates, guilty of irregularities. He was dismissed from public service before the trials. No bondsman lost a penny. If the government truly had lost, surely, others of its servants had been negligent in providing proof on which Federal attorneys could base a successful prosecution—had been guilty, in this, of irregularities.

Few Texans followed the course of the tedious cases. Many accounted Hall as not different from other faulty agents. Failure of the government to prove its charges in courts of law did not result in reïnstatement. Emmor Harston, who went with Hall on his visits to the Indians, and listened at night to the Agent's plans for his charges, perhaps, delivered the truest verdict:

"A deluded government saw fit to dismiss Hall instead of placing him at the head of the Indian Department." Harston was as powerless as the Agent's enemies were strong.

The Texas fighting stockmen, well under cover, had brought about discredit and dismissal. They had closed in and dealt Lee Hall a body blow from which he never could recover.[34]

---

on request to the Honorable W. H. Miller, Attorney General of the United States. A copy of this report was obtained for me through the kindness of Mr. Charles Moore of Gig Harbor, Washington, formerly of Washington, D. C.

[33] "A search of the old records of this Department reveals that the cases against Jesse Lee Hall were dismissed by the Court sometime in 1890 or 1891."— H. C. Donaldson, Chief Clerk, Department of Justice, Washington, D. C., to Senator Tom Connally, April 14, 1937. For this information I am indebted to Senator Connally.

[34] Mr. Emmor Harston to the author, San Antonio, Texas, May 29, 1937.

The Man They Left Behind Them

(1891-1898)

"Then we did agree to let each other be;
I was too much for him, and he was too much for me."

. . . .

"You go to the reaper
I'll go to the binder,
I've lost my true-love—
Where shall I find her?"

—Western Play-party Song.

XIX

The Man They Left Behind Them

AFTER LEE HALL's dismissal from the Agency he went with his family to San Antonio, where there had always been appreciation for his valor.

Its streets were as busy as in the smoky seventies, but its activities were commonplace. No longer the city of the Chihuahua trail, and of mule-drawn wagon trains, it was connected with the outside world by railways. The Southern Pacific linked it to San Francisco, and, on the south, the International and Great Northern went through to Laredo and connected with the Mexican Central. San Antonio was assiduously cultivating its reputation as a health resort! Men sat on sunny benches in its lazy plazas intent on keeping life. Seldom did there appear a swashbuckler of the range intent on taking it. San Antonio was developing a consciousness of Society, with its wheels within wheels, its cliques within cliques. The handsomest of its leaders, married now, was the girl in whom Hall had shown so keen an interest before he met Miss Weidman. Cattlemen of the seventies had grown in bulk, wealth, and in sobriety. Instead of carefree squandering, they bought homes and encouraged wives and daughters in the discriminating expenditure that they, themselves, lacked time or talent for. The city was tolerant of it all. It had as mayor, Bryan Callaghan, not so Irish as his name, but a Celt able to hold the diverse affections of Mexicans and Germans, to give good government, and to juggle the votes of a polyglot population.

It seemed the tempo of Hall's life had slackened so that it matched the tempo of the city. The business of making a living for a wife and family necessitated performance of routine duties. Lee Hall "would have been in his element as a knight in the days of chivalry,"[1] but a knight on a treadmill would give a poor performance. He now had a fourth daughter to provide for, little Mary. Successively, he was a wholesale coal merchant and a traveling passenger agent for the Santa Fé. In 1891 he assisted his brother, Richard Hall, in his unsuccessful campaign against James Stephen Hogg for governor.

The next year, as a deputy marshal, Captain Hall commanded 130 men sent against the strikers on the San Antonio and Arkansas Pass Railroad. His force manned trains, policed the shops, and guarded rolling stock. Netteville Devine was with him; "Baylor was second in command." Another deputy marshal was J. W. Bracken, an ex-Ranger who had served with Hall at the Agency. Bracken describes the men as a "hard bunch." Of them all, the Mexican, Juan Coy, was most powerful and most dangerous. Heavy-set, tremendous of stature, he was one of the fighting men of Butler's ranch in Karnes County. The road served part of the district where Hall's Rangers had scouted earlier—the counties of San Patricio, Bee, Live Oak, Karnes, Refugio, and Goliad—cattle country, feud country, where men could change a strike into guerilla warfare. Hall made his stand at Yoakum. As Bracken describes him, he was "head of everything"—and the only man who carried no pistol. He made Netteville Devine paymaster, bookkeeper, and timekeeper. Negroes brought in from Houston made up the switch crews. They had their own grudge against the union—it excluded them from membership. Hanging by one hand to the rails of a box-car and with his right on a Winchester, a "buck Negro" was of considerable assistance in getting a train through. For twenty-three days, Hall got them through. The engineers still served the company. Strike-breakers went with them in the cabs, but after a scab at the engine's throttle tore down part of the depot, Hall commanded that they keep hands off.[2]

---

[1] Letter to the author from Judge Duval West, San Antonio, Texas, February 27, 1935.
[2] Information from Mrs. Isham Keith.

THE MAN THEY LEFT BEHIND THEM

At the last, forty strikers stood beneath the coal-chute to dispute the right of way of an engine crew and its protectors. Five hundred shots were fired, so rapidly that ropes of fire illuminated the cold January night.[3] After this, the struggle ended. Lee Hall dismissed his force, and remained to arrange a settlement.[4] Strike-breaking was not his profession,[5] yet it was more congenial than "white collar" work. He could not sit at ease upon a swivel chair with long legs stretched beneath a desk while four walls shut away his view of far horizons. His gestures and his voice, his fearless eyes suggested windswept plains, the bitter tang and crispness of a norther. In moments of repose, he brought to mind the drift of sand dunes under quiet stars. Hall had dwelt with these, with rivers and great prairies. Death had been his neighbor.

Yet he could not go back, for the great days of the Rangers were over. The finest of the captains had resigned. If Lee Hall was to revive his reputation, it must be outside the state. And there was Bessie to think of — Bessie who had married a fighter and pledged him to peace; Bessie who had married one of the most noted of the idols of the state, one of its Ranger captains. She could not understand why he could not be equally a success in business. Her visits to Pennsylvania became frequent and protracted. In Lebanon with her mother and older sister, peace and security had their dwelling place.

Captain Hall felt these absences. His letters told of the children's friends in San Antonio; of plays that they were planning to enact when the daughters returned; of the pretty French doll he had given their cousin Sarah; of the new trotter he had bought, "faster than any other in the city," so gentle that Mama could drive her. He was pathetically eager for letters, begged that they remember his love for them. When his wife wrote that Jessie, in a fever, had cried for him, he was reminded of an illness in Corpus when he had kept her quiet and happy in his arms because she knew that her little head rested close to

[3] Letter to the author from the late John W. Bracken, May 25, 1935.
[4] *Dallas Morning News*, January 26, 1892.
[5] He expressed his distaste for this to Judge Duval West.

[263]

his great warm heart, "which belongs only to mama and you girls."[6]

Reunions were occasions of great joy, but Captain Hall's inability to mold himself into such a husband as the American woman expects became obvious. When his wife and the children, in 1894, went to Lebanon to visit, there was no hint of farewell in the parting, but from this time on the home was broken.

The husband's thoughts turned inward, and they were not happy thoughts. Outwardly, he seemed unchanged. By friends and certain winter visitors, he was prized as unique, charming in manner, a teller of tales always new. On the broad gallery of the San Antonio Club, overlooking the Plaza and the Alamo, in the lounge and smoking rooms, he still could dominate, but through urbanity.

It was here that he met Frederic Remington. As Hall would put it, there was man in Frederic Remington. He knew the West —sage brush and cactus, desert sands, the play of sunshine and its searing heat, the mysteries of night in an old land where arts had flowered and wilted before the European's coming. He knew the Indians, not in generic bulk as Indians, but as Comanches, Navajos, Apaches. He knew the good in each tribe, its history, its prospects for survival. And he knew horses.

Swiftly and surely through line and color he could endow with life a canvas, paper, whatever medium there was at hand. The life that he recorded was American life, stark hardihood of pioneers, heroism of men who died in combat without benefit of trumpet call or martial music; of men whose valor was above reward of stripes and epaulets. His was not an art of suavity. It was robust, ribbed, sharply pointed, without nuance, perhaps, but clean and fresh and true. In a country that was beginning to send its artists to study the technique and treasures of a Europe their forefathers had left behind, a sufficient number of the discriminating insured for Remington a sturdy popularity.

Lee Hall found him an avid listener. The Captain told him

[6] Captain Hall to Jessie Lee Hall, San Antonio, October 1, 1890; January 1, 1891.

stories that from others he withheld for fear hair-breadth escapes might seem imaginary. Remington remembered and recorded in *Harper's Magazine* parts of the conversation.[7] But he could not set down in words, the effect that Hall created. He suggested that the man of action turn writer and record his life.

"Lee," he urged, "my reputation is made. My pictures will start the sale of the book."[8]

Hall procrastinated. A book should have an ending—preferably a happy ending. He would not have a reader pause and peep, and ask of this and that. In the Nueces country, he had seen Mexicans attempt to follow *la luz del llano,* a dancing light that led to far off places, a beckon to rewards or to oblivion. Lee Hall was seeking, too, a pilgrim and a stranger. Until he found, his story was not ready. In Denver, he became a promoter, sure that soon he would delight his family by spectacular success.

"Truly I am going to surprise you very soon," he wrote to Jessie and Elizabeth. "This I tell you notwithstanding mama says 'Don't write anything but facts.' "[9]

The success remained a mirage, always just ahead. General Jesse M. Lee understood the matter when he wrote of Hall in after years:

"The qualities that fit a man for one career disqualify him for the other. Your father's ability to lead men, his disregard for danger and ability as a soldier did not go with the type that makes a financial success."[10]

In 1898, it seemed that the way was ready for the Ranger's return to his profession of fighting man—that he might command a regiment. A colonel's pay would keep the family together and with himself as its head.[11] War would bring tempo-

---

[7] Frederic Remington, "How the Law Got into the Chaparral," *Harper's New Monthly magazine,* December, 1896.

[8] Conversation repeated to me by Mrs. Isham Keith.

[9] Letter from Captain Hall, dated Denver, Colorado, January 11, 1898.

[10] This opinion General Lee expressed to Mrs. Keith at the time of Captain Hall's death.

[11] General King, Adjutant under the administration of Governor Ross, praised Captain Hall as "brave to the point of splendid daring." This was quoted in the *Galveston Tribune,* which suggested that the Captain be given command of a cavalry regiment for service in the Spanish American War. From an undated newspaper clipping in the collection of Mrs. Isham Keith.

rary separation, but chance for valor and promotion as well. His wife's consent would have to be won. Surely, Bessie would not always disapprove of a military career. His thoughts leaped forward to contingencies that might develop on the outbreak of a war.

For some years, its approach had been prepared. Lacking appreciation of the great debt the southwest owes to the rich culture of old Spain, the American public felt antagonism towards a country that they regarded as cruel, decadent, and, because of the possession of desirable islands, highly interesting. Our own country was rich. It had expanded from ocean to ocean. To the north, was peaceful Canada, daughter nation of old England, to the south, Mexico, much of whose territory had passed into our own possession. Under Diaz, it was strongly ruled and friendly to the advance of American capital—best left alone![12] And yet, a habit of expansion, possession of energy and rich resources pointed the way to new frontiers.

To citizens imperially minded, it seemed the manifest destiny of our country to serve humanity—and serve it with an economic profit—by redressing the wrongs of little Cuba. The island was in a state of insurrection against Spain. Early efforts to assist her were pacific. By sending the battleship *Maine* to Havana, the threat of force was added. The sinking of the *Maine* and the loss of 266 American lives made the nation clamorous for war. The correspondence of the Queen Regent and our Minister Woodford, withheld till long afterwards, shows that the Spaniards were not unreasonable toward our demands. At the last, they yielded the essence of almost all of them.[13]

In March, the committee investigating the destruction of the *Maine* reported that the explosion had occurred on the outside of the vessel. The Washington correspondent of the *Dallas News* was Colonel Bill Sterrett. He wired the Texas paper that war was inevitable. He found it nauseating "that Senators and

---

[12] J. Fred Rippy, "Some Precedents of the Pershing Expedition into Mexico," *Southwestern Historical Quarterly*, XXIV, (April, 1921), 292-316. Mr. Rippy cites the agreements made in the nineties between the two countries.

[13] Bertram D. Hulen, "When the Dogs of War Bayed at McKinley," *New York Times*, September 13, 1936.

members of Congress have been brought to this pass by pushing yellow journals."[14] In April, 1898, the Pope attempted to prevent the catastrophe of war. McKinley, exalted instrument of Providence, friend of Mark Hanna's, felt that he could do no more than assure the Vatican that he was extremely sensible of these pacific efforts.[15] Again, war was to be used to gain the objectives of peace and justice. Again, it was to end by gaining doubtful advantages of a character less abstract.

The stars and stripes flew from the staid cover of the *Atlantic Monthly*. Carl Schurz declared our actions the result of an untainted altruism.[16] The young Assistant Secretary of the Navy, Theodore Roosevelt, rejoiced that we were about to fulfill our duty of saving Cuba and driving Spain "from the Western world;"[17] many ministers and priests preached from their pulpits the beneficence of war. Most eloquent of these in Texas was Father Kirwin of Galveston, hero of the yellow fever epidemic of 1898 and rector of St. Mary's Cathedral. He eloquently exhorted American citizens to do their duty: his priestly calling and his God stood for peace, he said, but the time had come when to cry peace meant treason. He acclaimed it "a sweet and joyful thing to die for one's country."[18]

By the end of April, 1898, every youth had left the Cathedral School in Galveston and six hundred men were bivouacked in Cathedral Hall. They feared their services might not be accepted, for already the Texas quota of 4,000 troops had been filled.[19]

[14] Sam Acheson, *35,000 Days in Texas* (New York, Macmillan Co., 1938), 190.

[15] A dispatch from Rome announcing the failure was printed in *The Galveston Daily News*, April 19, 1898.

[16] Walter Millis, *The Martial Spirit*, 160.

[17] Theodore Roosevelt, "The Rough Riders," *Scribner's Magazine*, September, 1899.

[18] This address is included in the memorial volume of Father Kirwin, Father D. P. O'Connell, *Memoirs of Monsignor J. M. Kirwin* (Houston, Standard Printing & Lithographing, 1928).

[19] For the above and information as to the mustering of the Galveston regiment, I am indebted to Brother C. Raymond of the Kirwin High School, Galveston, Texas. It was due to the kindness of Father Kirwin's friend, Rabbi Henry Cohen, of the same city, that my requests for information reached Brother Raymond. Brother Raymond's information is based on a study of parish records and of files of the *Galveston Daily News*.

It was Lee Hall's idea to organize a unit so unique as to insure acceptance. He conferred in Austin with Governor Culbertson and Adjutant General Mabry. The press made the bad guess that the former Ranger expected trouble with Mexico, and asked command of a force for policing the border.[20] The Governor's telegram to Secretary of War Alger revealed a more important purpose: Captain Hall wanted to raise a battalion of scouts for service in Cuba, men of proven bravery, men who could speak Spanish; who could ride and who were acclimated and would be immune to yellow fever; men, in short, who could be sent immediately into action. The Governor commended Captain Hall as one whose services would be outstanding.[21] According to a newspaper account of subsequent date, it was Hall's idea to organize and command a regiment of not less than five hundred picked Americans and Mexicans, who were inured to frontier hardships and of proven skill in trailing, to be sent immediately to Cuba.[22]

The project was not received with enthusiasm in Washington. Colonel Bill Sterrett telegraphed that Hall had no chance to get an independent company. He could, asserted Sterrett, "muster his battalion into Ted Roosevelt's command," since this was to be brought to full strength in San Antonio. Sterrett had talked with Roosevelt and believed his regiment would make its mark. Cowboys and dudes were to be on equal footing. Any one who deserved promotion would get it, whether he had a million or never a dollar in his life. "It will be the very place for Hall and his men."[23]

It seemed that it might be the only one. When Congressman Slayden of the San Antonio district urged on the War Department the qualifications of Captain Hall, J. S. McNeill, and Cap-

---

[20] Dispatch of April 22, 1898, quoted in undated newspaper clipping in the collection of Mrs. Isham Keith; Houston dispatch of April 24, 1898, in undated newspaper clipping in same collection.

[21] Governor C. A. Culbertson to Secretary of War Alger, telegram dated Austin, Texas, April 22, 1898. A duplicate, sent Captain Hall by the Governor, is now owned by Mrs. Keith.

[22] Austin dispatch of April 25, 1898, quoted in undated newspaper clipping in Mrs. Keith's collection.

[23] Colonel W. G. Sterrett's Washington dispatch, quoted in undated newspaper clipping in Mrs. Keith's collection.

tain McKenzie, his claims were coldly received. Again it was Assistant Secretary Roosevelt, newly commissioned as a lieutenant colonel, who was encouraging. He declared that he knew by reputation the gentlemen on whose behalf the Congressman was working, and assured him that he would be happy to honor them in his own regiment. Mr. Slayden's opinion was that Roosevelt would be "not unhappy if some of the Northwest captains failed to respond to roll call at San Antonio and their places could be filled by Hall, McNeill and McKenzie."[24]

Colonel Leonard Wood, in command of the regiment, already was in San Antonio. He had selected the City not for its traditions, but because of its proximity to Fort Sam Houston, where was located certain equipment that he coveted. Organization was going forward rapidly, and, as Roosevelt's Rough Riders, the Regiment was becoming the favorite of the public.

Forthwith, Lee Hall went to San Antonio to present his plan to Colonel Wood. He found him encamped at the State Fair Grounds, a place well situated for the Regiment's maneuvers. Colonel Wood was very busy, punctiliously courteous and noncommittal. The matter could not be decided until the arrival of Lieutenant Colonel Roosevelt. Having waited in Austin several weeks for a reply from Washington, Hall waited in San Antonio a few days more.[25]

He found out what he could about the Regiment in which, with his men, he hoped to enlist. The Rough Riders were a motley aggregation and, for fighting purposes, a good one. Recruited, for the most part, from New Mexico, Oklahoma, Arizona, and Indian Territory, it had a sprinkling, as well, of star athletes from eastern colleges, and former Rangers and cowboys from Texas. Mining prospectors, hunters and policemen mingled with the rest. Among the men was great diversity.[26] One thing was common to officers and men—a belief in the prin-

[24] Washington dispatch of May 6, 1898, quoted in undated newspaper clipping in Mrs. Keith's collection.
[25] Austin dispatch of May 12, 1898, in undated newspaper clipping in Mrs. Keith's collection.
[26] Theodore Roosevelt, *op. cit.;* see also *Selections from the Correspondence of Theodore Roosevelt and Henry Cabot Lodge* (New York, Scribner's, 1925), I, 298, 299, 302, 305.

ciples of the Republican party.[27] Due to the unexampled energy of Colonel Wood and the fervent determination of Theodore Roosevelt, the men already were partially equipped. Some were in denim and some in city duds, but most wore slouch hats, flannel shirts, and uniforms of khaki.

While San Antonio companies did not have enough guns to go around, the Rough Riders had both arms and ammunition. Townspeople, standing beneath hackberry and sycamore trees that fringed the fair grounds, watched their dusty drills. There was nothing tame about them. Horses were newly broken and men were somewhat like their mounts. The precision and monotonous perfection of drills at Fort Sam Houston were not duplicated. In target practice, the Rough Riders had many who surpassed the men at the Post. Their firearms were the "Krag" and pistols. A few kept their new model Winchesters, which took the government cartridges. It was camp gossip that John Jacob Astor would soon join the regiment and bring a battery of six Maxim guns. A newspaper followed this report with the statement that "Captain Lee Hall, probably the most noted and experienced frontiersman of Texas," had offered to organize a squadron of Texas Rangers and frontiersmen and have them ready in a few days to march with the regiment. And this is significant. Fine as the regiment was, Captain Hall was not willing simply to be absorbed in it. He wished to bring his own men and serve as part of it. Even this would be less than the plan set before the Governor.

On the night of May 15, the Rough Riders sang new songs, not of the cow camps, "Ta-ra-ra-Boom-de-ay," "After the Ball is Over," and "Hot Time in the Old Town." They practiced the regimental yell:

> *"Rough—tough, we're the stuff!*
> *We want to fight and we can't get enough."*

Also, they cleaned, and they polished, to get ready for inspection, for the Lieutenant Colonel would arrive next day. He was from New York, and this caused some to shake their heads. It was better to know that he was a hunter and had ranched in

---

[27] "One—possibly two—Democrats," Millis, *op. cit.*, 219.

the Dakotas. He came, and at first the westerners were disappointed. No man who rode should wear glasses like a store clerk. All day long the officers from Fort Sam Houston and the good—and lonesome—Republicans of San Antonio kept him busy with their visits. Lee Hall, who fell in neither category, managed, nevertheless, to gain a conference.

Its result was not satisfactory. The former Ranger was always reticent about the matter.[28] One objection to Hall's plan of recruiting a battalion was immediately obvious to the Lieutenant Colonel. Roosevelt, earlier, had been refused permission to accept any of the companies offered by individual states. Only from the four territories could he take organized units. Twelve hundred men had been mustered in, and he had turned away as many more. For the rest, Hall's name had been much in the press, he was older than the Lieutenant Colonel and might prove difficult as a subordinate. Both men were strongly individual, though in temperament they differed greatly. Roosevelt had a vigorous and dental smile. His excess energy resulted in gestures and tones that, to quiet men, suggested the "r'arin', flarin', bucko, Dobie Bill." Hall may have shown irritation. He may not have been sufficiently tactful and deferential. Then, too, the Ranger was a Democrat, and the Spanish American War was fought on strictly party lines. Certain it is that in the tent of Lieutenant Colonel Theodore Roosevelt, the former Ranger remained a "pilgrim and a stranger."

In clouds of dust and enveloped in prophecies of coming glory, the regiment broke camp. Men, horses, and enviable equipment were entrained for Tampa. Lee Hall was not among the officers.

[28] This was told me by Mrs. Isham Keith. There is no record of what occurred during the interview.

XX
Captain of Immunes
(May, 1898-October 28, 1898)

"Come along and get your musket
For there's going to be a fight
Uncle Sam has pressed the button
And we think he's in the right.
"Well, well, well
We'll give the Spaniards hell
Well, well, well
We'll give 'em shot and shell.
When they try to break that Texas wall,
There'll be a hot time in the old town tonight,
My baby!"

—Campaign Song of '98.

In May, 1898, a modest advertisement in San Antonio papers, invited men between the ages of eighteen and fifty to join Captain Lee Hall's Company of First U.S. Volunteers. In fact, the Captain had secured authority to raise two companies to be mustered into the "Immune" regiment of infantry being organized in Galveston. One of the companies would be captained by the former Ranger, the other distributed throughout the regiment. Hall explained that the army was top-heavy with cavalry and that, for investing and capturing towns on the coast of Cuba, foot-soldiers were needed. Much as Texans disliked walking, he assured them that this was a war they could enter only on foot. As consolation, he promised that in thirty days they would be at the front,—perhaps would be within a captured city.

Immunes, he stated in an interview, were those who were born or had lived for a length of time in a section of country subject to yellow fever. His hope was to enlist many Spanish and English speaking Mexican-Americans, men who made magnificent soldiers, obeyed orders, and were always ready for duty.[1] The roster of his Company shows that he had no success in enlisting Mexican-Americans. Otherwise, it reflects the cosmopolitan character of San Antonio. The names are English, Jewish, Irish, German and French. Though many Rangers had enlisted in the Rough Riders and the other cowboy regiment, a number, who were valorously willing to walk, enlisted with the Immunes. Of these, Netteville Devine, first lieutenant, and Ben

---

[1] Captain Hall quoted in two undated newspaper clippings in Mrs. Isham Keith's collection.

Riely, second, had served under Hall before. Tom Little, Jr., another of his recruits, had fought in the Sudan with the British and been decorated for bravery.

Of the six hundred already enrolled in Galveston, some had left their business or professions, some were fresh from school, and some were without means of support. Food and shelter were given them, and to their families when they had them, until organization could be formally achieved. Since Texas had filled her quota, the Governor was forced to deny the Galveston regiment recognition. The men elected to stay on in the hope they would be needed. Quartered in Cathedral Hall, they drilled each night, studied their manuals, and got themselves in readiness. As colonel, they elected Charles S. Riché, graduate of West Point and member of an engineering corps stationed for some time in Galveston. Because he had recruited six companies from his former parish students of St. Mary's, because he was stout-hearted, jovial, a leader of men, the regiment chose Father Kirwin for its chaplain.[2]

The recruits were ignorant of the fact that the War Department intended to send the Immunes over only after Santiago had fallen. When National guardsmen had had the glory and peril of the capture, they would need to be relieved. The rainy season—and yellow fever—would last until October. Immunes, acclimated troops, would be useful.

Sherman, Alvin, Houston and El Paso added companies to Riché's Regiment. The last of May at San Antonio, Company M, Lee Hall's Company, marched to the depot of the Southern Pacific to entrain for Galveston. There were sixty-five men, instead of the two hundred Hall had hoped for.[3] Many of those who might have followed him had gone with the Rough Riders. The soldiers were in hilarious good humor. Ten or fifteen others, infected by their enthusiasm, enlisted at the last moment. Hall

[2] Brother Raymond's collection of extracts from *The Galveston Daily News* and *Galveston Tribune.*

A communication to Adjutant General Shafter from Adjutant General Corbin, Washington, D. C., July 13, 1898:

"Two immune regiments have been ordered to report to you for garrison duty after the reduction of Santiago." Adjutant General's office, *Correspondence Relating to the War with Spain,* I, 138.

[3] Newspaper clipping dated May 31, 1898, in Mrs. Isham Keith's collection.

put Devine in command and stayed behind, hoping for more. The *San Antonio Light* prophesied that the Company would "do some fine work in executing Spaniards."

It was routed to Houston, then brought to Galveston over the Santa Fé. The Regiment that had been waiting completion found the San Antonio troops inspiriting. As the Company marched to Hawley's Barracks, the men gave the Company yell:

> *"Lee Hall, Lee Hall, sis - boom - ah!*
> *Give us a chance to get to Cuba, ha!*
> *We drink, we yell,*
> *But we fight like—Lee Hall, Lee Hall,*
> *Ha, ha, ha!"*[4]

On a Saturday their Captain joined them at Camp Hawley. It was located a few hundred yards from the beach, and cooled by breezes from the radiant Gulf. Its sandy soil, planted in grass, was easily drained.[5] The men went swimming daily. Those who had leaves and carfare rode in three miles to Galveston, where there were such things as comfort soldier and sailor men, plus less necessary, but decorative, orange trees, magnolias, cape jessamine and oleanders, laden with blossoms, pink and white. Mosquitoes and the glare of the sun prevented conditions from being too idyllic, but of the 10,000 Texans who enlisted, probably, none were more favorably located during the training period than were these.

Early in June, the officers came up for medical inspection. Lee Hall and one other failed to pass.[6] The cause for Captain Hall's rejection was a hernia affliction which was found to have existed since 1872. In Palo Pinto County, he had swung himself upon a horse to follow an Indian trail. The horse had bucked, Hall had stayed on, and, there being need for it, had ridden without rest for a hundred miles. The men of Company M, when they heard he would have to stay behind, could not believe it. During the illness of Major Rogers, he had served as

---

[4] Undated newspaper clipping in same collection.
[5] Letter from Lieutenant Netteville Devine, quoted in undated newspaper clipping, Mrs. Isham Keith's collection.
[6] *Galveston Daily News*, June 9, 1898.

Acting Major and the men of the battalion had found him no weakling.[7] Sergeant Bracken, who had been with him at the Indian Agency and as a strike breaker in Yoakum, had many stories to tell of Hall's prowess and endurance. The records of his Ranger service were still remembered. He called his troops his "boys," as he had his Rangers. He was "Lee" to them, when not on duty. Officers and privates and the citizens of Galveston petitioned that the two officers, rejected by the doctors, be commissioned. At the end of the month, the petition was granted.

There was no further cause for excitement until July, when the regimental flag was flown in celebration of the Colonel's wedding. The bride was a young beauty whose picture had appeared in *Godey's Magazine*. Lee Hall had introduced her to his Colonel when she visited the camp with relatives from Denison. The romance was hastened by orders for departure.[8]

In hourly expectation of the surrender of Santiago, Adjutant General Corbin, on July 13, sent an order that the regiment sail for Cuba and report to General Shafter.[9] This, like many such embarkation orders, was canceled. On July 22, the regiment was directed to entrain for New Orleans. Officers expected that from there, in a few days, it would embark for Cuba. At the last minute, fifteen men, who had expected to form part of Colonel Swain's Louisiana regiment, joined Captain Hall's Company in impatience to be sent into action.[10]

Cuba, Puerto Rico, Hawaii, the Philippines! The correspondence of Henry Cabot Lodge and Roosevelt shows that the administration was "grasping the whole policy at last"—avid for territory that could not be gained and held without the use of many regiments.

On July 23, 1898, the Regiment arrived in Algiers across the Mississippi from New Orleans. It was a Saturday. Many of the troops that night crossed on the railroad ferry to see the sights.[11]

[7] Account of her father written for Mrs. Isham Keith by Mr. Netteville Devine, November, 1928.
[8] The bride was Miss Susan Horton Gadberry, according to an undated newspaper clipping in Mrs. Isham Keith's collection.
[9] Adjutant General's Office, *Correspondence Relating to the War with Spain*, I, 138.
[10] Undated newspaper clipping in Mrs. Isham Keith's collection.
[11] "Riché's Regiment of Immunes," *New Orleans Daily Picayune*, July 24,

New Orleans was not squeamish about informing men of what she had to offer. There were certain districts as proud of their women of ill-repute as Austin had been of Ben Thompson, or Laredo, of King Fisher. The men wandered here and there, and encountered some Negro officers, who demanded a salute. They got it, but not the kind they had expected.[12] When the men of the First returned to Algiers, they laughed over this, and they told tales of a section known as Storyville, titillating bed-time stories, not for the young. And Monday would be pay day.

Sunday was quiet. Father Kirwin preached, reminded the Regiment of the humanitarian character of their Cuban mission, spoke of dangers they would encounter, of the need for each to make his spiritual peace. The Chaplain's athletic build, out-thrust jaw, full lower lip, the hearty tones of his rich Irish voice, showed him to be a fighting man himself. The men surmised that he had his score of personal demons, but kept them well in hand. The soldiers wrote letters to wives, sweethearts, sisters. Captain Hall wrote, too, addressing his letter to Lebanon, and then he telegraphed that he expected to leave "tomorrow evening or Tuesday," adding "Goodbye."[13]

The hours went slowly, more slowly for the Captain than his Company. Would she come? Would she not come? For two years he had not seen his wife.

That night again, men ferried to New Orleans. Perhaps some of the troops bought the *Sunday Sun* and the *Mascot,* lascivious chronicles of scandal; perhaps they scanned the advertisements of *The Blue Book.*[14] It was long since pay day, and even for those of evil inclinations, the Sunday visit could have allowed little more than reconnoitering.

1898. I am deeply grateful to the late Miss Jean Myers of New Orleans, an alumna of Sweet Briar College, for having examined for me the files of the *Picayune* and *Times Democrat.* She supplied the dates for clippings from these papers in Mrs. Keith's collection, and copied and summarized articles having to do with the Immunes.

12 *New Orleans Daily Picayune,* July 25, 1898; *New Orleans Evening Item,* July 25, 1898. A white private struck the Negro lieutenant across the face with a revolver.

13 Telegram in Mrs. Isham Keith's collection.

14 For reference to the part of New Orleans that seems chiefly to have interested the Immunes, see Herbert Asbury, *The French Quarter* (New York, Knopf, 1936).

On Monday, Captain Hall was happy. His wife had come. She had started as soon as possible after receiving the laconic telegram, and the Captain knew that, in spite of the long absence, she truly loved him. He introduced her proudly to his Company. It was a time when the interest of the men could not be held by the wives of their officers.

The Immunes were wondering, some of them, whether they could win the money offered the first one who could thaw the notorious "Josephine Icebox." They were thinking of the not-so-blue women whose ample pulchritude was pictured in the *Blue Book*. And the pockets of the men had an unaccustomed weight of coins that jingled pleasant promises. For pay had been distributed—ten thousand dollars. Orders were that at ten that morning they were to board the *Berlin*. The transport was scheduled to sail at two, to leave New Orleans with its forbidden and so luscious fruits untasted!

The men marched to the wharf and saw the great steel hulk of the transport anchored off Slaughter Point. They discovered that Colonel Hood's Regiment had preceded them. The transport was already crowded. From its hold, came a stench that boded ill for those who would be quartered there. Hammocks to serve as bunks had not arrived. The surgeon of the Regiment examined the water supply and insisted that pure water be supplied.

Colonel Riché was absent. It was reported that at this critical time he had been called before the examining board for promotion; the Quartermaster had been relieved from duty, due to the sudden illness of his wife; Major Levy was hampered in giving orders because he had been insufficiently informed of the plans of his superior.[15] The officer who boarded the vessel to inspect her reported the transport over-crowded and advised that Riché's men be disembarked. Lieutenant Riely remembered that, against Lee Hall's judgment, Colonel Riché had failed to assist this inspector's son to be appointed to a commission in the First U.S.V.I. The Lieutenant suspected that the decision as to the transport was a nice retaliation.[16]

[15] *New Orleans Daily Picayune*, July 26, 27, 1898. *The Times Democrat* of July 27, 1898, carried an editorial on the overcrowding of the *Berlin*.

The men, slowly being embarked, were restless. A double sentry line was stationed to keep them on the ship. Quietly, the Texans broke through. When orders were given to sail at midnight, many were not present to hear them. Before that hour, a cable from Secretary of War Alger advised Major General Shafter at Santiago that the *Berlin* was under way with two regiments of the Immunes aboard. The Secretary of War was mistaken. Fourteen hundred hammocks for two thousand men arrived on an afternoon train and were hung in sleeping quarters on the transport. A generous woman of the city supplied the ship with fresh water. Most of Colonel Hood's Regiment embarked, Major Levy's Third Battalion was aboard. The roll was called and three hundred men of the Immunes "turned up missing"—two-thirds were Texans.[17]

Captain Lee Hall was detailed as Provost Marshal late that afternoon to get the men aboard. The Sunday papers had devoted much space to recounting his Ranger exploits.[18] None in the past equaled the present round-up. He sent patrols throughout the city, and personally searched wherever he was able. The missing three hundred were simultaneously exhibiting to New Orleans all possible types of inebriation. Some men lay prone on the window sills of the Pickwick Club; most of them found that the French Quarter could furnish all their needs. From notorious parlors and "boudoirs," hideouts with extravagant furnishings and bulbous chandeliers, from door-steps and beneath lamp-posts, from the colonnade of the Arlington Annex, from beer-dripping tables, and from under them, from all the haunts of Customhouse, Villere and Marais Streets, the Marshal and his men retrieved the missing men. They hauled and pulled and carried them to waiting patrols, speeded them down the levee to the wharf, tossed them, howling and struggling or heavily quiescent, into the busy tug that plied between transport and river bank, and returned to the tenderloin to search for more. The language that Hall used brought some of

16 Conversation of Lieutenant Ben Riely with Mrs. Isham Keith, Charles Town, West Virginia, May, 1935.
17 *New Orleans Daily Picayune*, July 26, 27, 28, 1898; Also special dispatch from New Orleans, July 26, *The Galveston Daily News*, July 27, 1898.
18 Biographical sketch in *New Orleans Daily Picayune*, July 24, 1898.

[281]

the men, blinking, to consciousness. Reporters in attendance jotted down smoking words of brimstone. "Ladies of the Queer Zone" parted draperies of shaded windows to cheer the chase. When one group of the derelicts had been hustled into patrols, news would come of the superior antics of another. The Provost Marshal would rush off in pursuit. Theirs was a jag that was continuous, and the soldiers, with gusto and originality, saw to it that excitement did not stale. No one was thinking of deserting, but none of the three hundred meant to board a stinking transport and sail away to shoot Spaniards until he had shown what a hot time could be had in the old town of New Orleans.

They fell in with the "Razzy, Dazzy Spasm Band," and commandeered the boys' instruments. They crooned through gas pipes, fiddled on cigar boxes, beat kettles and rang cow-bells. They rattled gourds till the fillings of pebbles burst through and scattered on the sidewalk. With "hi-de-hi's" and "ho-de-ho's," they outshouted the bandmaster, and then tiring of outrage upon music, they flung money to the boy-band and went on to something else.

After Hall and his force had worked five hours, there were sixty men whose whereabouts were still unknown.[19] The *Berlin* was scheduled to sail at midnight. Overcrowding, the excitement of hooking soused soldiers back into the tug when they leaped or tumbled out, made the night memorable even for the well-behaved. It was too much for poor John Emmert, bridge builder of Sherman, who for several weeks had been unwell. He died on board in the early morning, of suffocation, it was reported. Except for seven cents, they found his pay still in his pockets.[20]

To the pleasure of his young bride, who was in the city, Colonel Riché determined not to sail without the full complement of his Regiment.[21] He dispatched a telegram to the War Department to register formal complaint as to the condition of the transport.[22] The *Berlin* was moved to the head of Mande-

---

[19] *Galveston Daily News*, July 27, 1898.
[20] *New Orleans Daily Picayune*, July 28, 1898.
[21] *Ibid.*, July 28, 1898.
[22] *Times Democrat*, July 28, 1898; *New Orleans Daily Picayune* of same date.

ville Street and the men of the First were disembarked. At two
on a hot July afternoon, they set off for camp, loaded down with
equipment. The day was sultry; as the troops marched down
Esplanade Street, kindly disposed citizens handed them buck-
ets of ice water. Men were overcome by heat and fell out of
line. Others dropped out to rejoin the missing sixty. Those who
trudged on for two hours reached the site of their camp at the
Fair Grounds. It was opposite that of the Negro regiment
whose officers, on Saturday, had demanded the deference of a
salute. The troops of the First began setting up shelter tents to
the accompaniment of a drenching rain. Guard mount was carried out in rain. Enough dry wood was got together to make
sputtering, protesting fires. The men brewed coffee. They had
not had a warm meal for days.[23]

Before night, dozens reported to the hospital. The cowboys
were not used to army shoes, they were not used to marching,
not used to ice water. For some of them, these novelties were
combined with the stale results of the Monday celebration. A
heavy guard was set about the camp. Again the men broke
through. They searched out the redoubtable sixty who had
eluded the efforts of the Provost Marshal. By midnight, they
deployed upon Canal Street. Two and three and four abreast,
arms linked, feet wavering, they marched and sang, lamented
the girls they'd left behind them, praised the perennial charms
of Adeline. Some were overcome by their emotions and frankly
wept. Some turned surly.

In the neighborhood of Customhouse and Burgundy, two privates started a fraternal quarrel. Others joined in and there was
a good, healthy rough and tumble. The police tried to take a
hand in it and the men forgot personal grievances and were
animated by an unexpected *esprit de corps*. The fracas turned
into a riot. One soldier mounted a chair, declared Wenger's
Theatre under martial law, and began appointing officers. Another, impatient of the punctilio of seniority, proclaimed himself a general. After that, there were no privates left—and no
civilians, for the soldiers began shooting out the lights, a signal
to the rest of the wanderers that a first-class scrap was under

---

[23] *Times Democrat*, July 27, 1898.

way. Those who heard came jubilantly and as rapidly as their uncertain legs would carry them. Reporters hurried off to get the thing in headlines: *"RICHÉ'S MEN TOOK IN THE TOWN."*[24]

As for Colonel Riché, he was spending the night with his bride at the Grunewald Hotel.[25] To the relief of the police, other of the Regiment's officers arrived to stop the proceedings. No more policemen's heads were broken by their own billies. Orders were given for arrest of stragglers.

The work of the searching squads continued. Police Chief Foster and his men assisted intermittently. When they met with a group of twenty or thirty on a street corner in Storyville and heard a Sergeant give the command, "Squad load!" the police remembered duties elsewhere.[26] Riché's men were too busy painting the town red—turkey red—to be particular about where the color splashed. They did not like the stylish helmets and neat uniforms of the police. They had observed them for four nights. The city didn't like the police of the Storyville section either. They were Boss Anderson's men, not guardians of the law for New Orleans. Quarters and dollars were left on dingy doorsteps by drabs who needed their protection. The *Evening Item* was served by some of Boss Anderson's reporters. They gave the soldiers a generous rubric of publicity. Obligingly they furnished to Galveston papers crimson news of the Regiment's activities.[27]

By two in the morning, the streets of New Orleans, if not innocuous, were normal. The *Picayune* recorded that Captain Hall had been too occupied with onerous duties to devote time to his wife, and added that Mrs. Hall was patriotic and philosophic.[28] She hoped, as did her husband, that the Regiment's reputation could be repaired.

The Captain of Company B, a former newspaperman, re-

---

[24] *New Orleans Daily Picayune*, July 28, 1898: "Riché's men took the town last night. They came in to take it, and take it they did, with the police force thrown in for *lagniappe*."

[25] *New Orleans Daily Picayune*, July 28, 1898.

[26] *Ibid.*, same date.

[27] *Ibid.*, same date; also the late John Bracken's conversation with author, Austin, Texas, August, 1935.

[28] *New Orleans Daily Picayune*, July 26, 1898.

minded a reporter from the *Picayune* that the conduct of Louisiana troops on pay day in Mobile had been as reprehensible,[29] although their misdemeanors had been less protracted. On Thursday the "round-up" still continued. Two squads of men with side arms worked throughout the day, and a special detail was sent out in the evening to deal with soldiers still inclined to break the peace. The Central Police Station returned the three it had held in custody and made a list of all reported in the French Quarter. With Major Levy presiding, a summary court began its sessions at the Fair Grounds.[30]

On Wednesday, July 27, the *Berlin* sailed with most of Colonel Hood's Regiment. In the Convent of the Ursalines, Father Kirwin preached a funeral sermon over poor John Emmert. The body was laid to rest at Camp Chalmette with military honors.[31] Those events are past history, not so the misdemeanors of the First U.S.V.I. To this day, they have so tinged, or tainted the remembrance of Immunes that no other regiment is thought of when the word, "Immunes," is used. Stories of the three hundred are told to cub reporters in Galveston and in New Orleans as part of the background every servant of the press should have. Those who can recount no single circumstance of those perfervid, moonlit July nights shake their heads at mention of the Immunes. Posterity accepts the verdict that the men were a "hard lot."[32]

A grace note, perhaps, may be added to the processional of history by recording the events of the days from late July of 1898 to the disbanding of the First Regiment, U.S.V.I. It was supposed that their stay at the Fair Grounds in New Orleans would be brief—that soon they would embark for Santiago.[33] The majority of the men had been drilling and waiting since April. After their first hectic nights in the city, they were more

29 The newspaperman was Captain F. J. Cook of Company B. *New Orleans Daily Picayune,* July 28, 1898.
30 *Ibid.,* same date.
31 *Ibid.,* same date.
32 "It was gossip at Galveston police headquarters when I was a reporter on the *News* there some twenty-eight years ago."—Meigs O. Frost to the author. letter dated *Times-Picayune,* New Orleans, May 17, 1937.
33 *New Orleans Daily Picayune,* July 28, 30, 1898.

than ever eager to get away.[34] The Regiment was angry at criticism printed in the *Evening Item,* eager to prove its heroism by action in Cuba.

At the Fair Grounds of New Orleans abundant, if unwanted, opportunity existed to display the milder virtue of fortitude. There was rain, and rain and rain for sixteen dreary days— mocking, frolicsome showers, and long, slanting, drenching slithers of the stuff that fell hard to the ground and plopped in puddles. Camp streets were churned to a morass by passing and repassing footsteps. Reporters for the *Picayune* and *Times Democrat* floundered through the mud and gratefully returning to their offices, recorded that the race-tracks where the First encamped were hog wallows. Shelter tents sagged and became sodden. At first in intervals of sunshine, men tried to dry their shoes and coats, to oil and polish guns, but efforts lessened as the rains increased. The troops became accustomed to heavy walking in wet shoes, to sleeping in clothes so damp that even August air was chilled. Drills were abandoned, for companies could not keep step on oozy, sliding ground.[35]

Much equipment had been lost in transit from Galveston to Algiers, from Algiers to the *Berlin* and from the *Berlin* to the Fair Grounds.[36] Many things, lamentably, the Regiment had lacked from the beginning. There were myriads of mosquitoes and no mosquito netting. Drainage was defective. Typhoid developed. Slight colds became deep seated. Men shivered as rain trickled down soaked collars to their skin. At night, they burned and tossed with fever. A barn was turned into a hospital. There were no cots for the sick, no hammocks. Their diet was hard tack, bacon, canned goods, coffee without milk—a diet enervating even to those who were well.[37] Officers, who had

[34] *Times Democrat,* August 4, 1898; *New Orleans Daily Picayune,* August 6, 1898.

[35] *New Orleans Daily Picayune,* August 4, 15, 1898. "The grass at their camp is several feet high and in the morning the dew makes the camp almost as wet as a river. ... Officers did not feel it their duty to buy scythes out of their own money," *ibid.,* July 28, 1898.

"One was compelled to step about as if he were walking on pins and needles, so uncertain were the moving propensities of the mud," *ibid.,* August 7, 1898.

[36] *Times Democrat,* July 30, 1898.

[37] *New Orleans Daily Picayune,* August 9, 11, 1898. Efficiency in administration did not parallel advance in medical science. In the Civil War, 66 6/10%

received no pay for weeks, drew from reserve funds or borrowed to supply camp needs. Each captain, the newspapers stated, contributed from five to seven hundred dollars, much of it for medicine.[38] Before the end of the fortnight, the sick list had lengthened to one hundred a day. The women of New Orleans organized a war relief association and gave the assistance which was lacking from a country ripe for overseas expansion.[39] Help came slowly and only after many stories had been published describing the hardships at Camp Houston. When the fog rose at night and settled higher than a man's head over the dreary place, lights struggled feebly, as though discouraged at revealing constant suffering. The camp seemed a shadowy outline of some land of torment.[40]

Often the men managed to extract laughter from mishaps, as on the day when the officers finally unpacked their long expected uniforms. They had paid for them and sent in measurements. When they tried to wear the suits, they encountered difficulties. Major Levy's trousers were so tight that they could be removed only with the aid of an orderly. Colonel Riché's were lavish of cloth above the knee and skimpy below. They ended above the shoe tops, discouraged by inadequacy.[41] Puddles widened into pools within the tents, and the men told stories of playful bull frogs and friendly spiders.[42] They boasted that they could fish in the privacy of their boudoirs. The middle barn was turned into a bathhouse. One private disregarded the order for bathing. A sergeant showered and scrubbed him in the presence of a gleeful company. "So uncertain were the moving propensities of the mud" that men slipped and went

---

of the deaths were from disease. In the Spanish American War, according to Secretary Alger's figures, 88 1/10% were from disease, *(Philadelphia Medical Journal,* October 15, 1898, in a collection of Spanish American War clippings compiled by George Kennan, now in the New York Public Library).

[38] *New Orleans Daily Picayune,* August 7, 1898.

[39] *Ibid.,* August 14, 1898.

[40] "Major Levy thought much of the sickness was due to the heavy mist or fog that rose about seven feet from the ground every night two hours after sunset." *Ibid.,* August 15, 1898.

[41] *Ibid.,* August 6, 1898.

[42] Major Levy told reporters that he had found in one of his pockets a spring frog, a cricket, and spider. *Ibid.,* August 15, 1898.

down to other baths that left them the color of the Negroes encamped across the way.[43]

Of the proximity of this neighbor regiment, the men of the First were steadily and grimly conscious. Its presence accounted for whatever breaches of discipline occurred after the early misbehavior of the Regiment.[44] Discipline was rigorous. Only five men from each company were allowed to leave camp each day. On pay day, the number was no more than doubled. Sentries were instructed to make sure orders were obeyed.[45] On July 27, one man was induced to stay in camp only after he had had two ribs broken by the sentry. On August 1, another, seeking to slip by through a heavy mist, was shot and killed on refusal to answer to a challenge.[46] The First was to prove its ability to obey commands. Every rumor of lack of discipline must be dispelled.

When General Shafter's discouraging report on sanitary conditions in Cuba was published, Colonel Riché telegraphed that officers and men asked that they be allowed to go "where they could render the greatest possible service to the army and their country."[47] Four days earlier, but after the much reported "spree," General Corbin had cabled Shafter to hurry the *Berlin* back to New Orleans for the Regiment.[48] This, the First did not know, so that when Corbin telegraphed his answer to Riché the men were jubilant at finding that the *Berlin* was en route, and that, on arrival, the Regiment was to embark without awaiting further orders.[49] They believed Corbin's statement that this was in appreciation of their "ready response for duty in Santiago." The fateful telegram was posted in front of headquarters.[50] Singly and in squads, the men tramped by to read it. They slapped each other on the back, jigged and went sprawl-

---

[43] *Ibid.*, August 7, 1898.

[44] Conversation of Lieutenant Riely with Mrs. Isham Keith, Charles Town, West Virginia, May 1, 1935.

[45] *New Orleans Daily Picayune*, July 30, 1898, and August 7, 1898.

[46] *Times Democrat*, August 1, 1898.

[47] *New Orleans Daily Picayune*, August 6, 1898, quoting telegram of August 4.

[48] Adjutant General Corbin to General Shafter, cable dated August 1, 1898, Washington, D. C., *Correspondence Relating to the War with Spain*, I.

[49] *Times Democrat*, August 6, 1898; *New Orleans Daily Picayune* of same date.

[50] *New Orleans Daily Picayune*, August 6, 1898.

ing. Some slushed away to think of this thing so long hoped for and so portentous. In the hospital barn, men with fever-bright eyes and dry, lack-lustre skin hoped desperately that they, too, could embark when sailing orders came.

Pay was distributed on August 6, and Lee Hall designedly was made Officer of the Day. Guard lines were tightly drawn and soldiers were exemplary in conduct. Each man had $15.60, minus fines checked against him by Major Levy's court. Every additional offense had doubled the original amount. A few of the Regiment were down to zero. The others went about getting change and paying off small debts. Some sent the remainder home to their families.[51] At night guards were trebled. The men with passes to the city gave police no trouble. Instead, they assisted in the arrests of such Negroes of Crane's Regiment as ran amuck.[52]

Only once did a sentry find it necessary to appeal to Hall as Officer of the Day. He reported that a man on horseback was riding at break-neck speed on the part of the race-track within the lines. When the rider came within hailing distance of one sentry, he would wheel and gallop through the fog towards the bewildered sentinel on the other side. Captain Hall stationed himself in the place of one of them, and suddenly out of the blackness saw a huge figure coming towards him at full tilt. Captain Hall jumped to one side.

"Halt! Who goes there?" he demanded.

"Begorra, and it's the Colonel himself, sor!"

"Guard, put that Colonel in the guard-house and lock up that horse!"

Lieutenant Colonel McCaleb, as a result of the arrest, was temporarily deprived of the services of his orderly, one Murphy.[53]

On Sunday, in an end of the barn that served as hospital, Father Kirwin celebrated mass. The few who attended knelt on bare boards to pray and listened to the Chaplain chide that money was the root of evil, and that if the men had not re-

---

[51] *Ibid.*, August 7, 1898.
[52] *Times Democrat*, August, 1898: "The police were powerless."
[53] Undated clipping from Mrs. Isham Keith's collection.

ceived their pay they would have all been present to make peace with God before the time for sailing to war against the Spaniards.[54]

Those who did not attend service wrote letters, tried to get their blankets dry, and read newspapers. Again the stories in the *Item* rankled. There was no Sabbath calm for the men of the First so long as these had circulation. The scurrilous papers were torn to bits. A group determined to settle the quarrel with the paper's staff. Lieutenant Colonel McCaleb called the Regiment together, and its two most popular officers, Major Levy and Captain Hall, talked to the men. The speakers made no attempt to palliate the offense of the newspaper, but emphasized the need for restraint. Marching orders might be to railroad trains instead of to a transport, if discipline was not maintained. Hall had discovered the plan for a visit to the paper's offices. He would go too.

"Boys, I'm going down there." He pulled his coat open and exposed two six-shooters. "I'll kill the first man that shows up."

Tacitly the men relinquished the idea of their expedition. It is claimed that the articles were written, or inspired, by Major Duncan B. Harrison of the Negro Regiment. He was a brawny officer who had once been a professional wrestler and promoter of prize fights. He detested the officers and men of the First Immunes severally and as a regiment. Captain Hall, having saved the soldiers from letting their wish for revenge get them into the guard-house, adopted their quarrel as his own. He strode across to the neighboring camp and, in the presence of Colonel Crane, called Major Harrison a liar, adding such epithets as seemed appropriate. The Colonel withdrew rather than reprimand Hall for the tongue-lashing that he must have considered was Harrison's desert.

"I can't listen to this," said the retreating Colonel.[55]

According to newspapers, Captain Hall wished to settle the matter with pistols at whatever time and distance the Major

[54] *New Orleans Daily Picayune,* August 7, 1898.

[55] This story has been pieced together from what was told to Mrs. Isham Keith by Lieutenant Riely and to the author by the late John Bracken.

might select[56]—a challenge not in accordance with the military code. The matter was allowed to drop. The Major's reportorial career ended. He might have fared worse.

On August 9, the *Berlin* was rumored to be nearing Port Eads. She had sailed from an infected port and would dock in quarantine.[57] Since a hundred of the First U.S.V.I. were on the sick list, thirty being in the hospital, the interval would give time for recovery or, more probably, for increase of malaria and typhoid. The camp grounds were so wet that men were permitted to sleep in the barns. Because they could not take mosquito bars inside, they preferred to bunk in mud. While still there were no milk and no cots in the improvised hospital, bugles arrived, a round dozen of them. The men caught frogs and crawfish and cooked them according to the recipe of a recruit from New Orleans.[58] And the rain continued.

Orders came to the Quartermaster to pack and store all equipment that would not be needed before the voyage, and the men set about their individual preparations.[59] Line officers drew for seniority, Captain Hall placing second.[60] Next day, August 10, he was ill and the newspapers, remarking on his hardiness, reported that this illness, more than anything else, was proof of the dreadful condition of the camp. Colonel Riché for some time had been unwell in New Orleans. Major Rogers had contracted typhoid.[61] Forty-two privates were in the hospital. Father Kirwin appealed through the newspapers for cots. Then the tide of public opinion changed. Before night, twenty-five cots were brought into the hospital, and the good ladies who sent them sent ice, soups, and milk as well.[62] Tributes to the discipline and fortitude of the Regiment had been appearing in the newspapers since the beginning of August, and now the reporters, it appeared, had won effective sympathy.

Saturday fell on the thirteenth, and the night threatened to

56 Newspaper clipping, *Statesman* [Austin], in possession of Mrs. Keith; judging from the context, the date is August 14 or 15, 1898.
57 *New Orleans Daily Picayune*, August 10, 1898.
58 *Ibid.*, August 10, 13, 1898.
59 *Ibid.*, August 15, 1898.
60 *Times Democrat*, August 11, 12, 1898.
61 *Statesman* [Austin], August 14 or 15, 1898.
62 *New Orleans Daily Picayune*, August 11, 13, 14, 1898.

be of ill omen. A private of the First was beaten up by some of Colonel Crane's men. At the corner of Franklin and Customhouse, a group from his company retaliated by attacking a Negro dance hall. A telephone call from the Chief of Police brought Major Levy to the scene in twenty minutes with thirty men and one hundred and fifty rounds of ammunition. Captain Hall was on sick leave. However, the news of Major Levy's approach was, alone, enough to restore order.[63] The men had learned that disobedience brought heavy penalties. It was the Negro regiment that the people of New Orleans, at this time, petitioned General Corbin to remove.[64]

Meantime the boilers and machinery of the *Berlin* were overhauled and coal was stoked into her bunkers. On August 15, marching orders reached Camp Houston. The Regiment was to traverse Esplanade Street in route step; two stops of ten minutes were to be allowed because of heavy equipment carried by the men. New belts, bayonet scabbards, canteens, iron pans and platters had arrived. The men very busily assembled their kits, cleaned and oiled their guns. And over all their varied activities, the sun was smiling.[65] After sixteen days of rain, its beams seemed to show that an errant God had come back to His Heaven.

Next day a change of orders came from Washington. The *Berlin* was to sail for Cuba, but the regiment to be embarked was the Negro regiment of Colonel Crane.[66]

The First U.S.V.I. was ordered to entrain for Galveston.[67] No reason was given and the men were bitter. Next day, Adjutant General Corbin was quoted as saying that Riché's men lacked discipline.[68] Citizens of New Orleans who had come to

---

[63] *Ibid.,* August 15, 1898.

[64] Lieutenant Riely's conversation with Mrs. Isham Keith cited *supra.*

A New Orleans paper of August 13, 1898, reported that no order had been received concerning the transportation of Colonel Crane's regiment of Negro troops, "but it is quite safe to say that the people of New Orleans will be heartily glad when the regiment leaves the city." (Mrs. Keith's collection of newspaper clippings).

[65] *New Orleans Daily Picayune,* August 15, 1898; *Times Democrat* of same date.

[66] *New Orleans Daily Picayune,* August 16, 1898.

[67] *Ibid.,* August 16, 1898.

[68] *Ibid.,* August 17, 1898.

know the Regiment suspected it to be more sinned against than sinning.[69]

Lee Hall obtained a leave of absence and at the time the men entrained was on his way to Washington to plead their cause.[70] Six hundred, a half of the Regiment, had organized for Cuban service as early as April. The months of waiting and training, as well as the government's expense, he hoped might still be justified by splendid service. The First U.S.V.I. had shown itself undisciplined when sorely tried. He wished, in Washington, to call attention to its later conduct. He found General Corbin determined to muster the Regiment out, and yet was cheered by a postponement until the President should return to Washington.[71] A dispatch from that city credited Hall with keeping the First in the service and stated that he had made a favorable impression "from General Corbin down."[72] Yet he succeeded in winning only a reprieve. One rumor, credited by Lieutenant Riely of Hall's Company, was that the First was the victim of the animosity of Secretary of War Alger for General Nelson A. Miles, Commander of the Army. Miles was considered partly responsible for the charge of cowardice against Alger in the Civil War. Miles wanted the First to sail, but when the people of New Orleans petitioned that the Negro regiment be removed, Alger had his opportunity, and by ordering the First to Galveston thwarted the wish of the Commander-in-Chief.[73] Until late October, the Regiment marked time in the city where it had been organized, then a Washington dispatch recorded that "Adjutant General Corbin overruled General Miles and forced Secretary Alger to refuse to revoke the mustering out of the

69 "Endurance was taxed beyond bounds and when paid off they sought their cheer. Since then, however, a more soldierly or better behaved regiment has not been in New Orleans. The police had not a single complaint to make Saturday night. The men assisted the police in rounding up and capturing the negro hoodlums and roust-about 'soldiers' that terrorized the back of town tenderloin Saturday night."—Undated newspaper clipping in Mrs. Isham Keith's collection. From the context the date must be about the middle of August, 1898.

70 *New Orleans Daily Picayune,* August 18, 1898. The leave was for seven days, but in a special order Colonel Riché gave the Captain the privilege of requesting its extension for another seven days.

71 Telegram to Colonel Riché from Captain Hall, dated Washington, D. C., August 28, 1898.

72 *Houston Post,* August 30, 1898.

73 Lieutenant Riely's conversation with Mrs. Isham Keith, cited *supra.*

First Immunes." Thereby, the dispatch continued, Major Wild-er, of the Second Regiment of North Carolina Volunteers, would be deprived of his promotion to colonelcy of the First. As a result, there was criticism, amounting to abuse, of Corbin.[74]

'Twixt this and that, the search for truth is difficult. However, one thing is apparent. The reason that the First U.S.V.I. did not cross to Cuba and returned instead to Galveston with an impedimenta of typhoid and malaria was not primarily due to wild nights in New Orleans. The order for the *Berlin* to return immediately for the First was sent to Shafter by Corbin on August 1, when the facts connected with the Regiment's misdeeds were known.

It had been the first of the Immunes to be mustered in. On October 28, it gained a second distinction. It became the first of the Immunes to be mustered out. The memory of its misdemeanors lingers. For the rest, like other victims of futility, its men are only footnote persons—pedestrians of history who humbly march into oblivion.

[74] Special dispatch to *The Observer*, dated Washington, D. C., October 11, 1898, newspaper clipping in Mrs. Isham Keith's collection.

XXI
In Pursuit of Aguinaldo
(July, 1899-December, 1899)

"Am I the boss, or am I a tool,
Am I the Governor-General or a hobo,
or a hobo;
Now I'd like to know who's the boss
of the show,
Is it I or Emilio Aguinaldo?"

—Army Song of the Philippines.

"There were gallant deeds done in the Philippines by
those Western fellows of the State regiments which volun-
teered for the war with Spain that would have made the
little fighting around Santiago look like thirty cents."

—James Henderson Blount, *The American*
Occupation of the Philippines.

In Pursuit of Aguinaldo

WHEN LEE HALL attempted to secure a second commission, he wasted no time in Texas, but exerted his efforts in Washington. There, with other impecunious would-be officers, he stayed in a boarding house where the southern landlady was lenient about her weekly bills. When he was not cooling his heels in ante-chambers, or conferring in corridors, he hung around the old Metropolitan Hotel. One of his younger cronies was William C. Harllee, later a colonel of the Marines. The two tried to reach the hotel early enough to get chairs on the sidewalk where the haughty room clerk could not worry them, and Hall could roll his cigarettes and talk in peace of Ranger days. Whenever either was in funds, the two would walk proudly past the clerk, stock up on Duke's tobacco and adjourn to the bar.[1]

A recent army bill had provided for mustering twenty-four regiments of volunteer infantry. One of these Captain Hall aspired to command. His strongest recommendation was a letter addressed to General Joseph A. Wheeler. Its statements were not routine. On its reverse side, the General added his endorsement, and thus strengthened, it reached the office of Adjutant General Corbin.[2] In July, 1899, the persistence of the former Ranger was rewarded by a commission as first lieutenant. It was only one grade above that of a stripling graduate of West

---

[1] Colonel William C. Harllee, Marine Corps, retired, has been so kind as to tell me of these difficult days; conversation in Washington, D. C., April, 1938. A Washington dispatch in the *New Orleans Daily Picayune*, March 8, 1899, stated there were 20,000 applications for the 101 appointments that could be made to the office of second lieutenant.

[2] Colonel A. M. Shannon to General Joseph Wheeler, letter dated Galveston, Texas, November 22, 1898, in the possession of Mrs. Isham Keith.

Point. None the less, it was something of an achievement to be assigned, even with lowered rank, to a picked regiment, the Thirty-third U.S.V.I.[3]

After farewell visits to his family, he returned to Texas, reported to the officer in charge at Galveston and asked for instructions and the necessary blanks for recruiting in nearby towns. He was turned over to Sergeant Rogers S. Clarke. The Sergeant found him far from an enthusiastic student. The old Ranger denounced the "whole rigmarole" as a "damned lot of poppycock." In a short time, he declared that he was sufficiently prepared and took along a clerk to look after the official end of the business. He wanted to be free himself to talk to the men. In San Antonio he completed the organization of Company L. Its one hundred and six men were geographically a cross section of the Regiment. Until August 25 they were stationed at Camp Allyn K. Capron, the new name for the fair-grounds where the Rough Riders had encamped.

Lee Hall was forty-nine—old for a first lieutenant, and regarded as a bad risk by the regimental surgeon. To obtain his commission, the Lieutenant had to sign away all pension rights. Press photographs of officers of the Thirty-third showed the former Ranger erect, thin rather than spare, and of commanding presence.[4] Age was apparent in his eyes, in finely spun, faint wrinkles on his weather-beaten face, and in deep ridges furrowing his neck. In his army record his hair is described as fair, for white had mingled with its warmer coloring. No one had been designated captain of his Company. The men of the Thirty-third accorded him the rank the government denied, calling him always "Captain."

When Rogers Clarke came in from Galveston and reported to the Orderly's tent, he found Lee Hall and the First Sergeant going over daily reports by lantern light. The tent was crowded and the atmosphere hectic. Hall was anything but happy in his work. His second lieutenant had not reported. He was not of

---

[3] At the request of Mr. Charles Moore, then chairman of the Commission of Fine Arts, and of the Hon. R. E. Thomason, M. C., summaries of Captain Hall's service records were sent to the author by Major General E. T. Conley. A more detailed statement of the record was sent to the author by Mrs. Isham Keith.

[4] *St. Louis Post Dispatch; San Francisco Chronicle*, September 21, 1899.

much assistance when he did report. Hall assigned Clarke the duty of maintaining order at the mess shack, and when he found that the noncom could control "the human wildcats" even at feeding time, he made him Quartermaster Sergeant. The former Ranger himself had few ideas as to discipline, knew nothing of the manual of arms nor of infantry drill. His First Sergeant had attended a southern military school, but was not capable of commanding a lot of untamed men, many of them veterans of the war in Cuba. Lee Hall followed the unmilitary dictates of common sense and turned Company L over to Sergeant Clarke to be drilled. The arrangement was thoroughly satisfactory to Clarke and to the men. One morning an officer whom Clarke did not recognize stopped the drill, inquired the name of the Company and the whereabouts of its officers. He proved to be the regimental commander, Colonel Luther R. Hare. He sent for Hall. Clarke says that he regretted having to stand out of earshot:

"If possible, Colonel Hare used more picturesque English than Captain Hall. It was a long time before I again drilled the Company."

When the Third Battalion was sent to Fort Clark in August for target practice, Second Lieutenant John W. Healey, a former regular, was assigned to Company L and did wonders as a drill-master. Hall remained indifferent to straight lines, right dress, present arms, and all the rest of it, but he was expert with rifle and revolver. The men brought satisfactory results from the range, and made him happy.[5]

When reveille sounded the morning of September 15, 1899, the Regiment broke camp. Blankets and wearing apparel were made into rolls, and haversacks stuffed with what remained. Already the tents had been shipped. The men entrained for the Presidio. Hall was in the battalion that was first to depart— that of Major John A. Logan. Hundreds were at the depot to wave good-byes. The Thirty-third looked warlike. Privates swung aboard carrying their rifles, their bodies strapped with

[5] Mr. Rogers Stanley Clarke to the author, letter dated Seattle, Washington, July 28, 1937. Mr. Clarke, Secretary of the Thirty-third U. S. V. I. Association, has given me the best material available on Captain Hall's service in Galveston, San Antonio and Fort Clark.

[299]

Mills belts, well filled with ammunition. Officers were equipped with swords and pistols. The crowd said that the Regiment resembled the Rough Riders.[6]

It was to render service equally distinguished, although less publicized. Its colonel, Luther R. Hare, had previously commanded the First Texas Volunteer Cavalry, one of the regiments not sent to Cuba. His valor already had been proved in the Western Campaign with Custer, when, fresh from West Point, he served as Lieutenant of the Seventh Cavalry. At the battle of Little Big Horn, he had been in charge of a party of Indian Scouts.[7] In the Thirty-third, also, there were Indians—excellent marksmen, hardy and sinewy.

Although it came to be known as the Texas Regiment, it was recruited from New Mexico, Arkansas, Arizona, Oklahoma, and Indian Territory. Some contingents were from Illinois, Indiana, Tennessee, Missouri, Louisiana, and Mississippi. There was one small group from New Jersey. Most of the men were accustomed to heat and privations.[8] They could ride and they could shoot. Colonel Hare boasted that more than half were able to kill a running deer at 125 yards with a revolver. Officers represented twenty-three states. Some were graduates of West Point and some, like Hall, had been trained only in the hard school of experience.

At a Texas station which the train passed at midnight, a crowd waited and clamored to see Red Hall and say good-bye.[9] The town had not forgotten his work there as a Ranger. California papers lavished praise on the Regiment while it was training at the Presidio. Subalterns found to their surprise that, of the officers selected for special mention, none was more often chosen than a lieutenant—Lee Hall.

[6] Undated clipping from San Antonio paper in Mrs. Isham Keith's collection.
[7] *San Francisco Chronicle*, September 21, 1899; unidentified magazine clipping enclosed in letter to author from the late John Bracken.
[8] Letter from Mr. R. S. Clarke cited *supra;* "Will Help Otis," *New York Herald*, September, 1899; *Munsey's Magazine*, January, 1900, quoted in *Jawbone*, June, 1937. *Jawbone* is the lively publication of the Thirty-third U. S. V. I. Association.
[9] Lieutenant A. E. Gebert to author, letter dated Chicago, June 29, 1937. Mr. Gebert was sergeant major of the Regiment and has written its history for *Jawbone*.

The *San Francisco Chronicle*, ignoring military precedence, told first of him, then paid respect to Colonel Hare.[10] The chief characteristic of the anecdotes related of the Ranger was emphasis on his ability to make arrests without the use of firearms. One story told of his going alone to the retreat of six train robbers, arresting them at the pistol's point, and marching them thirty miles to jail through a district eager for their rescue.

At target practice he showed good reason for the preference of his antagonists for peaceable arrest. It was recounted that Hall once used as his range two rows of figures, each the size and shape of a man. He galloped through the lane they formed, reins in teeth and a pistol in each hand. Only when the figures were shot in the heart region was a bull's eye claimed. The score was surprisingly high and the publicity it gained assisted Hall to increase his number of peaceable arrests. Helped by his training, his Company broke the record at the Presidio for marksmanship. This was fact. It could not compete with the deeds that imagination added to the very real prowess and daring of Lee Hall.

Also old records were refurbished. A syndicated article stated that in one year he and his men had captured seventy-six murderers and forty-five highway robbers—had made in all 479 arrests.[11] Such statistics were not supplied by Hall. Some were the contribution of one of his former Rangers, Napoleon Augustus Jennings. What Jennings wrote for the *New York Herald* was quoted as valuable for stimulating recruiting. Friends of Frederic Remington knew of the artist's project to illustrate an autobiography of the former Ranger. News of this reached the press. It was chronicled that *Harper's* was eager to sign a contract.[12]

Target practice, battle exercises with blank ammunition, and daily drills revealed that the Thirty-third was well prepared for action. The good ladies of San Francisco had only eleven days to tamper with the Regiment's digestion by sending cakes and

---

10 *San Francisco Chronicle*, September 21, 1899.
11 This article probably first appeared in a September issue of the *New York Herald*, 1899.
12 *San Francisco Chronicle*, September 21, 1899.

pies.[13] On September 30, the 1,200 embarked for Manila on the transport *Sheridan*. The days at sea were long, year-full of monotony for men of action. Lieutenant Hall continued in command of Company L until October 25, when, on a surgeon's certificate of disability, he was granted ten days leave. This was probably not because of illness, but that he might familiarize himself with certain conditions before being assigned the very special service for which he hoped. The day he was granted leave, Captain Edward Davis was transferred from Company E to take command of Company L. The ex-Ranger found him difficult as a superior. On one occasion the Captain, while taking his bath, sent for Lieutenant Hall and started to give orders. The Lieutenant, with a steely look in his blue eyes, contemplated the wet, recumbent, and somewhat adipose figure in the tub, then announced that he would withdraw and return for instructions later.[14]

On October 27 the *Sheridan* docked at Manila. For two days the Regiment contemplated from shipboard a low and beautiful skyline, and in the foreground, ugly hulks of sunken Spanish warships protruding above blue waters.

Lieutenant Hall was the subject of several telegrams before the Regiment disembarked. The first came from Colonel Clarence B. Edwards, acting assistant to Adjutant General Elwell Otis. It was an inquiry to General Lawton's headquarters as to whether Lee Hall should be sent to join Batson's Scouts or kept for service with scouts of the Thirty-third.[15] The answer came promptly: if Lee Hall was "anxious to come," General Lawton directed that "he be sent along for duty with Batson."[16]

Hall was "anxious."[17] On October 30 he received his orders. By command of Major General Lawton, he was to proceed, via

[13] General Frederick Funston, *Memories of Two Wars* (New York, Charles Scribner's Sons, 1911).

[14] This story was amusingly told me by Captain Carroll Power, Washington, D. C., then a lieutenant of the Thirty-third.

[15] Telegram sent to Colonel Starr, San Isidro, P. I., dated October 28, 1899, copy in collection of Mrs. Isham Keith.

[16] Lieutenant Colonel Starr to Colonel Edwards, October 28, 1899, source cited *supra*.

[17] Telegram to Colonel Edwards, October 29, 1899, source cited *supra*.

San Isidro, and report to the commanding officer of Batson's Macabebe Scouts.

The struggle he was to engage in was not against Spain, but against Spain's insurgent subjects. Between the spring of 1898 and the fall of 1899, Uncle Sam had executed a somewhat curious *volte face*. To Emilio Aguinaldo, President of the Republic of the Philippines, he seemed a malevolent weathercock who, after prophesying smiling weather, threatened storms, death, and destruction.[18] The demand for cession of the Philippines, made during negotiations for peace with Spain, confirmed the leader's fears. In a proclamation, published at the turn of the year, he reviewed his dealings with Admiral Dewey and American consuls at Singapore and Hong Kong, and accused them of breach of faith. In February, 1899, he began hostilities against the United States. The one hundred and fifteen pounds of Aguinaldo were one hundred and fifteen pounds of the dynamics of revolution.

War in the eastern islands was far more formidable than press accounts disclosed. A presidential election in the United States was in the offing. The censor's orders were to let nothing through that would injure the administration: the Filipinos must be described as always fleeing, as bandits, unkempt, cowardly ladrones, whose complete defeat would soon be chronicled. In July, 1899, newspaper correspondents, via letters to Hong Kong, got through a protest of the censorship.[19] Soothing statements from placid General Otis forthwith were questioned in the States. Indeed, plenty of fighting remained for the

18 J. T. McCutcheon records that after Aguinaldo came down from Hong Kong on the *McCulloch*, Admiral Dewey put him and his staff ashore and gave them guns and ammunition captured from the Spaniards. The insurgents organized an army that made rapid conquests. In early September, 1898, U. S. commanders reported from Manila that Filipinos were in control of all the island except Cavite. When the United States called halt, Aguinaldo became a formidable enemy, Millis, *Martial Spirit*, 181.

Phelps Whitmarsh in "The Men Behind the Plow," *Outlook*, December 15, 1900, claimed the United States needed to send over 100,000 men. See also *The American Occupation of the Philippines* by James H. Blount (New York, Putnam's, 1913).

19 This was published in U. S. newspapers July 17, 1899. Lieutenant Blount says that the newspapermen had an unsuccessful interview with General Otis. The censor said "My instructions are to let nothing go that can hurt the administration."

regiment in which Hall served. After a little guard and patrol duty at La Loma Cathedral in line of defense of Manila, the Regiment was ordered to join the expeditionary force of Brigadier General Lloyd Wheaton. The General was slender and quick and could make himself heard "above the roar of the stiffest fight." General Funston has described him as "the most striking individual and the most interesting character who served in our army in the Philippines."[20] With the Thirteenth Infantry, the Thirty-third embarked on the transports *Sheridan* and *Aztec* for the port of Dagupan on Lingayen Bay. Gatling guns, field guns, and a naval convoy indicated the importance of the expedition. Its object was to attack the Philippine army from the rear and prevent its retarding the main American advance in northern Luzon. Generals Wheaton and Lawton were to make simultaneous attacks in widely separated divisions; General MacArthur, with the cavalry, was to clear the territory between. A junction of the American forces at Dagupan was to be effected, and on the western coast, roads leading north were to be blocked. By the forces of General Lawton, Wheaton, and MacArthur, the enemy was to be prevented from defiling through the passes of the Carabello Mountains and making its escape.[21]

To volunteers from our Southwest, the plan seemed in the nature of a round-up, like those on the ranges of many counties in the spring. If it succeeded, guerilla tactics would be impossible. War would cease.

Above all realization of tactical objectives, the success depended on the scotching of the insurrection incarnate—of capturing or slaying Emilio Aguinaldo. For this, the main hope rested on the expedition of General S. B. M. Young, who on October 11 began a march that was to take him more than 300 miles.[22] The rigors of the chase increased the value set upon the prey. The diminutive rebel leader with the bristling pompadour

[20] Funston, *op. cit.*

[21] "To Dagupan with the Texas Rangers," *Colliers Weekly*, December 2, 1899; special to *Times*, Manila, November 5, 1899, *New York Times*, November 6, 1899; Adjutant General's Office, *Correspondence Relating to Affairs in the Philippine Islands*, November 6, 1899.

[22] James A. LeRoy, *Americans in the Philippines*, II, 122 ff.

was worshipped by his followers. Even his name had mystic power; they scribbled it on parchment and in battle held it beneath their tongues, and so believed themselves invincible. He was in command of excellent regiments and maintained headquarters at his capital, Tarlac.

During a torrential downpour, Hall reported for duty at San José, November 4, 1899. Batson's Scouts had been reconnoitering in advance of Young's men and south of Aliaga, going so rapidly that they captured ordnance and other property before it could be removed or destroyed, reporting steadily on the movements of the enemy. The scouts were in an ugly mood because two days before their officer, Lieutenant H. M. Boutelle, had been killed while fighting on the soggy Carmen trail south from Aliaga.[23] He had been the friend of Major Batson, and the sight of their leader's grief made them vindictive. Also, some of the insurgents had escaped punishment from General Young's men by pretending to be Batson's Scouts. The General ordered 450 campaign hats to be sent the battalion to avoid any further difficulties as to identity.

The loss of young Boutelle, the men thought, was not repaired by the appearance of Lee Hall. He was erect and alert, but he was elderly. It was the season of rains and monsoons. The scouts were wading in rice paddies, ploughing through swamps and the mud sloughs of river valleys, living on scant handfuls of rice and fish or fowl scooped up on plantain leaves. When they found that their new Lieutenant filled his canteen with *vino* and drank it neat, they changed their opinion and respected his endurance. For himself, he had heard much of the Macabebes and liked them at sight. Their appearance would have dismayed a West Point lieutenant. They were Malays, wiry and small, no higher than Hall's epaulets. They wore shirts and pants and by preference went barefoot. They used their own boats, rationed themselves, and secured their own rifles. For their services, they received one-half the pay of privates.[24]

23 General Otis's report, dated November 3, 1898, *Correspondence Relating to Officers in the Philippines*.
24 The Macabebes were paid from civil funds. The arrangement for this is recorded in General Otis's report of September 29, 1898, *Correspondence Relat-*

It was not this that urged them on to deeds of valor. Money was little valued by a people who went clothed only when they were soldiering and whose wants were few. The emotion that impelled them was hatred, intense and tribal, for the Tagalogs. According to legend, these had lured leaders of the Macabebes to a great feast. The feast had ended with their murder. The Tagalogs had taken the best of their land. On what remained the descendants of the slaughtered chiefs lived and nourished their hatred. As a secondary matter, they grew hemp, a little very choice tobacco, and much rice. Neither tribe asked quarter. After Aguinaldo's capture of Samal, his men had massacred one hundred and fifty of the Macabebes. General Lawton decided the little men could be used profitably as scouts. To organize and lead them, he selected Lieutenant Matthew Batson, who had handled natives admirably in Cuba. Batson formed the Macabebes into a battalion, became its Major and the idol of the tribe. Women helped him in recruiting, for they, too, hated Tagalogs, and he was able to make choice of the best —little men with feet almost as hard as the hooves of carabaos, keen eyes to pierce through cogon grass and bamboo thickets,

---

ing to Affairs in the Philippine Islands; Will Levington Comfort describes the Macabebes with more flavor than accuracy in his account, *Our Islands and Their People,* II, 617. Mr. Comfort's claim that the Macabebes wore long hair in braids to the waist is denied by United States troops who saw service in the Philippines. General Funston pays high tribute to the Macabebes in his volume, *Memories of Two Wars.* Colonel William O. Smith and Captain Carroll Power in conversation have given me valuable information on these scouts. This is supplemented by a letter from Mr. R. S. Clarke, dated August 8, 1937.

Inquiry of authorities at Washington revealed the belief that the records of the Macabebes Scouts prior to 1901, when they were taken into the United States Constabulary, were destroyed by the Insular Government. The military service of the tribe in 1899 is best described in the report of First Lieutenant Matthew A. Batson, Fourth U. S. Cavalry, *Annual Reports of War Department for Fiscal Year Ended June 30, 1900,* I, Part V, 123-37 (Washington, Government Printing Office, 1900). In subsequent references it will be called *Batson's Report.*

A picture of the Macabebes faces page 385 of the volume cited. They wear shirts, trousers, cartridge belts, and large hats. Two wear sandals. One wears gloves!

It is regrettable that though Batson mentions the regiments from which his other officers and noncoms are drawn, he omits to mention that of Lieutenant Jesse Lee Hall. Hall's initials are given as J. D. Hall, which accounts for the fact that in the index his exploits are wrongly listed under D. Hall, Second Lieutenant, Twenty-first Infantry. Fortunately, abundant source material exists to correct the error.

nostrils that could distinguish, amid the tropical odors of a heavy night, each alien scent.

Shortly after Hall was placed in command of the First Company of Macabebes, General Young gained permission to move independently. With five days' rations and preceded by the Macabebes, the General cut loose.[25] With him were two companies of the Third Cavalry including some men who lacked mounts. The blue fungus that in the morning appeared on shoe and saddle leather had little time for growing, since his troops turned night to day. Behind him tramped Ballance's battalion of the Twenty-second, footsore and uncomplaining. In Young's command, exclusive of the Macabebes, were less than a hundred men. As nearly as possible, he adopted the method of the enemy, leaving behind all transportation, marching swiftly and with light equipment. Ahead went the Macabebes under Major Batson, Lieutenants Hall, Quinlan, and Blount. At every village, the Americans were met with welcomes and assurances of friendship. Inquiries as to the whereabouts of Aguinaldo ended verbosity. There were blank looks and head shakings. The rain that dripped from palm leaf roofs of nipa huts, and the closed thatch-shuttered windows were not more enigmatic.

From the Macabebes, no questions came. They had another method of extracting information—a way that evoked a torrent of words, a confession, instead of ambiguous and halting answers. It was a practice that had existed on the Islands long before the insurrection. Americans called it the "water cure." Lee Hall thought its effects no worse than unwise consumption of native *vino*. The latter accomplished waste of man power, the former brought material results. For instance, a Macabebe sergeant sent to bring in rifles admitted that he got them by using a carabao horn as a funnel to connect throat and stomach of his victim with a constant stream of water. The Americans were engaged in war and, in this matter, let the nature of the Macabebes take its course. And yet, as must be Christian men who serve as warriors, the officers were inconsistent. General

25 "Leaving behind all transportation," General Otis's dispatch, received in Washington, November 13, 1899, *Correspondence Relating to Affairs in the Philippine Islands;* Colonel R. Howland, "The Philippine Insurrection of 1899," *Infantry Journal*, January-June, 1927.

Lawton ordered that the natives be treated considerately, since later "they would be our people." The Macabebes were contemptuous when the wounds of Tagalogs were dressed, and sullen when prisoners were paroled after no heavier punishment than the beating of rice.[26] Those scouts who were left behind, due to wounds or other disabilities, retaliated by brutal crimes. These were reported to Aguinaldo and stiffened his resistance.

While General Young and his men splashed in oozy mud and plunged into the tropic night of jungles, General Otis at headquarters read and dictated dispatches.

They were of different mettle—the two generals. The one superior in rank had eyes that were kindly and ineffectual; hair that strove to cover his head, and, too, was ineffectual; side whiskers, laxly recalling the hirsute embellishments of President Arthur. The other was pure fire, so that one noted his personality, his spirit, rather than the body that it animated. General Elwell Otis found the impetuosity of this cavalry officer perturbing. Young was out to catch Aguinaldo. Otis lacked confidence that he could do it and was parsimonious in his assistance—he sent horseshoes without nails, and sometimes cavalrymen without horses. Comfortably he dispatched his prediction: if Young did not catch Aguinaldo, "he would at least make him unhappy."

The complacence of General Otis, coupled with his lack of vigor, prompted officers and men to ridicule him in forbidden song. They pretended that he boasted after this fashion:

> *"The rebels up in Tarlac town*
> *Three men to every gun,*
> *I say the war is almost o'er*
> *They say it's just begun—*
> *Well I want to know who's boss of the show,*
> *Is it I or Emilio Aguinaldo?"*

General Young prevented the Filipinos from occupying San José, then scouted westward into Pangasinan to cut off a march

---

[26] Information as to the "Water Cure" and the quotation from General Lawton are derived from Captain Hall's testimony before the Senate Committee on the Philippines, *New York Times*, May 16, 1902; *Philadelphia Times*, May 16, 1902, quoting Washington dispatch of previous day.

by Aguinaldo up the course of the Agno. On November 10, and on the eleventh, Young tried to effect communication with General Wheaton on the Tayug Road, and occupied Asingan across the Agno.

Next day the Macabebes, pressing ahead to Humingan, were fired on by two hundred of the insurgents at about five hundred yards range. Lieutenant Quinlan was sent around the town to the right to prevent escape of the insurgents by way of the Tayug Road. Lee Hall was sent to the left to intersect the Rosales Road. Batson, with the other two companies, attacked the Tagalogs. They fled, leaving their breakfast behind them, and the Macabebes feasted on rice and roast hog. An hour later General Young and his cavalry passed through on their way to Tayug. That afternoon they captured it.[27]

On the night of the eighth, the insurgent leader, his cabinet, military staff and escort had abandoned Tarlac, their temporary capital, to escape the converging movements of the Americans. His army followed five days later. Batson and his scouts, with General Young and the cavalry, swam the swollen torrent of the Agno and occupied Asingan; the scouts pressed on alone to Urdaneta, where they engaged in a skirmish. Throughout the march, rain was continuous. Hats went first, then shoe leather rotted, and Americans as well as Macabebes were barefoot. In brambly undergrowth a trail of khaki cloth and flannel accounted for tattered coats and torn shirts. Any bamboo hut, built four feet above the sodden earth, with a bamboo ladder leading to its slanting door, appeared to the heavily marching men as an abode of paradise.

Lee Hall added to his knowledge of Texas northers the experience of a Philippine typhoon. Undeterred by weather, his Macabebes pushed on. A few days after leaving Asingan, General Young, following more slowly, reached Pozorrubio, where he conferred with General Lawton.

They had passed beyond telegraphic communication—a fact that caused more anxiety to headquarters than it did to them. Young was glad to hear of the success of Lawton's part of the "round-up." The northern advance had scattered the insurgent

27 *Batson's Report*, 135.

army, and Lawton was free to march south to attack the rebels near Manila. He counseled Young that since Otis disagreed as to the location of the rebel President, the only remedy would be to prove him wrong by bagging Aguinaldo. As they talked, the rains ceased, stars shone out and fireflies rose slowly upward from tall grass.

Next day General Young started north,[28] General MacArthur preceding him by a few hours. The fog lifted and vegetation steamed beneath a torrid sun. The Macabebes knew their prey was close, and panted on in hot pursuit. At San Rosario, their outpost captured Aguinaldo's official communications. The agile *Presidente* with four hundred soldiers had been in the town the day before. Thirty insurgents retreated toward Tulao and the Macabebes, fagged and footsore, followed by mountain trails. There they left a squad to care for weary stragglers who were being brought in by Lieutenant Bell and the rear guard. The main body reached the river Aringay at nightfall, November 19. Brush was burned at different points and revealed the enemy entrenched upon the other side. Batson, who could fire in the swing of his arm, ordered a part of his battalion to cover the crossing of the rest. In the darkness, the Macabebes were facing crack troops behind strong entrenchments—the rear guard of Emilio Aguinaldo. Lieutenant Hall led his men to the bank of the Aringay. They waded the river under fire of the enemy in front, and on the side from sharpshooters stationed in the hills on the left. Some Macabebes were carried off their feet by the strength of the current. One was killed. The rest followed Lee Hall in his attack on the Insurgents' trenches.

The impetus of the advance and the skill of Macabebe marksmanship demoralized the Filipinos. Hall and his men dislodged them and they fled toward the town of Aringay. Not until then did Batson collapse. At the beginning of the engagement, a spent bullet had shattered his left foot, breaking four bones and causing great pain and loss of blood. With Hall and his men in pursuit, the retreat of the Tagalogs became a rout.

[28] General S. B. M. Young's movements are described in LeRoy's *Americans in the Philippines*, II, 122-50. General Young's report is contained in *Annual Reports of the War Department for Fiscal Year Ended June 30, 1900*, I, Part IV, 262-288.

After the Macabebes captured the town of Aringay, some of the little men remained and "hustled for chow," for they had long been marching and fighting without food. Lieutenant Hall with twelve cavalrymen and twenty Macabebes pushed on and occupied Tulao. Ahead of Aringay, trenches had been constructed to defend the coastal road. In the black night they were not visible. Before sunrise the force that occupied them had escaped, and was fleeing towards the mountains. Others of the Insurgents were hiding in the jungle. Some were prisoners.

According to a dispatch of General Young's the order was given to Captain Hall at Tulao to return to Aringay and remain with the "overworked Macabebes," and troopers whose horses had gone lame[29]—sixty of the weariest men who ever played at fox and hounds with Aguinaldo. Next day Hall convoyed his charges to shelter at Asingan. It was safer. Insurgents had an unpleasant way with Macabebes whom they captured. They beat them over the head and body and burned on their wrists the mark of Aguinaldo's desperate followers, the Katapunan.[30] On November 20, the day that Hall safely delivered the spent and wounded men, the forces of Generals MacArthur and Wheaton occupied the Insurgents' deserted capital, Tarlac.

From Asingan, Hall and his men pushed on to Naguliang. There the Lieutenant received orders from Colonel Wilder, Batson's successor,[31] to march his company over mountain trails direct from Naguliang to San Fernando. General Young and a remnant of his men, thirty-seven troopers, arrived there at eleven the night of November 21, his cavalry crippled for want of shoes. Lieutenant Hall arrived after midnight. The Macabebes were disconsolate over the loss of Batson. Many were ill and all were footsore. Leeches on the trails had in-

[29] Dispatch to Major General Lawton, dated Aringay, November 19, 1899.

[30] The program of the Katapunan was death or expulsion of all Spaniards and members of religious orders, and confiscation and distribution of their estates to the people. A communistic republic was to be established.

[31] "Have placed Colonel Wilder in temporary command of Macabebe battalion," General Young to Major General Lawton, November 19, 1899, *Correspondence*, etc.; Colonel Theodore Schultz, *The Operations of the Thirty-third U.S.V.I. Association*, quoted in his letter to author, dated Phoebus, Virginia, June 8, 1937.

creased their suffering. Stone cuts had festered and remained unhealed in the tropical climate. That day Aguinaldo passed through a village only twenty miles away, Managpacan. Could they have known, the men would have followed on. They had pursued so long that they could almost see a flittering specter just ahead. Above them loomed Arayat, the giant mountain of Luzon. Below were rice paddies and trails soft as paste. A thick, wraith-like mist made the men seem like ghosts. Their stamina was real enough.

On November 23, Lieutenants Hall, Quinlan, and Blount, officers of the Macabebes, with General Young and the Third Cavalry reached Managpacan, but Aguinaldo was safely away, on a right turn that led to Bayombong across the mountains. In the village the *Presidente*, it was said, had talked defiantly: he would take refuge until messengers could rally his people to his support; the war would continue. To guard his trail, he left a picked force under young Gregorio del Pilar, his Secretary of War. In Washington, Senator Henry Cabot Lodge evoked laughter by describing the "honorable *Presidente*," as having retired to permanent headquarters in the mouutains with his "government concealed about his person."[32]

The men who trailed Aguinaldo were not able to regard the refugee as a subject for jest. On November 26, General Young arrived at Managpacan, was provisioned by a naval gunboat, and continued his march next day, reaching Kandon, there to hear again that Aguinaldo had preceded him. From thence, the General advanced into the mountains of Ilokos Sur. From November 29 to December 6, Headquarters had no news of him.

The complacency of the Commanding General was somewhat shaken. The force was a small one and operating with scant supplies in hostile territory. The hatred felt by Tagalogs for Young's scouts made perilous the position of the advance guard. Evidence of the crimes of those Macabebes who had been left behind was now incontrovertible. If Young's troops were defeated, they could expect no quarter, and such a defeat would be a bad end for a year preceding the election of a presi-

---

[32] Quoted by Blount, *op. cit.*

dent in the United States. Additional forces were hurried to Young's support.[33]

From the military standpoint, the General was not faring badly. He had captured Aguinaldo's official press, his personal baggage, and part of his escort. As he continued his march, he occupied the towns along the route, and from them provisioned his small force. He rescued Americans and Spaniards, long held prisoners. Early in December at Narvacan, he encountered a large force and drove it into the cañon of San Quintin. Nearby was Vigan, where on December 5 he halted his advance and established headquarters.[34] The city was the chief port on the coast of the China Sea, and was approached by land by the *Camino Real* that ran through fertile country. Here Young could block the route over which General Tinio wished to march to Aguinaldo's aid. The Insurgent leader was somewhere in the cloud-screened mountains that stretched afar to the great headland of Cape Bojeador. Forests extended to the mountain tops and deep ravines splashed heavy lines across their green.

The main body of Young's troops had traveled 308 miles since they began their march, October 11.[35] The Macabebes, since they scouted in many directions, had gone much farther. So thoroughly had the expedition reduced the northwest portion of the Island that it remained for years a model province, the First District of Northern Luzon.

It was fortunate the work was durable, since to the title gained by military conquest the United States added a second claim. At the price of $20,000,000, Spain agreed to cede the Philippines. The work of treaty drafting was begun while Young was still on his march.

On the day that the General established headquarters, Lieutenant Hall with his company was at Narvacan. Each of the little men and all their officers burned with the wish to bag the *Presidente*. None was more ardent in the quest than Lee Hall,

---

[33] Both General Wheaton and General Lawton came to General Young's support.

[34] Dispatch of General Otis, received in Washington, December 7, 1899, *Correspondence*, etc.

[35] General Otis's dispatches to Washington, November 20, 22, 24, 25, 27, and 29, 1899, *Correspondence*, etc.

the oldest trooper in the battalion. Whether he caught him or not, the Thirty-third was proud of the quiet work Lee Hall was doing. One of its officers, who had served as captain in the First Immunes, wrote back to Galveston that the men of the Regiment gloried in Hall's fighting record.[36] Their letters, as well as official dispatches, flashed his name into the headlines of Texas papers: "Lee Hall After Aguinaldo."[37]

If he could capture this elusive adversary, success would flood out in bright light the injustice of his trials as Indian Agent, the disappointment he had suffered when the First Immunes were shuttled back to Galveston and then demobilized. To soldiers in the Philippines and to civilians across the Pacific, Hall would again become a hero. Never again would he be identified as "the old Texas Ranger." He could afford to count his years, all of them, and sometimes he was very weary.

He needed a glory of light—sun, moon and stars of it, to vanquish the blackness of years of absence from his wife and children. Bessie had filled a scrap-book with clippings that told of his exploits. How happily her face would flush if she could read the headlines:

"Lee Hall Captures Aguinaldo!"

She would come back to him. She loved him. She must come.

Beneath his consciousness, there swirled such longings as made him seem impervious to sensory impressions. Up zig-zag trails that mounted dizzily to mountain tops, he climbed persistently, descending into gulches and ravines and clambering out again to mount steep bluffs that by their lordly heights inspired him with the promise of dominion, a vision of the China sea, a hint of space illimitable.

A time would come, his grandfather had prophesied, when Hall would fear high places. He did not fear them, but he knew their treachery, knew that the higher one climbed the more dangerous must be descent. He knew with what swiftness mountains could retract high promises and send a shower of

[36] Letter of E. P. Bujac to Major Ike Stafford of Houston. The letter is dated January 23, 1900, undated newspaper clipping in Mrs. Isham Keith's collection.

[37] *San Antonio Express*, December 8, 1899; *Austin Statesman*, quoting Washington dispatch, December 9, 1899.

puny stones to scold and rattle against a slipping, sliding man. They could be sombre, too, these mountain fastnesses. Sometimes he stumbled in soft earth—a grave new made for Tagalog, *Americano*, or Macabebe, to turn from dust to dust. Some warrior scout lay there, who after pride and daring was now a cadaver, meek and serene in his possession of six good feet of mother earth.

On the twelfth of December, Lee Hall scouted on Tilad Pass, where Major March ten days before, in command of a battalion of the Thirty-third, had defeated the rear guard of Aguinaldo. In the action, the gallant Filipino, Gregorio del Pilar, had lost his life. The cleft towered 4,500 feet above the waters of the China Sea. A dizzily winding trail, too steep for native ponies, led to stone barricades where the Insurgents had made their stand.[38] A man climbed by digging his heels into the treacherous mountainside, clutching at twigs, grasping at rocks and boulders, slipping back, then advancing. So Lee Hall climbed until he fell. It was night when a group of Macabebes carried him on a stretcher into Kandon. In the lantern light his face was drawn with pain. He was more seriously injured than he allowed others to know. He eased his feelings by sulphurous comments on having had to smoke white paper cigarettes. His former sergeant, Rogers Clarke "rustled" brown paper for him[39] and men of his Regiment gave him news of recent exploits of the Thirty-third.[40] Through will and pluck, he soon resumed his work. An order reached him to report on the night of December 19 to General Lawton. Lee Hall was confident that the command presaged a special commission.[41] He traveled

[38] Report of Major Peyton C. March, *Annual Reports of War Department for Fiscal Year Ended June 30, 1900.* Colonel Wilder with fifty-five Macabebes followed Major March's trail. They were with him at Cervantes, December 7, 1899; information concerning this came to the author also from Mr. Robert R. Montgomery, a veteran of the Thirty-third, in a letter dated Galveston, Texas, June 25, 1937.

[39] Letter to the author from Mr. R. S. Clarke, Seattle, Washington, July 28, 1937.

[40] The Regiment deservedly had won the name of "The Fighting Texans." Their bravery and marksmanship has been too often extolled to justify a digression here.

[41] This information came to me from Mrs. Isham Keith, who had it from her father.

to Manila, but was not destined to carry out the order. Twelve miles from there, on that very morning, while driving back the enemy at San Mateo, General Lawton had been instantly killed.[42]

Next day, Hall reported at the Reserve Hospital, Manila. As a result of the fall at Tilad Pass, the hernia from which he suffered had made further service temporarily impossible.[43] On cloud-shadowed, sun-checkered mountains, the round-up continued.

One top hand was absent.

[42] General Otis conveyed the news in a dispatch ending, "A great loss to us and to his country."
[43] The report as to the effect of the fall was signed by E. F. Robinson, surgeon at the Reserve Hospital, Manila.

XXII
"Lee Hall, Fighting Man"
(January, 1900-October, 1900)

"In that land of dopey dreams, happy peaceful
        Philippines,
Where the bolo man is hiking night and day;
Where Tagalogs steal and lie, where Americanos die,
There you hear the soldiers sing this evening lay:

>   *"Damn, damn, damn the Filipinos,*
>   *Pock-marked khakiac ladrones,*
>   *Underneath the starry flag*
>   *Civilize 'em with a Krag,*
>   *And return us to our own beloved homes."*

                                —Forbidden Army Song.

                . . . .

>   *"Land of the morning,*
>   *Child of the sun returning*
>   *With fervor burning*
>   *Thee do our souls adore."*

                        —Philippine National Hymn.

XXII
"Lee Hall, Fighting Man"

FOR THE TIME, Lee Hall was on the side lines. He spent the latter part of December, 1900, in the First Reserve Hospital in Manila. Christmas was a season he had often passed in strange places and under strange conditions, seldom in repose. Manila, with its electric lights and street railways, its hundreds of squatting, filthy beggars and its moated walls of the sixteenth century presented no contrasts more peculiar than the idle man of action. By the time that General Theodore Schwan had completed preparations for an expedition to the south, Lee Hall's two weeks of painful quietude were ended. He was ready to scout again with the Macabebes.

The military objectives of the new campaign were the reduction of the southern provinces of Luzon: Cavite, Laguna, Batangas and Tayabas.[1] Under command of General Mariana Trias, scattered forces and a hostile populace persisted in resistance. In southern ports, great numbers of rifles and ammunition were being distributed for use against Americans, and 1,500 prisoners there were waiting for release. The campaign was of sufficient importance to justify the plans of two generals, one column to be led by Wheaton, the other by Schwan. The regiments were chosen from newly arrived volunteer infantry. Their orders were to establish a line east and west through the province of Cavite, and confine the forces of Trias

[1] The objectives and result of the expedition are described in General Schwan's report: Brigadier General Theodore Schwan, Santa Cruz, P. I., February 8, 1900, to Adjutant General, First Division, Eighth Army Corps, Manila, P. I., *Correspondence Relating to the War with Spain*, II. A more detailed report by General Schwan is in *Annual Reports of War Department for Fiscal Year Ended June 30, 1900*, Part V, 387-564. This last will be referred to in subsequent citations as *General Schwan's Report*

to a middle stretch of territory by sending one column to subject the coastal region to American control and begin from there a policy of "squeeze."

Schwan's column was organized at San Pedro Macati, six miles from Manila. There, Lee Hall reported for duty. He was assigned the command of the First Company of Macabebe Scouts in the detachment attached to the Thirtieth Infantry and commanded by Lieutenant W. C. Geiger.[2] The Second Company was under the command of Lieutenant James H. Blount.[3]

The little warriors were as eager as Hall to begin the march. They raced by heavy carabaos, frightening them, so that the animals ran as fast as horses, dragging their two-wheeled carts behind. They peered into escort wagons, and perilously examined the harnessing of government mules. They got themselves infernally in the way of swarming Chinese coolies, the human pack animals that were to accompany the expedition. They listened to the talk of groups of soldiers, eager to hear speech of Macabebe cruelty and daring. With the curiosity of veterans, they inspected mountain artillery; they appraised cavalry mounts, raised the lids of camp kettles, and passed judgment on the strange tinned food that came from overseas and, somehow, kept from spoiling. There were about one hundred and forty Macabebes, but so omnipresent were they at San Pedro Macati that they seemed two thousand.

On January 4, the expedition began its march, Hall's Company scouting in front of the First Battalion of the Thirtieth Infantry. The little men went with more than usual eagerness, for they were to invade Cavite Province, the birthplace of their enemy, Emilio Aguinaldo. Next day, near Muntinlupa, the column was fired upon by sharpshooters in rice fields and behind the brush of a small hill. Hall and his men fought a half-hour skirmish with Filipinos who were entrenched in an irrigation

---

[2] The chief source for Lieutenant Geiger's operations is his report in *Annual Reports of War Department for Fiscal Year Ended June 30, 1900*, Part III, Appendix XXV, 546, 547. This will be subsequently cited as *Lieutenant Geiger's Report*.

[3] Of interest in connection with this expedition is Lieutenant James H. Blount's *The American Occupation of the Philippines*.

ditch beyond a screen of thick bamboo. Fifteen of the enemy
were killed and wounded, two hundred retreated toward Binan
on Laguna de Bay. On the outskirts of the town, the Macabebes
fell upon other entrenched Filipinos and drove them on to join
the rest. From Binan, the trail led southwest through Cavite
Province to Silang.[4] At the arsenal the Americans took possession of Mausers, modern mountain guns, and ammunition. They
found there brass and copper field pieces of ancient Spanish
make and bamboo cannon, wound round with wire—cannon
that had been used in the campaigns of 1896 and 1897; one-
pounders, also, ancient "lantankas."[5]

At Silang, Lieutenant Hall with a picked detachment of fifteen Macabebes was ordered to join Colonel Gardiner, Thirtieth
Infantry, and proceed by way of Alfonso and Bailen to Naic.
On January 9, they marched to Indang. The town was thoroughly hostile but unable to muster forces for adequate resistance.
Most of the citizens deserted before the troops' arrival. Schwan
and Wheaton for a time joined forces and sent detachments
from Silang and Indang to break up the Insurgent bands that
operated south of the two cities. Hall and his men were sent to
scout ahead of Major Hartigan, commanding the Third Battalion. The trail they followed, too tenuous to be shown on military maps, led towards Magallanes. Near that town Hall and
his Macabebes surprised and captured two outposts and several
prisoners. Immediately after this, the enemy was discovered
rapidly advancing in a column. The United States troops
adopted battle formation, Hall and his men and the advance
guard composing the first line.[6] Their fire at first was returned,
but soon the Filipino column broke and fled. Among those taken
prisoners was Colonel Riel of the Second Regiment of Insurgents. He told his captors that the force they had attacked was
the rearguard of General Trias. The Macabebes continued to
pursue until stopped by a ravine. The column then marched towards Magallanes, and in a deep gorge came upon the main

---

[4] *Lieutenant Geiger's Report.*
[5] Information as to Spanish arms was given me by Colonel William O. Smith,
who for long was stationed in the Philippines.
[6] Report of Major Thomas L. Hartigan, *Annual Reports of War Department
for Fiscal Year Ended June 30, 1900*, Part III, 512, 513.

force of the enemy. Under a covering fire of a company of the Thirtieth, the Macabebes' advance guard, together with Company L, rushed through the gorge and routed the enemy. Magallanes was entered without opposition.

On January 12, in the service of the Thirtieth, Hall's men made a thirty-three mile march. Before rejoining the main body of the Macabebes at Tanuan, they scouted under the immediate command of General Schwan.[7] Since leaving San Pedro Macati they had been constantly on the march. The trails followed by the Macabebes ascended rocky peaks and dropped to deep cut gorges that sheltered mountain streams. Passage through the trails was disputed, guerilla fashion, by Tagalogs of the regular force, by religious fanatics, and by bolo men.

The Americans were approaching Batangas, capital of the province and chief port of Verde Island Passage. It was from here that the Filipinos were receiving the greatest amount of arms and ammunition. It was the port, too, that Schwan designated as the best one to which headquarters could dispatch much needed rations and supplies. The ships transporting them engaged in a little preliminary shelling to facilitate the attack by land. Lee Hall with twenty of his bravest Macabebes set off before the rest of the command were stirring and reached Batangas at about nine on the morning of January 16. There were 15,000 townsmen and a number of troops within the city. They could not surrender to a force so small. Lee Hall proved that neither could they rout it. For three hours, until the American forces appeared, he and his Macabebes alone held the enemy at bay.[8] What strategy he used has never been described, but the achievement, chronicled officially by General Young, remains

[7] Lieutenant Hall to First Lieutenant William C. Geiger, Commanding Macabebe Scouts, Schwan's Expeditionary Brigade, *ibid.*, Part III, Appendix XXVI, 547.

[8] The American forces were commanded by Colonel Gardiner, Thirtieth Infantry. Report of Major General J. C. Bates, *ibid.* General Bates had succeeded to the command of General Lawton's old division.

"The twelve days of continuous marching and fighting of the Brigade in its operations from San Pedro Macati to Batangas was strikingly evidenced by the torn clothes and worn out shoes of the infantry." *General Schwan's Report.* See also LeRoy, *Americans in the Philippines*, II, 166.

as amazing as any of the fictitious stories of the Lee Hall legend.

General Schwan remained in the city until his forces could be refitted and reprovisioned. During this period, he issued a proclamation inviting Philippine coöperation. There was no response. Long after his expedition ended, the city and province continued to resist. When the column set off to the northeast to invade the province of Laguna, the towns along the line of march—San Rosario, San Pablo, San Diego—seemed silent and deserted. Their fighting men either lurked on the outskirts or were racing to Mahaihai[9] to dispute the passage of a narrow gorge that they esteemed impregnable. On January 22, the Macabebes camped on the heights west of Mahaihai. By reconnoitering, they found the Insurgents' flank was unprotected. Due to this information, the troops of the Thirtieth were able to descend the sides of the gorge by means of ropes and attack at an unexpected place.[10] The Filipinos abandoned the defense. The Macabebes scouted around Luisiana, and went into camp on January 25 at Santa Cruz, on the western estuary of Laguna de Bay. From there, they deployed through San Antonio, Pieta, Lumbang, and Caventi, returning on February 3.

A month had passed and the advance was ended. The brigade traversed, between towns, 650 miles. The Macabebes, starring out in many directions, had traveled many more. Though there were not enough troops to garrison and hold all territory conquered, there were enough to prevent the southern end of the province from serving as a gateway through which the Tagalogs could reënforce the rebels to the south. Insurgent forces had been scattered, 12,000 rounds of ammunition captured by the Macabebes, towns garrisoned as outposts, and many prisoners released.[11] After this, it was possible by patience and a judicious show of strength to organize the southern provinces

9 Spelled Majayjay in *Lieutenant Geiger's Report.*
10 LeRoy, *op. cit.,* II, 167, 168.
11 Major General John C. Bates to Brigadier General Theodore Schwan, dispatch dated Manila, P. I., April 15, 1900.
The marching was done over steep, rocky mountain trails, through deep gorges and over bridgeless streams. "The Macabebe Scouts were well handled by their officers and always with the advance, and performed excellent service as Scouts." *General Schwan's Report.*

into districts under the command of American officers. It fell to the lot of the colonel of Hall's regiment, Luther R. Hare, to undertake such work in Cavite.[12]

When the advance ended, Lee Hall acknowledged illness.[13] Until March 19, he was incapacitated by fever. A part of the time was spent in a hospital on Corregidor Island in the narrows of Manila Bay. Swamps, rice paddies, and bamboo forests seemed far removed from the lofty island. From his window, he could see the lighthouse, batteries, and pleasant bits of turf. On either side, ships passed, bearing their cargoes to Cavite and Manila or returning with disabled soldiers to the States. Among the passengers on one were members of the First Philippine Commission, men of many minds, incapable of acting as a unit. Always there were sea gulls flying. Hall watched them with a lassitude so great that if with the flip of a finger he could have turned life's page to see what next adventure would befall, the page would have remained unturned.

The sick man was much talked of in the States. His national reputation had burgeoned, due to the ministrations of the volatile Philadelphian of Hall's former Company, he of the grandiloquent Christian names, Napoleon Augustus Jennings. Jennings was no less picturesque as a journalist than as a Ranger. He had enhanced his reputation by entering the lions' den of Barnum and Bailey's circus, and if he did not beard the animals, he at least smoked a cigar in their august presence and

[12] This work is described in Dean C. Worcester's *Philippines, Past and Present*, I, and in Blount, *op. cit.*, 261, 262.

[13] Items regarding physical disability are recurrent in Lieutenant Hall's service record. Had his health been good, the commendation he received for leadership of the Macabebes would have insured promotion:

"These officers [Lieutenants Geiger and Hall] were frequently exposed to fire and displayed courage and coolness."—*Colonel Cornelius Gardiner's Report.*

"The work of Lieutenant Hall, Thirty-third Infantry, during the whole expedition was of the highest order."—*Lieutenant Geiger's Report.*

That the memory of Lieutenant Hall's service persists is shown by the posthumous praise of Brigadier General Joseph C. Castner, retired, in a letter to Mrs. Isham Keith, dated August 11, 1937:

"Your father's splendid standing as a man and a soldier was well known to me and thousands of other soldiers. In my opinion, Batson's battalion of Macabebes did more to suppress the insurrection by their great work in the fall of 1899 and later, than any other single battalion in the United States Army. I refer any one who doubts this last statement to the official records of the War Department for that period."

won unlimited and undated passes for himself and friends. There was no telling what advantageous publicity might accrue from one of his visits. He was versatile. He supplied the American troops with their slogan of "Remember the *Maine*." He ridiculed Police Commissioner Roosevelt as "Teddy Toddlekins, the Boy Detective," came to admire the man prodigiously on his return from Cuba as Colonel of the Rough Riders, and, in the end, became his friend.[14] What Jennings did was talked of, what he wrote was quoted. He wielded a spirited and facile pen, writing regularly for *The New York World*, contributing sophisticated articles to *Town Topics* and hero-stories to *The Youths' Companion* and *The Saturday Evening Post*.

In these last, he extolled the Rangers and Lee Hall. No new experience was more vivid to him than adventures they had shared in Texas, no later leader more glamorous than his daredevil young captain. Under the caption of "Lee Hall, Fighting Man," he presented him to the multitudinous readers of *The Saturday Evening Post*, the 1900 approximation of an introduction over a national radio "hook-up":

"There is one fighting man who has gone with Uncle Sam's Army to the Philippines of whom the great American public knows little or nothing, but whose name throughout the State of Texas stands as a synonym for desperate courage and fighting qualities of the highest order. He is Jesse Lee Hall, now a Lieutenant in the Thirty-third U.S. Infantry, but he earned the rank of Captain in the Texas Rangers by years of the hardest kind of service on the border."[15]

"He earned the rank of Captain!" On March 19, 1900, Lieutenant Hall was able to report for duty.

In less than a month, he was again invalided. The surgeon reported him as suffering from the hernia that had reappeared and grown larger after his fall at Tilad Pass. The Ranger was a warrior, *hors de combat,* capable of fighting only against this ancient enemy and the malaria that shook his frame with chills

14 From an account written for Mr. J. Frank Dobie by Mme. Edith Helena, the opera singer, who is Mr. Jennings' widow. Mr. Dobie very kindly lent me this manuscript.
15 Jennings, "Lee Hall, Fighting Man," *Saturday Evening Post*, January 6, 1900.

and sapped his strength with fever. Until early June, he was again invalided in the hospital on Corregidor Island.

Returning to duty, he saw the beginning of a new chapter in the history of the Philippines. General MacArthur had superseded General Otis. A genial chuckle was heard throughout the land. It came from William Howard Taft. He, with other members of the Second Philippine Commission, was spreading the doctrine of good fellowship among the "little brown brothers." No longer were Filipinos to be described as banditti and ladrones.[16]

On June 9, Lieutenant Hall was informed his services with the Macabebes no longer were required.[17] For a few days, in Ilocus Sur, he served with his old regiment, the "Fighting Texans." Again, he was ordered to report for treatment, this time to the hospital in Vigan, the city where General Young maintained headquarters. Released,[18] a week's duty with his company, and then for a fourth time, he was pronounced unfit. He was ordered to present himself to the regimental surgeon in San Francisco, far enough away to prevent him from trying again to report for active service.

As finis, there was published the complimentary reference and recommendation in the official report of General S. B. M. Young:

> Lee Hall, First Lieutenant, 33rd, Infantry, U. S. V., to be breveted Captain of Volunteers:
>
> For gallantry and meritorious service in action at Aringay, Province of Union, Luzon, P. I., November 19, 1899, where, with great gallantry and good judgment, he led his Company forward in the dark, waded the river under a strong fire from a superior and intrenched hostile force, and materially assisted in demoralizing and completely routing the enemy and capturing the works and the town, I recommend that First Lieutenant Lee Hall, 33rd Infantry, U. S. V. be breveted Captain of Volunteers.
>
> At Batangas, a city of 15,000 inhabitants, Captain Hall, with twenty Macabebes, held the enemy at bay for three hours until

---

[16] Worcester, *op. cit.*, I.

[17] Order of Major General Bates by Arthur L. Wagner, Assistant Adjutant General, Headquarters, Department of Southern Luzon, Manila, P. I.

[18] He was transferred to his command for duty, June 22, 1900.

American troops came up. It was Company L, of the 33rd Regiment, under Captain Hall's command, who broke the record at target practice in San Francisco before they sailed for duty in the Philippines.[19]

Weeks lengthened into months while Hall's body took toll at last for excess labor and endurance. Perhaps, he would have mended more rapidly had a home awaited him. His family was his no longer. In Lebanon, a will was signed that gravely influenced his future. His wife had five little girls, the eldest fifteen, the youngest seven. The problem of making a home for them and paying for their education was one she felt their father could not solve. The will that was signed, December 4, 1899,[20] provided that the maternal estate, home and furnishings and interest on a sum of money, be left conditionally to herself and a Lebanon member of the family. The condition was that the two live together, until Mrs. Hall's youngest daughter, Virginia, should be fifteen. If the condition was violated, the estate would be divided into six equal parts. Bessie's would be too small to afford support. This kept the wife from her husband. They would grow old apart, but she would have shelter and a relative degree of comfort for Jessie, Elizabeth, Dorothy, Mary, and Virginia. The tragedy in the situation was that the man and his wife were lovers, that each had need of each and was shamed and unhappy through separation.

On September 20, 1900, the sick man was honorably discharged—the order to take effect on October 6. To gain his commission, he had renounced all claim to pay if disabled in consequence of his old malady. He left the hospital as Lee Hall, citizen, middle-aged, without employment or profession, battered and broken by service rendered in alien islands;[21] Lee Hall, widower, by grace of a strange will, humbly agreed to by an anxious, grieving wife; Lee Hall, pilgrim and stranger.

His needs had the effect of a pricking wind that whistled an old tune on an old theme—danger and the unknown. It was the

---

19 This citation was copied in numerous newspapers in the United States.
20 Mrs. Isham Keith kindly furnished me with a copy of this will.
21 "When he returned to San Antonio he was completely broken in health."—Letter of Mr. Netteville Devine to Mrs. Isham Keith, November, 1928.

time of the year when, in Texas, the first fresh northers sweep away the drowsy lassitude of heat, a time when breath comes quickly and seems again God-given. He would go back. And remembering his days there, Hall's spent body quickened. With clear eyes and head held high, he seemed a gallant Ranger. For little boys, who gloried in their new found hero in the *Post;* for men, inspirited by fellowship and brave example, he would still be a leader. No veteran to recount the past and prize a listener's tribute of attention! He would still be as Jennings introduced him to a million readers:

"Lee Hall, Fighting Man!"

XXIII
The Last Scout
(November, 1900-March, 1911)

"He was happy when he died
And brave and true alive.
God send the West a-many such
To make our country thrive!"

— STANLEY VESTAL, "Kit Carson's
Last Smoke," *Southwest Review.*

"Corner with your left,
Partner with your right,
Right and wrong, all night long,
Meet your partner and promenade home."

—Western Play Song.

The Last Scout

LEE HALL reëntered Texas at its western gateway, the border city of El Paso. The Rio Grande, dividing the city from Juarez, was an old friend to whose sins and vagaries he was accustomed. He was fond of the river in an ironical way, with a fondness of the kind a cowboy feels for some "widow-maker" of a mustang, when both have tested strength and grit. The range of Rockies near the city seemed not unlike a group of magnificent "old timers." Mount Franklin sprawled and stretched itself—a western mountain, appropriating sufficient space—a mountain that defied man to make free with it. Hall found human companionship in Sam Platt, a veteran of Special State Troops,[1] and each recounted adventures never told outsiders for fear of incredulity.

The Captain's headquarters were the law offices of Turney and Burges.[2] The younger member of the firm, William H. Burges, was the son of one of the prosecuting attorneys Hall had assisted in the Brazell cases. As a little shaver, Mr. Burges had listened in Seguin to tales of how the Rangers were carrying law into the chaparral. There was ample exchange now for his early pleasures. His library was one of the best in the state, and it offered opportunity for adventure into the land of books. Hall knocked at doors and opened wide the windows of peasants' huts and border Scottish castles. He had always hated hours spent within four walls. There were no walls in the li-

---

1 This information was given me by the late John Bracken.
2 Letter to the author from the Hon. William H. Burges, El Paso, Texas, March 30, 1936.

brary. He ranged at will through the years and through the world. Life had granted a better understanding of fantastic circumstance and humorous incident, of knave and hero, of star-crossed lovers and their sufferings, than could have been gained in a school room. The books were passports to the pleasant country of Cockaigne.

In May, 1902, the former Ranger went to Washington to appear before the Senate Philippine Commission. His testimony was neither sensational nor sentimental. He knew too much of war to think it could be made with rose-water. In the Insular campaign, it had been waged, at times, by water mixed with sand and grit and administered in the "water cure." He felt that American officers, in permitting their native allies to use the method, had done no more than take advantage of the barbarous custom of the country. He testified that Filipino prisoners, except for being required to beat rice, were treated as well as American soldiers. He said that General Lawton admonished the troops to remember in dealing with the natives that they, some day, would be "our people."[3]

Only in entertaining grandiose schemes for money making did Hall show lack of logic. Old age was close upon him. Scant time was left to win a fortune. Bessie, Jessie, Elizabeth, Dorothy, Mary, Virginia, even their names, as he said them, were a prayer. He would have encircled them in sweet security. With the white wings of his wishes he tried to hide realities. But the plans he made were of the earth and went astray. In Kansas City, he promoted a Texas road that he hoped the Missouri Pacific or the Rock Island Railroad would purchase from him.[4] In St. Louis, he worked for the sale of a tremendous acreage of Texas rice lands. The World's Fair was in progress, and Jessie was a secretary at the Texas building. There he saw old friends, could be sure of an eager audience. At noon, or thereabouts, it was his custom to visit the offices of Captain Caspar

[3] "Lee Hall is Called in Philippine Case," *San Antonio Express,* May 4, 1902, quoting Washington dispatch of May 3; *New York Times,* May 16, 23, and June 1, 1902.

[4] Letter to the author from Dr. B. Albert Lieberman, Kansas City, July 26, 1936. Dr. Lieberman was the surgeon of the Thirty-third, and had treated Captain Hall during his illness at the First District Hospital at Vigan Ilocos Norte.

Conrad of the Jefferson Guards, and with him to pour a bourbon libation to the goddess Chance. Yet again this jade turned against him, for his deal for the rice lands failed because the daughter-in-law of the investor, at the last minute, refused to live in Texas. He made money in real estate, lost more in oil, and even more by going surety for the notes of friends. Once, when his pockets were nearly empty, he visited members of the Thirty-third in line school at Fort Leavenworth.[5] At Another time, he traveled in Texas counties as an agent for sewing machines.[6] It was hard to credit to the quiet agent the personality of Red Hall of the smoking seventies. And yet the work of the Ranger had made possible the homes he visited—a multiplication of homes for others.

Again in 1906 the skies seemed roseate. In response to a telegram, Lee Hall contracted to organize and lead a force for the Giroux Consolidated Mines Company in the State of Sonora, Mexico. The corporation agreed to pay a good salary and allow a free hand in his selection and command of half a dozen men. He sent a check to his wife and a copy of the contract so that she would see this was no day dream.

Bessie answered his summons to come, and for a day in Washington the two experienced a second honeymoon. They had rooms at the Metropolitan Hotel, where, with young William Harllee, he had been an impecunious lobby and sidewalk guest in the anxious period when the two men were trying to gain commissions. Hall, in a letter to Jessie, spelled honeymoon in capitals.[7] He asserted that he was not allowed to write all that he wished and yet enjoyed the orders of his gentle tyrant. Darby and Joan, long separated and briefly reunited, busied themselves with readjustments. Hall found his wife stouter than before and was distressed by her gray hair. She wrote[8] that he was "more like himself" than he had been for

[5] Letter to author from Colonel Theodore Schultz, Phoebus, Virginia, July 6, 1937.
[6] Letter to the author from Mr. E. R. Dabney, Newspaper Division, Library of the University of Texas, March 5, 1936.
[7] Captain Hall to Jessie Lee Hall, Washington, May 14, 1906.
[8] Mrs. Bessie W. Hall to Jessie Lee Hall, Washington, May 14, 1906.

[333]

years, although he showed the wear and tear of time. It was the ending of her letter to Jessie that was memorable:

"Don't play with love, dear. Make up your mind to love one man and stick to him."

Next day the four daughters, Elizabeth and Dorothy, Mary and Virginia, met their parents in Philadelphia. Jessie could not come. She remained in West Virginia, held by the duties of her first position. Each girl received a banknote: "It has rained in my garden at last," their father told them.

He traveled on to Greensboro to visit his mother; then to San Antonio to begin recruiting. There *The Express*, commenting on the Mexican employment of the former border Ranger, spoke of him as one of the "gatling guns of civilization," whose work had proved so effective that Texas could afford to lend him to her sister nation—"reciprocity extraordinary."[9] The State of Sonora, in 1906, presented problems to Mexico like those which the Nueces Strip had presented earlier to Texas. In Bisbee there was talk of annexing Sonora to the United States. Mexican strikers endangered copper mines. Arizona Rangers enlisted in the Mexican army to restore order, until Diaz compelled them to withdraw. He sent to the scene Colonel Kosterlitzky with the *Cordada,* or flying column of the Rurales.

Hall bought tickets for himself and his men to Carbo in Sonora, and on arriving rode thirty miles to the Sultana Mines which he had come to guard. They were situated in mountains claimed for one hundred and sixty years by Yaquis. The Indians spoke Spanish and professed the Roman Catholic religion, but they spoke, also, their own language,[10] and the idols behind the altars of their new religion were plainly visible.

After pilfering implements and *tequila* from wagon trains, they made bold to attack the mines themselves. Before the Captain's arrival, they had killed the superintendent. Nor had danger come from Yaquis only. Indian strife with the Mexicans and unsettled conditions on the border had drawn to the region in the eighties revolutionists and bandits of every kind. The

[9] "Reciprocity Extraordinary," *San Antonio Express,* June 3, 1906.
[10] C. L. Lumholtz, *New Trails in Mexico* (New York, Charles Scribner's Sons, 1912).

native breed was influenced by the remainders of marauding bands.

One top hand added himself immediately to Hall's force— George Talley, the former Ranger, who had been "on the dodge," in Mexico since the killing of Peters in 1878.[11]

To reassure his mother, Hall wrote that he never saw the Yaquis except when they were scurrying off into the brush; he complained that the only dangers were those incident to childhood: one might fall off a bluff, get thorns in his knees, or have unpleasant encounters with rattlesnakes, centipedes, scorpions, and tarantulas. As for cut-throats and ladrones, he insisted that he was safer from them in Sonora than in Texas, and much safer than in Chicago or New York.[12]

There was interest, if not excitement, in the work. Silver ore was carried by the Mexicans to the surface by means of notched poles, six or eight inches in diameter. The poles were tilted, and supported in the shaft by timber-scaffolding.[13] Contact with the bare feet and the huaraches of the miners kept the poles smooth and polished. At the top, the ore was loaded into strongly constructed wagons. Fifty tons was the amount necessary to fill a freight car. When this had been collected, ten or twelve mules were hitched to each wagon and, with Lee Hall and his men as escort, the journey to Carbo started. It consumed two days and was uneventful, for the sight of the heavily armed Ranger and his followers discouraged depredations. So peaceful was his occupation that he invited his second daughter, Elizabeth, to come to Sonora and keep house for him.[14] Jessie had become engaged to a young Virginian, Isham Keith, and Hall sent money for the trousseau and the wedding.

It was one of his last gifts, for the region of the Sultana Mines became so peaceful that Hall and the guard were not needed.[15]

11 Mr. Kleber Miller's interview with former Ranger George W. Talley, Falfurrias, April, 1935.

12 Letter to Mrs. H. M. Hall from Captain Hall, Sonora, Mexico, August 4, 1906.

13 John Hays Hammond, The Autobiography of (New York, Farrar and Rinehart, 1935), Chapter I.

14 Letter to Mrs. H. M. Hall cited supra.

15 Frances Wier Hall in her manuscript claims that Captain Hall "was largely

After this, he worked in Mexico and Texas on a succession of projects designed to make his fortune; projects connected with oil leases, mining concessions and schemes for colonization. For a while, he was in Mazatlan. In 1910, he tried to promote the sale of a 1,235,000 acre tract in the territory of Tepic, Mexico. If the scheme succeeded, he planned to buy two million acres, over a five year period, at sixty cents an acre. On this, as impresario, he meant to settle fifty families of Germans that he would bring from Texas. These would make a nucleus. The promoters hoped to realize a profit of two millions![16]

Mexico, during the presidency of Diaz, exerted a peculiarly stimulating effect on the acquisitive instinct of Americans. Many made fabulous fortunes. Hall failed. As his clothing grew threadbare and his dreams grew dim, drink became more necessary as a solvent for his doubts, and a stimulus to his imagination. He was ill increasingly, but kept away from those whom this would trouble. He was lonely. And many times from childhood days, an old refrain was wafted back, "I'm a pilgrim, and I'm a stranger."

Cheap hotels and boarding houses, poor food and poorer drink were endurable. It seemed better to write no letters, since affection might discern on white paper the blackness of despair.

Very gradually, the shimmering hopes dwindled into a very humble one that he might not cause suffering to those who loved him. In Houston, he had a brief visit with his mother. He had been ill for two weeks before this, but he faced her in such happy fashion that she believed him well.[17] For a long time, there had been a pact between them that she must safeguard her health, since he believed that he was destined to reach whatever age that she did.

He gained a new reason to live, a wish to see his grandson. Jessie's child had been given a Virginia name, Isham Keith, Jr., but he was to be reared in the tradition of the Ranger. No

---

instrumental in quelling a rising of Yaqui Indians in Mexico." For this I have not been able to find references.

[16] Letter of Captain Hall to C. W. Ogden, Hotel Clendenning, New York. The Captain's letter is dated San Antonio, September 17, 1910.

[17] Letter of Mrs. H. M. Hall to Mrs. Isham Keith, June 12, 1911.

Texan could have been in heartier agreement with this than the boy's own father. The mother wrote to Lee Hall and urged that he visit her in West Virginia. The sight of his "red headed grandson" would make him young and well again. The letter was delayed, for the wanderer had left the place to which it was addressed.[18] It was given to him later by a Sister of Charity in Santa Rosa Hospital in San Antonio.

Lee Hall was too well-known for his illness at Santa Rosa to be unnoticed. The news that he was there brought to the place diverse men, the reasons for whose friendship would have told the story of his life. When his brother, Richard Hall, arrived from Dallas,[19] he found the gentle nuns had heard from visitors a score of incidents drawn from the Ranger's long career. Already, a telegram had been sent which brought Jessie to his bedside. It was not signed by the father, but by a regal woman who had cherished from her youth remembrance of things too vivid to be spoken of as though they were long passed. Of these, the nuns heard nothing. She was self-contained, somewhat aloof, worldly, but never trivial. She had known Lee Hall, loved him, some said, when he was at his best. She might have kept him there, or, walking at his side, drawn him to greater heights. She could do nothing now. His only interest was in a scout of which she was quite ignorant. He was about to leave her, as he had done before when they danced together at the Menger, and a summons from the Adjutant General had meant good-bye, and sent him running down the stairway, his thoughts already far afield.

John Bullis came to Santa Rosa. He had been a lieutenant on the border when Hall first knew him, a very famous Indian fighter. He was a general now, still slim, erect, weather-beaten, one of the citizens in whom an ancient city had high pride. The surgeon of the First Immunes, Dr. Hadra, who had discovered Hall's old malady in Galveston, attended the ex-Ranger with greater skill because of long knowledge of his disabilities. Two

18 Letter to Captain Hall from Mrs. Isham Keith, Mt. Clare, West Virginia, March 4, 1911.
19 *San Antonio Express*, March 18, 1911.

daily visitors were ranchmen from the Sherman district, men much younger than the Captain, but who had heard from their fathers stories of the days when Red Hall, as a young peace officer, made history. One of the ranchmen had run away to the Ranger camp when he was a little boy, and begged to be a member of the Company. He had been received kindly and returned to his father at the first opportunity.[20]

Judge T. S. Paschal came. People were beginning to call him "old Tom Paschal." He had served as a congressman in Washington and then established a law practice in San Antonio. He was almost bald, oratorical in speech, convivial in habit. However the two men may have appeared to the rest of the world, each saw in the other the remnant of a burning, valorous spirit, and each knew that the other's work would more surely live through the fact of their association. The Judge's decisions formed a part of the legal record of the state, and Ranger history could not be written without the name of Captain Hall.

Another who came was General Jesse Lee, whose friendship for the Captain had seasoned and mellowed through a quarter of a century.

At noon each day, there was a visitor that generals and judges did not know. He came, remembering a day when, as a very small urchin in Laredo, a little dirtier and more ragged than the rest, he had seen Lee Hall come riding by, and had run and clung to his stirrup, since he could reach no higher. In a torrent of Spanish, he had poured out his woes to the great *capitán*, telling him that the world was very hard for a little boy who had no father or mother and was starving and needed shelter. Lee Hall had swung him up to the saddle, and so he had ridden through the town and to the ranch in LaSalle County. From then on, Hall had befriended him whenever he was able. The Mexican did without his lunch to make the visits. When he left the hospital, it was to return to a news stand at one of the rail-

---

[20] Letter to the author from Mrs. Isham Keith, August 14, 1936. Mrs. Keith mentions as frequent visitors the Kampmans, the Reids, Mrs. Netteville Devine, Mrs. Eagar, Miss Flo Eagar, and Dr. Fred Hadra. Ranger visitors were Captain W. A. (Billy) Pitts, Captain Dave Wilson, and former Assistant Adjutant General E. M. Phelps.

road stations, and to try to do his work well, for Lee Hall had got him the place.[21]

Of the many visitors during the five days at Santa Rosa, one man, alone, could help in preparation for the final scout. For Hall was making ready to cross into a foreign country. The old Ranger knew the loops and turns of the Rio Grande, its bluffs and fords, its course—more tortuous than the tracks of fugitives whom, earlier, he had pursued. He did not fear the Rio Grande nor did he fear the land beyond. But always, when he crossed, he went prepared.

Beyond the Big Bend, was a land uncharted, *Tierra Desconocida,* Unknown Country. There were great bluffs on the Texas side, and a man might slip and plunge headlong. The cacti and the Spanish daggers would not leave him in good condition to find the ford and start a scout upon the other side. Some said it was a desert waste of mountain and of plain, and some that, if one persevered, he found green pastures, springs of sweet water, and shade of trees for rest.

Death stalked at the border. He had been close to Lee Hall many times, but on the Ranger's body there was neither knife wound nor bullet wound to show that He had noted him.[22] The sick man knew that he was destined now to meet Him—in a small room in a hospital. And yet the encounter would not be within four walls. From his pillows, Hall looked ahead and dimly saw the River—Rio Grande, Rio Bravo, Jordan, Styx—the name was nothing—and beyond, *Tierra Desconocida.* He wished to cross and make his scout as a good Ranger should, riding "tall, wide and handsome."

He needed a guide, one of his own people, one who knew him, one whom he could talk to. Father Kirwin was in the city and came to see him. Hall liked the Irish humor and the frankness of the priest. He knew him to have a stout heart in a manly body and to be possessed of enough of Adam's taint to give him understanding.

[21] Letter to the author from Mrs. Isham Keith, Ingleton Farm, Warrenton, Virginia, June 24, 1937.
[22] Letter to the author from Judge Duval West, San Antonio, Texas, February 27, 1935.

Father Kirwin persuaded the Captain to confess his sins. He received the absolution of the Church. He was baptized. Contact with the gentle strength of the brave priest was good, and a Ranger who had had over much of dogma and church attendance in his youth felt now the peace that, on occasion, could be bestowed by the Church of Rome, of Peter and of Paul, by "Father Kirwin's Church." From his parish in Galveston, the priest could not prolong his absence. Leaving peace behind him, he, too, carried peace with him.

"Do not grieve for your father," he told Mrs. Keith. "He has his faults, but there are elements of greatness in him."[23]

Soon after, it was decided that extreme unction should be administered. A Mexican priest officiated. Bell, Book, candles, intoning of Latin, use of anointing oils seemed, somehow, to contract the place Hall rested in, to close his vista. It seemed as though a little, alien man was striving to veil the austere majesty of Death—to fling about Him something flimsy, cozening, a little soiled.

Time was brief after this. When no longer he could speak, Hall sought by pressure of his hand to convey the solace that still he understood. On March 17, 1911,[24] soon after nine in the evening, his body ceased to live. In the plaza outside, a little wind was fluttering light flowers. Darkness made contrast with the glint of fireflies and the moon-white wings of moths. And above these little things, these pretty things, afar off there shone the splendid stars that had given Lee Hall his bearings when roads were lacking and the way was dark.

The funeral was a military one. There was a caisson for the body's final carriage, a battery of artillery for its escort and the National Cemetery for its resting place. A chaplain read the service and General Jesse Lee paid tribute. He praised the Ranger's bravery and tender heart.

"His heroic deeds," he said, "would fill a volume."[25]

---

23 This was told me by Mrs. Keith.

24 "Captain Lee Hall, Man Famous as a Former Ranger and Hero of Daring Exploits Yields to Illness," *Austin Statesman*, March 18, 1911; *San Antonio Express*, March 18, 1911.

25 "I have known him intimately for twenty-five years in peace and in war. No braver spirit, no more devoted friend ever passed from earth. He was the

THE LAST SCOUT

And then the notes of a bugle sounded, four times calling to the fallen warrior; falling, in a confession of human impotence, and rising in a last endeavor to go a little way with him upon his quest—the hail and farewell of the Army—a bugle sounding taps.

For a few days inaccurate obituaries lauded Lee Hall for his own deeds and for deeds of others. There were editorials and letters praising him as the best of the border captains, the one unequalled in making arrests through sheer persuasion, a man who had hidden his charities and mercies. Let one obituary stand for all:

"He did more to rid Texas of desperadoes and establish law and order than any officer Texas ever had. He has made more bad men lay down their guns and delivered more desperadoes and outlaws into the custody of the courts and used his own gun less than any other officer in Texas."[26]

A single tribute, could he have heard it, would have outweighed all others with Lee Hall. It was the wish his wife expressed to take her last rest at his side. He had a home for her now, one that would be enduring. When the time came for this, her body was brought from Jessie's home in Virginia and buried by his own. Hall had not feared Death, and Death proved kindly, bestowing on the body that had housed his restless spirit an earthy home and a still and constant bride.

The spirit still is ranging, not to be shut within the covers of a book, not to be walled into some chamber locked and barred by Time. It mingles now with others, merges with shadowy troops, the hoof-beats of whose phantom horses wake the dawn, whose cries and laughter faintly sound across the River. Too unique to perish, they have become a part of tradition, figures in the folklore of a prideful state.

As surely as Rangers are born, Rangers do not die.

---

bravest of the brave and his heart was as tender as that of the most lovable woman," *San Antonio Daily Express,* March 18, 1911.

General Lee paid tribute again to the Captain on Decoration Day, May 30, 1912. Letter to Mrs. Keith from General Lee, June 9, 1912.

[26] John E. Elgin in *San Antonio Express,* March 20, 1911.

Index

Index

INDEX